Reader's Guide
to
JONATHAN SWIFT

Reader's Guide to JONATHAN SWIFT

W. Cormier

CENTRUM PRESS
NEW DELHI-110002 (INDIA)

CENTRUM PRESS
H.O.: 4360/4, Ansari Road, Daryaganj,
New Delhi-110 002 (India)
Ph.: 23278000, 23261597

B.O.: No. 1015, Ist Main Road, BSK IIIrd Stage
IIIrd Phase, IIIrd Block,
Bangalore - 560 085 (India)
Tel.: 080-41723429
Visit us at: www.centrumpress.com

Reader's Guide to Jonathan Swift

First Edition, 2009

ISBN 978-93-80106-72-4

PRINTED IN INDIA

Printed at Salasar Imaging Systems, Delhi-110035 (India)

Contents

Preface

Jonathan Swift was born in Dublin. His father, Jonathan Swift Sr., a lawyer and an English civil servant, died seven month's before his son was born. Abigail Erick, Swift's mother, was left without private income to support her family. Swift was taken or "stolen" to England by his nurse, and at the age of four he was sent back to Ireland. Swift's mother returned to England, and she left her son to her wealthy brother-in-law, Uncle Godwin.

At school Swift was not a very good good student and his teachers noted his headstrong behavior. When the anti-Catholic Revolution of the year 1688 aroused reaction in Ireland, Swift moved to England to the household of Sir William Temple at Moor Park, Surrey - Lady Temple was a relative of Swift's mother. In 1695 Swift was ordained in the Church of Ireland (Anglican), Dublin.

Jonathan Swift died in Dublin on October 19, 1745. He left behind a great mass of poetry and prose, chiefly in the form of pamphlets. William Makepeace Thackeray once said of the author: "So great a man he seems to me, that thinking of him is like thinking of an empire falling." Swift's religious writing is little read today. His most famous works include The Battle of the Books (1697), exploring the merits of the ancients and the moderns in literature. The author himself pretends to be an objective chronicler of events, but his sympathies are more on the side of the ancients.

Author

Chapter 1

Introduction

Jonathan Swift (30 November 1667 – 19 October 1745) was an Anglo-Irish satirist, essayist, political pamphleteer (first for Whigs then for the Tories), poet and cleric who became Dean of St. Patrick's, Dublin.

He is remembered for works such as *Gulliver's Travels, A Modest Proposal, A Journal to Stella, Drapier's Letters, The Battle of the Books, An Argument Against Abolishing Christianity,* and *A Tale of a Tub.*

Swift is probably the foremost prose satirist in the English language, and is less well known for his poetry. Swift originally published all of his works under pseudonyms such as Lemuel Gulliver, Isaac Bickerstaff, M.B. Drapier or anonymously. He is also known for being a master of two styles of satire; the Horatian and Juvenalian styles.

YOUTH

Jonathan Swift was born at No. 7, Hoey's Court, Dublin, and was the second child and only son of Jonathan Swift (a second cousin of John Dryden) and wife Abigail Erick (or Herrick), paternal grandson of Thomas Swift and wife Elizabeth Dryden, daughter of Nicholas Dryden (brother of Sir Erasmus Dryden, 1st Baronet Dryden) and wife Mary Emyley.

His father was Irish born and his mother was born in England. Swift arrived seven months after his father's untimely death. Most of the facts of Swift's early life are obscure, confused and sometimes contradictory. It is widely believed that his mother returned to England when Jonathan was still very young, then leaving him to be raised by his father's family. His uncle Godwin took primary responsibility for the young Jonathan, sending him with one of his cousins to Kilkenny College (also attended by the philosopher George Berkeley).

In 1682 he attended Dublin University (Trinity College, Dublin), receiving his B.A. in 1686. Swift was studying for his Master's degree when political troubles in Ireland surrounding the Glorious Revolution forced him to leave for England in 1688, where his mother helped him get a position as secretary and personal assistant of Sir William Temple at Moor Park, Farnham.

Temple was an English diplomat who, having arranged the Triple Alliance of 1668, retired from public service to his country estate to tend his gardens and write his memoirs. Growing into confidence with his employer, Swift "was often trusted with matters of great importance." Within three years of their acquaintance, Temple had introduced his secretary to William III, and sent him to London to urge the King to consent to a bill for triennial Parliaments.

When Swift took up his residence at Moor Park, he met Esther Johnson, then 8 years old, the fatherless daughter of one of the household servants. Swift acted as her tutor and mentor, giving her the nickname "Stella" and the two maintained a close, but ambiguous relationship for the rest of Esther's life. Swift left Temple in 1690 for Ireland because of his health, but returned to Moor Park the following year.

The illness, fits of vertigo or giddiness now known to be Ménière's disease would continue to plague Swift throughout his life. During this second stay with Temple, Swift received his M.A. from Hertford College, Oxford University in 1692. Then, apparently despairing of gaining a better position through Temple's patronage, Swift left Moor Park to become an ordained priest in the Established Church of Ireland and in 1694 he was appointed to the prebend of Kilroot in the Diocese of Connor, with his parish located at Kilroot, near Carrickfergus in County Antrim.

Swift appears to have been miserable in his new position,

being isolated in a small, remote community far from the centres of power and influence. While at Kilroot, however, Swift may well have become romantically involved with Jane Waring. A letter from him survives, offering to remain if she would marry him and promising to leave and never return to Ireland if she refused. She presumably refused, because Swift left his post and returned to England and Temple's service at Moor Park in 1696, and he remained there until Temple's death.

There he was employed in helping to prepare Temple's memoirs and correspondence for publication. During this time Swift wrote *The Battle of the Books,* a satire responding to critics of Temple's *Essay upon Ancient and Modern Learning* (1690). *Battle* was however not published until 1704.

On January 27 1699 Temple died. Swift stayed on briefly in England to complete the editing of Temple's memoirs, and perhaps in the hope that recognition of his work might earn him a suitable position in England. However, Swift's work made enemies of some of Temple's family and friends who objected to indiscretions included in the memoirs. His next move was to approach King William directly, based on his imagined connection through Temple and a belief that he had been promised a position.

This failed so miserably that he accepted the lesser post of secretary and chaplain to the Earl of Berkeley, one of the Lords Justices of Ireland. However, when he reached Ireland he found that the secretaryship had already been given to another.

But he soon obtained the living of Laracor, Agher, and Rathbeggan, and the prebend of Dunlavin in St. Patrick's Cathedral, Dublin.

At Laracor, a mile or two from Trim, County Meath, and twenty miles (32 km) from Dublin, Swift ministered to a congregation of about fifteen people, and had abundant leisure for cultivating his garden, making a canal (after the Dutch fashion of Moor Park), planting willows, and rebuilding the vicarage.

As chaplain to Lord Berkeley, he spent much of his time

in Dublin and traveled to London frequently over the next ten years. In 1701, Swift published, anonymously, a political pamphlet, *A Discourse on the Contests and Dissentions in Athens and Rome.*

WRITER

In February 1702, Swift received his Doctor of Divinity degree from Trinity College, Dublin. That spring he traveled to England and returned to Ireland in October, accompanied by Esther Johnson now twenty years old and his friend Rebecca Dingley, another member of William Temple's household.

There is a great mystery and controversy over Swift's relationship with Esther Johnson nicknamed "Stella". Many hold that they were secretly married in 1716. Although there has never been definite proof of this, there is no doubt that she was dearer to him than anyone else and that his feelings for her did not change throughout his life.

During his visits to England in these years Swift published *A Tale of a Tub* and *The Battle of the Books* (1704) and began to gain a reputation as a writer. This led to close, lifelong friendships with Alexander Pope, John Gay, and John Arbuthnot, forming the core of the Martinus Scriblerus Club (founded in 1713). Swift became increasingly active politically in these years.

From 1707 to 1709 and again in 1710, Swift was in London, unsuccessfully urging upon the Whig administration of Lord Godolphin the claims of the Irish clergy to the First-Fruits and Twentieths ("Queen Anne's Bounty"), which brought in about £2500 a year, already granted to their brethren in England.

He found the opposition Tory leadership more sympathetic to his cause and Swift was recruited to support their cause as editor of the *Examiner* when they came to power in 1710. In 1711, Swift published the political pamphlet "The Conduct of the Allies," attacking the Whig government for its inability to end the prolonged war with France. The incoming Tory government conducted secret (and illegal) negotiations with France, resulting in the Treaty of Utrecht (1713) ending the War of the Spanish Succession.

Swift was part of the inner circle of the Tory government, and often acted as mediator between Henry St. John (Viscount Bolingbroke) the secretary of state for foreign affairs (1710–15) and Robert Harley (Earl of Oxford) lord treasurer and prime minister (1711–1714).

Swift recorded his experiences and thoughts during this difficult time in a long series of letters to Esther Johnson, later collected and published as *The Journal to Stella*. The animosity between the two Tory leaders eventually led to the dismissal of Harley in 1714.

With the death of Queen Anne and ascension of George I that year, the Whigs returned to power and the Tory leaders were tried for treason for conducting secret negotiations with France.

Also during these years in London, Swift became acquainted with the Vanhomrigh family and became involved with one of the daughters, Esther, yet another fatherless young woman and an ambiguous relationship to confuse Swift's biographers. Swift furnished Esther with the nickname "Vanessa" and she features as one of the main characters in his poem *Cadenus and Vanessa.*

The poem and their correspondence suggests that Esther was infatuated with Swift, that he may have reciprocated her affections, only to regret it and then try to break it off. Esther followed Swift to Ireland in 1714, where there appears to have been a confrontation, possibly involving Esther Johnson. Esther Vanhomrigh died in 1723 at the age of 35. Another lady with whom he had a close but less intense relationship, was Anne Long, a toast of the Kit-Cat Club.

MATURITY

Before the fall of the Tory government, Swift hoped that his services would be rewarded with a church appointment in England. However, Queen Anne appeared to have taken a dislike to Swift and thwarted these efforts. The best position his friends could secure for him was the Deanery of St. Patrick's, Dublin. With the return of the Whigs, Swift's best move was to leave England and he returned to Ireland in disappointment, a virtual exile, to live "like a rat in a hole". Once in Ireland, however, Swift began to turn his pamphleteering skills in support of Irish causes, producing some of his most memorable works: *Proposal for Universal Use of Irish Manufacture* (1720), *Drapier's Letters* (1724), and *A Modest Proposal* (1729), earning him the status of an Irish patriot. Also during these years, he began writing his masterpiece, *Travels into Several Remote Nations of the World, in Four Parts, by Lemuel Gulliver, first a surgeon, and then a captain of several ships*, better known as *Gulliver's Travels*. Much of the material reflects his political experiences of the preceding decade. For instance, the episode when the giant Gulliver puts out the Lilliputian palace fire by urinating on it can be seen as a metaphor for the Tories' illegal peace treaty; having done a good thing in an unfortunate manner.

In 1726 he paid a long-deferred visit to London, taking with him the manuscript of *Gulliver's Travels*. During his visit he stayed with his old friends, Alexander Pope, John Arbuthnot, and John Gay, who helped him arrange for the anonymous publication of his book.

First published in November 1726, it was an immediate hit, with a total of three printings that year and another in early 1727. French, German, and Dutch translations appeared in 1727 and pirated copies were printed in Ireland. Swift returned to England one more time in 1727 and stayed with Alexander Pope once again.

The visit was cut short when he received word that Esther Johnson was dying and Swift rushed back home to be with her. On 28 January 1728, Esther Johnson died, though he prayed at her bedside, even composing prayers for her comfort. Swift could not bear to be present at the end, but on the night of her death he began to write his *The Death of Mrs. Johnson*.

He was too ill to attend the funeral at St. Patrick's. Many years later, a lock of hair, assumed to be Esther Johnson's, was found in his desk, wrapped in a paper bearing the words, "Only a woman's hair."Death became a frequent feature in Swift's life from this point. In 1731 he wrote *Verses on the Death of Dr. Swift,* his own obituary published in 1739. In 1732, his good friend and collaborator John Gay died. In 1735, John Arbuthnot, another friend from his days in London, died. In 1738 Swift began to show signs of illness and in 1742 he appears to have suffered a stroke, losing the ability to speak and realizing his worst fears of becoming mentally disabled. ("I shall be like that tree," he once said, "I shall die at the top.") In order to protect him from unscrupulous hangers on, who had begun to prey on the great man, his closest companions had him declared of "unsound mind and memory." However, it was long believed by many that Swift was really insane at this point. In his book *Literature and Western Man,* author J.B. Priestley even cites the final chapters of *Gulliver's Travels* as proof of Swift's approaching "insanity". In 1744, Alexander Pope died.

Then, on October 19, 1745, Swift died. After being laid out in public view for the people of Dublin to pay their last respects, he was buried by Esther Johnson's side, in accordance with his wishes.

The bulk of his fortune was left to found a hospital for the mentally ill, originally known as St. Patrick's Hospital for Imbeciles, which opened in 1757, and which still exists as a psychiatric hospital.

EPITAPH

Jonathan swift wrote his own epitaph:

Hic depositum est corpus
Ionathan swift s.t.d.
Huyus ecclesiæ cathedralis
Decani,
Ubi sæva indignatio
Ulterius
Cor lacerare nequit,
Abi viator
Et imitare, si poteris,
Strenuum pro virili

Libertatis vindicatorem.
Obiit 19 die mensis octobris
A.d. 1745 anno ætatis 78.
Which william butler yeats translated from the latin as:
Swift has sailed into his rest.
Savage indignation there
Cannot lacerate his breast.
Imitate him if you dare,
World-besotted traveller.
He served human liberty.

WORKS

Swift was a prolific writer, notable for his satires. The most recent collection of his prose works (Herbert Davis, ed. Basil Blackwell, 1965-) comprises fourteen volumes. A recent edition of his complete poetry (Pat Rodges, ed. Penguin, 1983) is 953 pages long. One edition of his correspondence (David Woolley, ed. P. Lang, 1999) fills three volumes.

MAJOR PROSE WORKS

Swift's first major prose play, *A Tale of a Tub*, demonstrates many of the themes and stylistic techniques he would employ in his later work.

It is at once wildly playful and funny while being pointed and harshly critical of its targets. In its main thread, the *Tale* recounts the exploits of three sons, representing the main threads of Christianity, who receive a bequest from their father of a coat each, with the added instructions to make no alterations whatsoever.

However, the sons soon find that their coats have fallen out of current fashion and begin to look for loopholes in their father's will which will allow them to make the needed alterations. As each finds his own means of getting around their father's admonition, they struggle with each other for power and dominance. Inserted into this story, in alternating chapters, Swift includes a series of whimsical "digressions" on various subjects.

In 1690, Sir William Temple, Swift's patron, published *An Essay upon Ancient and Modern Learning* a defence of classical writing (see Quarrel of the Ancients and the Moderns) holding up the *Epistles of Phalaris* as an example. William Wotton responded to Temple with *Reflections upon Ancient and Modern Learning* (1694) showing that the *Epistles* were a later forgery. A response by the supporters of the Ancients was then made by Charles Boyle (later the 4th Earl of Orrery and father of Swift's first biographer).

A further retort on the Modern side came from Richard Bentley, one of the pre-eminent scholars of the day, in his essay *Dissertation upon the Epistles of Phalaris* (1699). However, the final words on the topic belong to Swift in his *Battle of the Books* (1697, published 1704) in which he makes a humorous defence on behalf of Temple and the cause of the Ancients.In 1708, a cobbler named John Partridge published a popular almanac of astrological predictions. Because Partridge falsely determined the deaths of several church officials, Swift attacked Partridge in *Predictions For The Ensuing Year* by Isaac Bickerstaff, a parody predicting that Partridge would die on March 29th. Swift followed up with a pamphlet issued on March 30th claiming that Partridge had in fact died, which was widely believed despite Partridge's statements to the contrary.

Drapier's Letters (1724) was a series of pamphlets against the monopoly granted by the English government to William Wood to provide the Irish with copper coinage. It was widely believed that Wood would need to flood Ireland with debased coinage in order make a profit.

In these "letters" Swift posed as a shop-keeper a draper in order to criticize the plan. Swift's writing was so effective in undermining opinion in the project that a reward was offered by the government to anyone disclosing the true identity of the author.

Though hardly a secret (on returning to Dublin after one of his trips to England, Swift was greeted with a banner, "Welcome Home, Drapier") no one turned Swift in. The government eventually resorted to hiring none other than Sir

Isaac Newton to certify the soundness of Wood's coinage to counter Swift's accusations. In "Verses on the Death of Dr. Swift" (1739) Swift recalled this as one of his best achievements.

Gulliver's Travels, first published in 1726, is Swift's masterpiece. As with his other writings, the *Travels* was published under a pseudonym, the fictional Lemuel Gulliver, a ship's surgeon and later a sea captain. Some of the correspondence between printer Benj. Motte and Gulliver's also-fictional cousin negotiating the book's publication has survived.

Though it has often been mistakenly thought of and published in bowdlerized form as a children's book, it is a great and sophisticated satire of human nature based on Swift's experience of his times. *Gulliver's Travels* is an anatomy of human nature, a sardonic looking-glass, often criticized for its apparent misanthropy. It asks its readers to refute it, to deny that it has not adequately characterized human nature and society.

Each of the four books recounting four voyages to mostly-fictional exotic lands has a different theme, but all are attempts to deflate human pride. Critics hail the work as a satiric reflection on the failings of Enlightenment modernism.

In 1729, he published *A Modest Proposal for Preventing the Children of Poor People in Ireland Being a Burden to Their Parents or Country, and for Making Them Beneficial to the Public,* a satire in which the narrator, with intentionally grotesque logic, recommends that Ireland's poor escape their poverty by selling their children as food to the rich: "I have been assured by a very knowing American of my acquaintance in London, that a young healthy child well nursed is at a year old a most delicious, nourishing, and wholesome food..." Following the satirical form, he introduces the reforms he is actually suggesting by deriding them.

Therefore let no man talk to me of other expedients ... taxing our absentees ... using [nothing] except what is of our own growth and manufacture ... rejecting ... foreign luxury ... introducing a vein of parsimony, prudence and temperance ... learning to love our country ... quitting our animosities and factions ... teaching landlords to have at least one degree of mercy towards their tenants.

Therefore I repeat, let no man talk to me of these and the like expedients, 'till he hath at least some glympse of hope, that there will ever be some hearty and sincere attempt to put them into practice.

According to other sources, Richard Steele uses the personae of Isaac Bickerstaff and was the one who wrote about the "death" of John Partridge and published it in *The Spectator,* not Jonathan Swift.

ESSAYS, TRACTS, PAMPHLETS, PERIODICALS

Swift as depicted on the Irish £10 banknote, issued 1976–1993.

- "A Meditation upon a Broomstick" (1703–1710)
- "A Critical Essay upon the Faculties of the Mind" (1707–1711)
- The Bickerstaff-Partridge Papers (1708–1709)
- "An Argument Against Abolishing Christianity" (1708–1711)
- *The Intelligencer* (with Thomas Sheridan) (1710-????)
- *The Examiner* (1710)
- "A Proposal for Correcting, Improving and Ascertaining the English Tongue" (1712)
- "On the Conduct of the Allies" (1713)
- "Hints Toward an Essay on Conversation" (1713)
- "A Letter to a Young Gentleman, Lately Entered into Holy Orders" (1720)
- "A Letter of Advice to a Young Poet" (1721)
- *Drapier's Letters* (1724, 1725)
- "Bon Mots de Stella" (1726): a curiously irrelevant appendix to "Gulliver's Travels"
- "A Modest Proposal", perhaps the most notable satire in English, suggesting that the Irish should engage in cannibalism. (Written in 1729)

- "An Essay on the Fates of Clergymen"
- "A Treatise on Good Manners and Good Breeding"

POEMS

An 1850 illustration of Swift.

- "Ode to the Athenian Society" 1692 (first published work)
- Poems of Jonathan Swift, D.D. Texts at Project Gutenberg: Volume One, Volume Two
- "Baucis and Philemon" (1706–1709)
- "A Description of the Morning" (1709)
- "A Description of a City Shower" (1710)
- "Cadenus and Vanessa" (1713)
- "Phillis, or, the Progress of Love" (1719)
- Stella's birthday poems
    - 1719. Full annotated text
    - 1720. Full text
    - 1727. Full text
- "The Progress of Beauty" (1719–1720)
- "The Progress of Poetry" (1720)
- "A Satirical Elegy on the Death of a Late Famous General" (1722)
- "To Quilca, a Country House not in Good Repair" (1725)
- "Advice to the Grub Street Verse-writers" (1726)
- "The Furniture of a Woman's Mind" (1727)
- "On a Very Old Glass" (1728)
- "A Pastoral Dialogue" (1729)
- "The Grand Question debated Whether Hamilton's Bawn should be turned into a Barrack or a Malt House" (1729)
- "On Stephen Duck, the Thresher and Favourite Poet" (1730)
- "Death and Daphne" (1730)

- "The Place of the Damn'd" (1731)
- "A Beautiful Young Nymph Going to Bed" (1731)
- "Strephon and Chloe" (1731)
- "Helter Skelter" (1731)
- "Cassinus and Peter: A Tragical Elegy" (1731)
- "The Day of Judgment" (1731)
- "Verses on the Death of Dr. Swift, D.S.P.D." (1731–1732)
- "An Epistle To A Lady" (1732)
- "The Beasts' Confession to the Priest" (1732)
- "The Lady's Dressing Room" (1732)
- "On Poetry: A Rhapsody" (1733)
- "The Puppet Show"
- "The Logicians Refuted"

CORRESPONDENCE, PERSONAL WRITINGS

- "When I Come to Be Old" Swift's resolutions. (1699)
- *The Journal to Stella* (1710–1713)
- Letters:
  - Selected Letters: JaffeBros
- 'The Correspondence of Jonathan Swift, D.D'.

SERMONS, PRAYERS

- Three Sermons and Three Prayers
- Three Sermons: I. on mutual subjection. II. on conscience. III. on the trinity.
- Writings on Religion and the Church.
- "The First He Wrote Oct. 17, 1727."
- "The Second Prayer Was Written Nov. 6, 1727."

MISCELLANY

- *Directions to Servants* (1731)
- *A Complete Collection of Genteel and Ingenious Conversation* (1738)

- "Thoughts on Various Subjects."
- Historical Writings: Project Gutenberg
- Swift Quotations: JaffeBros many choice, well-documented Swift quotations here
- Swift quotes at Bartleby

LEGACY

John Ruskin named him as one of the three people in history who were the most influential for him.

Chapter 2

Jonathan Swift's Voyage to Lilliput

Of the four parts of Gulliver's Travels, the third, the Voyage to Laputa, is for many the least satisfying and least understood. The conventional critical take on Part Three is that the entire series of episodes is fundamentally pointless and artless in comparison. It does of course satirize the new trends in mathematics and theoretical science and politics but does so with less finesse than Swift does in his accounts of Gulliver's three other voyages.

The centre for these criticisms focus on the episodic character of the third voyage, the multiplicity of themes and the lack of clear philosophical intuition in the voyages to Lilliput and Brobdingnag or the savage attacks on the human condition in the voyage to the Houyhnhnyms. The three themes that critics find distasteful are the curious combinations of mathematics and music displayed by the Laputans, the lack of unity displayed by the Balnibarians especially the series of experiments at the Grand Academy of Lagado, and the so-called magical apparatus the Flying Island a device Swift borrowed from other sources.

The simplest defence I think of these charges that Swift does not equal in Part III the standards of the rest of the voyages is to argue that this structure is quite deliberate. The word Laputa is derived as out text reminds us in a footnote on p.135 from the Spanish La Puta the whore. It is about a people and a place that deals unnaturally with its physical nature. If the structure and themes in this part of the story strike as unnatural, fragmented and incoherent it might well be that this is what Swift intends. Unnatural and disjointed and impractical philosophies make for unnatural, fragmented and impractical social structures. The third voyage I argue is meant not as a blanket condemnation of new sciences or new philosophies but as a warning to this imprudently over optimistic era to keep its eye on the past and its head out of the clouds. We need to notice too that the work here is not purely fanciful, even though on first reading it may not seem so. Swift draws nearly all of his satirical material from the genuine articles.

Most of the ideas he presents are based on real experiments reported in the literature of his day and particularly on reports published in the Philosophical Transactions of the Royal Society during the last third of the 17th century and the first quarter of the 18th up to and including material published in 1726 the year Swift composed Part III.

Swift uses this material extrapolated of course to ludicrous extremes-which he then blends with the then prevalent attitude that all mathematical and theoretical learning was "useless," to weave his underlying message that the "virtuosi" of his day had lost sight of the world at large. Modern society is not entirely unfamiliar with this still persistent view.

Public perception still portrays absent minded unworldly scientists sporting pocket protectors pursuing unrealistic goals. Whether Swift intends this as a viscous attack on the new science or a call for balance depends on how we read the text. One of his sources for his satire on the Laputan fusion of geometry and music, to the exclusion of everything else, was the celebrated scientist Christiaan Huygens.

In 1677 Huygens had written that, "no matter how inhabitants of other planets might differ from man in other ways, they must agree in music and geometry, since [music and geometry] are everywhere immutably the same, and always will be so."

As satisfying as such a "universal" idea might seem and it is intriguing the role of the satirist is to make sure such ideas are seen in proper relief. Worshipping circles, ellipses, parabolas, oboes and violins and praising the beauties of the world in like fashion is after all an unbalanced response. Furthermore, the "new philosophies" of Swift's time-political, moral and natural-might not last-and history has shown this. New philosophies do not always endure. Everything has its fashion-everything has its day.

Lucian-a satirist living in the second century who Swift greatly admired had done the same thing on the "old" philosophies 1,500 years earlier. Lucian had once written a work called "Philosophies Going cheap." In it, Pythagoras and Socrates, among others, were parodied with wit equal to that of Swift in his day.

Swift's astounding "discovery" of the two moons of Mars known now as Phobos and Deimos 150 years before they were first discovered by Hall in 1877 was nothing more than a lucky guess: but the guess was a good one and showed that Swift was no slouch he did careful research and based his other speculations in the third voyage on real evidence. As for Mars, Swift knew that earth had one moon and Jupiter four Galileo has demonstrated that in the "Starry Message."

In his day Cassini had reported 5 moons around Saturn. What about Mars? Well, the sequence ran one for Earth, blank for Mars, four for Jupiter, and five for Saturn. For Mars, the "blank," he might have guessed 2 or 3. He guessed two. Swift was not a mathematician but he could handle Kepler's laws, so he devised orbital periods for those two moons with simple to handle times of 10 and 20 hours which placed them at the distances he used in the story these are a fair guess but far from an exact approximation to the 9,300 and 23,500 km distances they actually are.

Those moons are by the way quite small if you placed the largest, Deimos, in downtown Nanaimo, its outer edge would extend only to the Departure Bay Ferry terminal. The Laputans fear of the sun and of comets was rooted in some very real anxieties. That the earth might be swallowed by the sun or that the sun would be "encrusted by its own effluvia" was a general and genuine concern. No less than the mighty Newton himself had, in his Principia, noted that the balance between the earth's orbital velocity, and its fall toward the sun, was extremely delicate. Any disturbance in that, Newton had said, would be disastrous. Although Newton concluded that any slowing of the earth as it moved about the sun through whatever was in its way was indeed small others were not so sure.

This fear was tied up in the seemingly unrelated discussions about the nature of light. If light was some kind of a wave motion, it would require some sort of medium to get from the sun to the earth all waves known then needed something to be waves in! However, if light was made of particles or corpuscles as Newton called them no medium was necessary.

Newton an advocate of the particle or corpuscular theory needed no medium but Robert Hooke an opponent of Newton believed light was wave like. If Hooke was right, the earth was in trouble the stuff whatever it was that light needed to move through would slow the earth down and we would fall into the sun! History has shown that Newton was half right for the wrong reason and that Hooke was also half right also for the wrong reason light is both a particle and a wave but requires no medium to get from the sun to the earth.

The concern over the sun's demise was also genuine, in the context of the times. Galileo had discovered those embarrassing spots on the sun in the beginning of the 17th century. By Swift's day speculations on the nature of the spots centered on the possibility that they were caused by sub-solar volcanic eruptions a form of smoke indicating that the sun was consuming itself up at a prodigious rate. Modern calculations confirm this.

The sun's mass is reduced by something like four million metric tonnes every second! Had Swift's contemporaries known that they would have freaked. They knew nothing of course about nuclear energy in 1726. Lucky they did not--a little knowledge is a dangerous thing. The sun's gradual loss of mass through nuclear conversion, means that the gravitational attraction weakens over time-heralding a widening orbit and perhaps a spiraling away from the sun.

The fear of comets was yet another source of genuine

social anxiety. Employing Newton's newly expounded theory of universal gravitation Edmund Halley has forecasted that the comet of 1682 known now as Halley's comet would return in 1758. Remember Swift is writing here in 1726 and projecting in his reference to a Laputan comet 31 years in the future. That comet did, by the way, return spotted first on Christmas day in 1758 and became a source of universal amazement of the exactitude of Newton's science.

In fact, it was a bit late, caused we know now, by the perturbing effects of the planets Uranus and Neptune which were undiscovered in Newton's day. The social anxiety around the comet's return was occasioned by none other than Halley himself who in 1694 had written a paper speculating that the biblical flood described in Genesis might have been occasioned by the shock from a near miss from a comet. Halley noted in his writing that a near miss could indeed reduce the earth to its "ancient chaos."

It was nail biting time in Europe. Is there any wonder Swift enjoys playing on those fears? Swift has most of his fun playing with the work of the projectors at the Academy of Lagado. Their work is in the main drawn from real stuff but he takes real experiments a step beyond their original intent or combines cleverly work reported in two different experiments. The conversion of human excrement back into the original food was not one of those. That example was based on a work written by Rabelais called "Archasdarpenin."

The novel building methods Swift talks about building from the roof down was loosely written around architectural ideas advanced by Christopher Wren the designer of St. Paul's Cathedral. Surprisingly, the example of the blind projector who was able to feel colours was based on a real paper.

In a condensed version of Robert Boyle's Philosophical Works published the year before Swift wrote, there is a report of a blind man at the city of Maestrict who could distinguish colours by the touch of his fingers. A careful series of experiments in which the man was given a collection of colored ribbons and blindfolded don't ask (he was supposed to be blind) confirmed the man's ability to identify the primary colors: red, blue, green and yellow, as well as black, white and gray. He described the feeling as being particularly acute in his right thumb and described the effect as due to "aspirations" from the material. Black felt like tingly points. Red felt smooth.

There was actually some credible "science" here. Or there may have been. Boyle is skeptical about the feeling bit and ventured that the ability was due to the man's sensitivity not to colour but to the scents in the dyes used to colour the ribbons. He noticed that the blind man's capacity to detect colour was affected by eating. Dogs he also noticed had their sense of smell reduced after eating too.

The story about spiders spinning naturally colored silk stockings also has some basis in fact but is a classic blending by Swift of two unrelated reports. In 1710 Emile Pons published an account called "The Silk of Spiders" in the Philosophical Transactions. His paper described how he actually made gloves and stockings from the threads that short legged spiders used to wrap around their eggs-not the webs used to weave their webs. He also offered that this spider material easily "took colour."

The second source Swift uses here was one by a Dr. Hall who described in a 1708 paper how pismires (ants) in the East Indies could convert tree saps and natural gums into excrement-excrement that retained the natural colors of those saps.

This conversion, Hall noted, was unique in nature and probably caused by a chemical conversion involving formic acid. It was Swift who tied the two ideas-spider silk to ant "poop," into the novel method for weaving naturally colored silk stockings.

The story about converting calcine ice (hailstones) into gunpowder was based on a 1693 description, again in the Transactions, of investigations on the explosive noises made by the bursting of hailstones after being thrown into fire. The bursting was caused by the sudden fractures in the crystal structure of the ice, and I'm sure the original investigations were learning that-but Swift decided to place another spin due perhaps to an allusion in that same paper that some hailstones had dark matter at their centers. Swift decided to infer that the bursting and dark matter was connected-possibly a natural source of gunpowder? The wonderful research on sunbeams and cucumbers was derived from a 1693 paper by Halley on the "Circulation of Watery Vapours" and also a lot of other pioneering work at the time on the nature of light, heat and the respiration of plants. As satiric as that episode may have seemed to his 18th century audience, we know now that cucumbers do work like that-store solar energy through photosynthesis as plant material and release it as heat and food energy when it is consumed. Perhaps Swift knew this intuitively at the time?

Swift's idea for using 600 hogs simultaneously furrowing and manuring a field was drawn from a 1702 paper on the Culturing of Tobacco in Zeylon where Buffaloes were used in a similar fashion.

Swift's universal artist whose designs included the propagation of naked sheep may be directed at Robert Boyle. There's lots of other great stuff.

This marvelously clever computing device is eerily prophetic of a time-our time perhaps when society would place more value on "instrumental reason" than the more natural forces of reason at our disposal.

The bits in Chapter VI on the political researches are clearly directed at Thomas Hobbes' Leviathan and the natural resemblance between-in Swift's words, the "strict universal Resemblance between the natural and political body."

What better justification for carrying out political experiments drawn from this analogy? My favourite bit there was a proposal to sever and exchange the half brains of quarreling politicians leaving them to debate matters "between themselves within the space of one Skull!" Swift's description of experiments designed to analyse the odor, Colour, consistence, and taste! of human excrement as a means of detecting threats to the state is exquisite madness-Swift at his piercing best. "Men are never so serious, and intent, as when they are at Stool." Swift's visit to Glubbdubdrib-the island of sorcerers and magicians--where he is able to call back the dead-is a transparent copy of Lucian of Samosata's True Histories where similar encounters with the dead were described. In his story Swift describes Homer-who legend had always treated as blind as having the most quick and piercing eyes I ever beheld." Lucian in his story written 1,500 years earlier says that he had no need to ask Homer if he was really blind for, "I could see for myself that he was nothing of the sort." Lucian-in this same episode also describes a fanciful voyage to the moon-a voyage that involved encounters with moon men every bit as strange and metamorphic as Swift's.

Swift most certainly based much of his style on his. Whatever the validity of the criticisms of the Voyage to Laputa, its lack of unity, and multiplicity of themes, this adventure does paint a picture of an age which although optimistic and heady over its recent achievements, is clearly anxious about the future. Swift is clearly wistful for ancient virtues and solid values, and indicates so often, but I don't see this story as an injunction to regress.

What he offers us is a series of cautions and warnings about modern times. The human project is off and running-Swift knows that-as much as a parent knows that the child who finally leaves the nest is not going to return. But like the young adult-incautious and fearless about taking on the world, Swift is shaking a finger at his age-be prudent-keep your head out of the clouds-look both ways before crossing the street-and above all remember your parents and those virtues we taught you!

Chapter 3

Measurement, Irony and the Grotesque in Gulliver's Travels

Postmodernity is obsessed with the Eighteenth Century. As an example of how our nostalgia for that period manifests itself, Hans Kellner has pointed out that a genre of novels and films set in Eighteenth century has exploded in popularity: Lempriere's Dictionary, Perfume, "The Madness of King George III." We could also point to the ongoing revision of scholarship on the period, of which GEMCS itself is an example.

In considering what generates this contemporary fascination I have given some thought to the aesthetic and political issues surrounding the beginnings, and perhaps also the end, of the bourgeois social sphere. A conviction, argued most aggressively by Jean Baudrillard, is beginning to take hold, in and out of the academy, that this sphere, after an almost totalizing expansion, is now in decline.

The panic over the loss of the social, whether supportable or not, offers a possible explanation for the contemporary nostalgia for the period in which Swift wrote Gulliver's Travels. In this age of dissolution, what do we see when we look back at the age of our creation? One thing we observe is the development of a peculiar kind of irony which we can't help but distinguish from our experience of this trope in the age of its dominance.

The satirical effect of the irony in Gulliver's Travels read by the Postmodern will be precisely what it was not at the time of its production. The historical distance between Eighteenth

Century and Contemporary readers can be understood by way of Hayden White's use of the master tropes in "Foucault Decoded." White assigns one of the master tropes to each of the four archeological periods described by Foucault in The Order of Things. In White's system, Foucault's Renaissance was metaphorical, locating truth in similarity.

Swift wrote in what Foucault considered the Classical Period, which, for White, had metonymy as its overriding mode of reason, because a new transparency of representation made it possible to organize knowledge by a standard and represent it symbolically on a table.

The Modern period was characterized by synecdoche, in that the subject of knowledge, Man, was now included in the study of the world, in a part-whole relationship. Finally, the Contemporary or Postmodern mode is ironic, characterized by a questioning of the foundations of knowledge and a Dionysian disappearance of the subject of that knowledge.

It is in this epistemological space that Baudrillard can argue that representation is no longer transparent, or even opaque, but impossible, as the world of signifieds has been swallowed by the world of signifiers, leaving only signifiers.

Given a depthless world of signs, or if you wish, given The Age Of Irony, it seems fitting that Foucault should have privileged literature within the system of The Order of Things, because literature is the world of signifiers that admits readily that its connection to the signifieds of the Real is only suggested and always deferred.

While Foucault and White show the sciences of each period to be trapped within a single trope, literature enjoys a singular ability to step outside, move between, or encompass more than one of these modal tropes. Literature invites its reader to draw metaphorical connections between the prose and what the reader sees as his or her own personal experience.

Gulliver's function as a measuring stick is metonymic: he comes from the British world ostensibly the land of the Real and so the British reader feels he can be used to establish differences between the Real and the fantasy worlds he visits. This process reflects the ideological construction of the British

Subject in the Colonial period. The aspect of the observed that can be measured by Gulliver serves to organize and name the whole, excluding whatever remains. In other words, just as a thermometer does not measure intelligence, the yardstick of rationality Gulliver finally brings down on the Yahoos fails to measure warmth, or any other human or British quality, if I can rightly call warmth a British quality.

Gulliver's journey becomes synecdochic when he serves a role in the visited society and this role has a reciprocal effect on his own character; he no longer can be said to function as a constant or impartial measure.

His trustworthiness as narrator is undermined and his representations become opaque or fall under suspect. This blow to representation brings the grotesque into play. As Gulliver changes scenes, the multiplicity of perspectives forces an ironic mode on the reader, in which the grotesque gains destabilizing power.

To clarify what it means that the grotesque destabilizes in an Age of Irony, we can examine, for contrast, the role of the grotesque in the aesthetic of Swift's time, in the Age of metonymy, measurement, and of course, Reason. In The Politics and Poetics of Transgression, Stallybrass and White document the active role played by literary artists in the creation of a public sphere in the late-Seventeenth and early-Eighteenth centuries. Dryden, Pope and Swift are given as examples of artists who use the grotesque as a domesticated sign of the low intended to embarrass the audience into self-regulation.

This device was part of a larger Programme to create a rational space for discourse, a social sphere aligned with the coffee house and in direct opposition to the participatory carnivals and rowdy playhouses. So, while readers could enjoy the comedy of Swift's obscene portrayal of the body, as a rule they would have projected this disgust away from themselves and at the unfit audience of the popular playhouse, associating themselves with the rational social sphere or the coffee-house.

The political-aesthetic of the time could not allow a freely or multiplicitously ironic reading of Swift's irony. Rather, the rhetorical effect of Swift's irony was actually metonymic, reaffirming bourgeois values by employing the bodily grotesque as a signifier for the undesirable playhouse and carnival. This metonymic dissassociation of the self from the body in aesthetics was aligned with the rise of scientific rationality. Despite the fanciful nature of Swift's writing, Swift's ironic descriptions of science should not be read as broadside attacks against science and rationality, but against human fantasy when it intrudes on the careful empirical progress of knowledge.

Frances Louis argues in Swift's Anatomy of Misunderstanding, in a chapter section significantly entitled "The Real Thing," that Swift, like the Royal Society friends he would have met in the coffee houses, believed in "an unquestioned physical reality to be approached straightaway".

His irony, then, could not have the effect of undermining any of the basic ideological assumptions of his readers in The Age of Metonymy. Rather, his irony warns them away from the very ridiculousness you find in his writing and calls them back to the safety of the metonymic ideology of species-genus analytics: it guides them back to "The Real Thing."

Jean Baudrillard argues that the radical expansion of this social sphere, which provided the environment in which Gulliver's Travels could be written, has led to the loss of The Real Thing. The mechanical reproduction of the Real, made socially possible by the communicative freedom of the social sphere, the invention of mechanical and electronic reproduction, and, importantly, the construction of a self-regulated audience, capable of receiving rational discourse, has produced an excess of information.

The social grew and grew until the information it produced was more than it could digest. We are in a period of social implosion, analogous to the run on the commercial banks that occured before the Great Depression, when it became clear that there was not enough capital for everyone to withdraw their funds. There is not enough Real to guarantee the representative capacity of our representations of the Real. The return of the Postmodern imagination to an earlier time, before the disappearance of reality, represents an ideological bum rush on the fountain of reality.

The use of representation to regain reality, of course, only creates more excess, exasperating our depression in the economy of signs.

Significantly, Baudrillard links the proliferation of signs to nuclear proliferation, because just as the nuclear threat provides a deterrence against warfare, the excess proliferation of signs creates a psychological deterrence against any meaningful use of these signs, particularly against the political use-value of signification. Given this change in the economy of signs, it becomes clear that the use-value of Swift's employment of irony and the grotesque in Gulliver's Travels could not be constant throughout these historical changes, that its consumption now will mean precisely what it did not at the time of its production.

Harold Bloom noted in a 1986 introduction that, in the fourth voyage of Gulliver's Travels, "Swift rather dubiously seems to want it every which way at once, so that the Yahoos both are and are not representations of ourselves, and the Houyhnhnms are and are not wholly admirable or ideal. Or is it the nature of irony itself, which must weary us, or finally make us long for a true sublime, even if it should turn out to be grotesque"?

In the metonymic political-aesthetic of the early Eighteenth Century, this ironic trap had a fixed satirical message: separate and temper body and mind. As Gulliver says: When I behold a Lump of Deformity, and Diseases both in Body and Mind, smitten with Pride, it immediately breaks all the Measures of my Patience.

However, the contemporary reader knows far less about how we would enforce this dualism of good Behaviour. The satirical function of irony has transmuted into a pastiche, devoid of ideology. The reigning metonymic structure of Classical thought ordained that no message, not even one more difficult to interpret than Gulliver's, could have failed to reify the developing bourgeois ideology circulated within the early social sphere. Now, reading within the suction of the implosion of the bloated social sphere, meanings proliferate endlessly in excess, an excess which is indistinguishable from lack, and which causes even Harold Bloom to throw up his hands at the problem. In the words of this Postmodern reader, "Swift audaciously plays at the farthest limits of irony, limits that make satire impossible, because no norm exists to which we might hope to return". Gulliver's Travels signifies everything and nothing.

If the rhetorical power of irony has developed in accordance with the social sphere's explosion and implosion, so has the intertwined relevance of measurement and the grotesque. The political and aesthetic regulation of measurement and the grotesque represented an alienation of the shared space of the body in favour of a new, singular empiricism which harnessed the power of vision as never before.

The hidden origins of thought, the smallest particles, the previously unspeakable biology, the physical laws, even our unconscious motivations have all been brought to the surface by Gulliver's powers of observation and measurement. But, saying everything is visible at the surface now amounts to the same as revealing the absence of depth. No unconscious, no invisibility, nothing unspeakable, because if these things existed, they would be in view.

There is no postmodern grotesque or sublime, because these suggest a source of values that can differentiate between the acceptable and the grotesque and an unknowable that can be suggested by the sublime. We have the amplified state of the grotesque and the sublime, the ob-scene: after the absolute success of metonymic reasoning, everything is more visible than visible.

It is tempting, in the desire to maintain a responsible form of social criticism, to reject Baudrillard's line of reasoning out-of-hand as an apolitical or even regressive form of uncritical hype. But, in his words, his writing is not apolitical but hyperpolitical. It is because everything is political that no political difference can be grasped and put to use: Consider this passage from Baudrillard's Fatal Strategies:

We thought we discovered something subversive when we affirmed that the body [was]... political. We have only precipitated their indifferentiation into an analytical and ideological fog a little like discovering that all illnesses are psychosomatic. A wonderful discovery, but one which gets you nowhere: it just assigns them to a more poorly defined category.

Everywhere the widely accepted obviousness of a generalization of this order political, cultural, social, sexual, psychological marks its death sentence (57-8). So, what shall we make of our own quasi-objective revision of the Eighteenth Century? Why are we wading through the textual evidence like so many Gullivers, colonizing the radical Otherness of the past? Is this the death drive of the metonymic subject? In what Baudrillard reminds us is the most important master-slave relationship, we are subjects inspecting objects, like Gulliver among the Houyhnhnms.

Why does the Gulliver, who should have been the master, bow down before these horses? Why does he prefer them to his own land and kind, forsaking the Real? Though no meaning can be made of this in our Age of Irony, we can recognize this same passive seduction by the object in our nostalgia for the Eighteenth Century.

Chapter 4

Modes of Reading, and Modes of Reading Swift

Over the past few years it has become clear to me that I don't know nearly as much about reading as I once did. For instance, ten years ago I was sure I knew what one did with a passage like the one I'm going to quote here. In fact, what I did know was what one was supposed to do with it, and it was fairly direct (if not exactly uncomplicated): one was to find out what its real meaning was.

I now think, however, that the act of reading is a lot more complicated than that model allowed for, perhaps especially when you're dealing with a text that is as rich and rewarding and endlessly engaging as the one I'm going to cite here (or, perhaps, as rich as most of the texts we've all agreed to call "classics" of literature). Thus I'm no longer nearly so sure I know the appropriate way to deal with this text.

These days, I can think of at least four quite different ways in which one might read it. It's an excerpt from a book published anonymously in London in the year 1726. In it, a world traveller who identifies himself as one Lemuel Gulliver describes a custom he's observed in one country he visited. He calls the participants "Rope-Dancers":

This Diversion is only practised by those Persons who are Candidates for great Employments, and high Favour, at Court. They are trained in this Art from their Youth, and are not always of noble Birth, or liberal Education. When a great Office is vacant either by Death or Disgrace (which often happens), five or six of those Candidates petition the Emperor to entertain his Majesty and the Court with a Dance on the Rope, and whoever jumps the highest without falling, succeeds in the Office. Very often the chief Ministers themselves are commanded to shew their Skill, and to convince the Emperor that they have not lost their Faculty.

Flimnap, the Treasurer, is allowed to cut a Caper on the strait Rope, at least an inch higher than any other Lord in the whole Empire. I have seen him do the Summerset several times together upon a Trencher fixed on the Rope, which is no thicker than a common Packthread in England. My friend Reldresal, principal Secretary for private Affairs, is, in my opinion, if I am not partial, the second after the Treasurer; the rest of the great Officers are much upon a Par.

In an article in *College English* in 1987, William Dowling, a respected scholar of eighteenth-century literature, pointed out that when he studied Swift in university, this in part is what was offered by the notes on that passage in the text he used (it was also the one I used when I studied Swift as an undergraduate):

Flimnap represents the famous Whig statesman, Sir Robert Walpole, head of the government from 1715 to 1717 and from 1721 to 1742. His political dexterity is here satirized. Swift disliked him both as a man and a politician.... Reldresal [is] possibly Lord Carteret, Secretary of State in 1721 and later Lord-Lieutenant of Ireland;... Also suggested as Reldresal: Lord Townshend, Secretary of State and a chief ally of Walpole.

Now, Dowling can't for the life of him understand nor can I how we ever came to like the eighteenth century and its literature in the face of the assumptions ab out reading that seem to be implicit in that note. As Dowling phrases it, "The most unrepentant biographical-historical critic who ever lived might see, one supposes, the sense in which this sort of thing spells death in the classroom".

It is clear, though, that Louis Landa, who wrote the notes to that edition, believed and we must agree that the reasons he believed it were not trivial ones that it was important for students to follow the complex political and social allegory of Gulliver's visit to Lilliput.

Still, it is apparent that that note invites you to read as though the text were primarily a source of information about the eighteenth century, an example of literary history, or evidence about the author's life. Looking at Gulliver in Lilliput in such a way you are likely to find interpretations like this appropriate: Gulliver represents Lord Bolingbroke, "tied down" (politically immobilized) by a legion of (morally or intellectually) tiny bureaucrats and packthread laws.

Lilliput is England, and Blefescu, across the channel, is France. The Emperor of Lilliput is George I. (One of the problems with this sort of allegorizing is exemplified by Arthur Case's classic footnote: "The Emperor represents George I, although much of the description of his physical and mental characteristics is inconsistent with the facts" [14-15]]. Any student must wonder, as I did, if the description were so inconsistent with "the facts," how anyone ever recognized the allegory.)

It was, of course, true that most teachers agreed with Landa that knowing about all those obscure details of the history of English parliamentary politics was justified because it helped us enjoy Swift. And as it turned out, Dowling and I, and a few other people, must have enjoyed him: we apparently did, in fact, go on to read lots of other eighteenth-century texts, and build up our knowledge of the background, and sometimes even became experts on the political allegory of *Gulliver's Travels* and professors of eighteenth-century literature.

Most people, though, responded exactly as you might expect. Dowling phrases it this way: "The dense circumstantiality of so much eighteenth-century poetry and prose, the relentless allusion to people and places and acts of Parliament one never heard of, puts off the inquiring undergraduate student". And, even for those of us whom it didn't put off, it certainly tended to render Swift a writer whose concerns seemed far distant from our own.

One important problem with that sort of focus on information is the way in which it affected how I and other students actually read and responded to Swift and other writers. At the time, of course, none of us knew that Louise Rosenblatt, in 1938, in *Literature as Exploration* a book hardly anyone in traditional university English studies was to notice until the seventies (cf. Suleiman and Crosman, and Clifford) had distinguished between two kinds of reading one might do with literary texts. She called one of them *efferent* meaning that you wanted to take something away from the reading with you to remember and the other *aesthetic* meaning that you wanted to live through an experience with the text.

That distinction and even more basically, the important idea that reading might not be a unitary, unproblematic phenomenon, but different things entirely in different situations allows me now to think more clearly about the reading I was doing then.

It was possible to read the Flimnap and Reldresal passage aesthetically with Landa's footnote staring you in the face, but it wasn't easy. And since eighteenth-century literature was so circumstantial anyway, and thus more difficult to begin with, it was pretty easy to lose sight of what Rosenblatt called the aesthetic, the "lived-through experience," and just find a way to rejoice efferently in the biographical, historical, and political details. (Or, of course, to give up on Swift altogether, which is what most people did.)

What I now suspect was particularly important about reading in this way was that it was a distancing procedure. Once I had mastered it, I could read Swift without being directly involved at all; I could admire his skill, even gasp at his rhetorical brilliance, and still hold myself quite aloof from the implications of his ideas.

Thus I never understood at all why so many nineteenth-century literary figures the most well known was William Makepeace Thackeray were so outraged, even angry, at Swift for being cynical and occasionally obscene and outrageously skeptical about human dignity. I thought of myself and my colleagues as pretty enlightened and tolerant to be able to read Swift with a cool appreciation of his brilliance.

All this was a long time ago, and in another country. Though many of us graduate students weren't exactly aware of it then, a revolution was not only underway, but had in most circles long before been won (and in fact the new regime was already under counterattack). Among people who argued and cared about literary theory and criticism, the critical approach that had come to be called New Criticism had long before swept the field, and the fruits of that revolution were already apparent in many classrooms.

(It is not entirely irrelevant, by the way, that the dominance of the New Critical defence of literature as something approaching an "objective science" was one of the main reasons so few people knew of the existence of *Literature as Exploration*.) Among lots of other changes, the New Critics offered us a new way to read *Gulliver*.

It's no simple matter to describe exactly the difference New Criticism made to the classrooms of the late fifties and early sixties. It's difficult partly because so much of what it proposed became so widely accepted that soon we didn't know we believed it any more: it became almost immediately the new common sense. Dowling presents an excellent description of the impact of New Criticism on the way he (and I) taught Swift and the other eighteenth-century writers. At the same time it suggests something more general about what the New Criticism was.

What New Criticism said, in a word, was that this episode wasn't about Robert Walpole, head of the government from 1721 to 1742: it was about politicians, who are still there, walking tightropes, in this morning's *New York Times*. Flimnap was a politician, but he was not Walpole; he was, as Fielding says about the lawyer in *Joseph Andrews*, someone who has been alive these four thousand years.

Though New Criticism said, of course, quite a lot more than that, what is relevant here is the way it convinced us all that the historical origins of a work of literature, or what you might find out about what its author thought he meant to do in it or through it, or with it, couldn't tell you what the work actually *did*: only the work could tell you that. The result of believing that was that all the work those generations of scholars had done in identifying Flimnap, and Reldresal and even the cushion that Gulliver says once kept Flimnap from breaking his neck (Queen Caroline) was rendered, apparently, irrelevant to the classroom. What mattered now was what the work meant, said, and did, in and of itself. This led us toward designating as our central critical and pedagogical activity what we called then what we still call "close reading of the text."

Rather than trying to look through the text to what might lie behind it what it might tell you about Swift's political opinions, or the character of the age he lived in, or even about Swift's psychological adjustment or lack of it we were to look at "the text itself."

This had some good effects and some bad ones. At the time, most of us who were teaching undergraduate courses in eighteenth-century literature thought the results were pretty much all to the good. Now, we thought, we could ask our students to read *Gulliver* in the faith that the text would make everything clear if only we all just read it hard enough we wouldn't have to go through that long, distracting, boring period of preparation, of filling in historical and social background, before our students would be "ready" to read Swift.

If you read the Flimnap and Reldresal passage carefully and closely enough, we said, it just sort of "automatically" became a comment on politicians in general. What else could it possibly mean? Another effect of buying into New Criticism was that we focused our attention on different kinds of passages (and, in fact, often even on different works altogether as, for instance, Donne's poetry replaced Milton's as the central work of the seventeenth century).

In the case of Gulliver, for example, different events and passages became central. Klaus Zöllner has shown how the choices of passages that scholars quoted from Gulliver to prove their various contentions changed over the course of this period how, for instance, passages concerned with *text* gradually replaced passages concerned with *philosophy*. For us as teachers, the Flimnap and Reldresal passages became more like background, and they were replaced in the centre of our lens by passages like the wonderful, ironic attack on war, when Gulliver explains to the poor, dumb king of Brobdingnag why he ought to be happy to have the secret of gunpowder. Poor Gulliver doesn't understand the king's appalled response.

The King was struck with Horror at the Description I had given of those terrible Engines and the Proposal I had made. He was amazed how so impotent and groveling an Insect as I (these were his Expressions) could entertain such inhuman Ideas, and in so familiar a Manner as to appear wholly unmoved at all the Scenes of Blood and Desolation, which I had painted ...

A strange Effect of *narrow Principles* and *short Views*! that a Prince possessed of every Quality which produces Veneration, Love and Esteem; of strong Parts, great Wisdom and profound Learning, endued with admirable Talents for Government, and almost adored by his Subjects, should from a *nice unnecessary Scruple*, whereof in Europe we can have no Conception, let slip an Opportunity put into his Hands, that would have made him absolute Master of the Lives, the Liberties, and the Fortunes of his People. Neither do I say this with the least Intention to detract from the many Virtues of that excellent King, whose character I am sensible will on this Account be very much lessened in the Opinion of an *English* Reader.

What New Criticism did with a passage like that, of course, was to direct our attention to its exquisite and elegant irony to the facts, for instance, that Gulliver had just previously betrayed himself to the king as a member of what the king now called "the most pernicious Race of little odious Vermin that Nature ever suffered to crawl upon the Surface of the Earth", and that Gulliver himself clearly has not the least idea why the king is beloved by his people, or what makes him an excellent king.

Teaching this, then, we didn't have to bother with the historical background the fact, for example, that gunpowder had been a common example of the evils of technology in the arguments between traditionalists and progressives ("Ancients" and "Moderns"), arguments that Swift had been engaged in most of his adult life. We could skip all that background and get right to the literature. Dowling says this "appeared to scholars and teachers of my generation as a kind of classroom salvation".

But, as it turned out, we weren't to be so readily saved. I now think we were deluding ourselves. That we weren't conscious of our historical and social background didn't mean it wasn't conditioning and determining how (and what) we read. It did, however, mean that when we told students that it was "just them and the text," when we assured them that if they just read closely enough they'd get it, what we really did was to make it seem like magic to most of them.

We made reading seem, even more than it had, something that only the really brilliant, the inexplicably initiated, could do. The students simply didn't have access to the contextual information we were tacitly bringing to bear on our reading and, moreover, didn't have any way to know that that was the problem.

So, just as a previous generation had done, they relied on us to tell them what the text said and, now, even to tell them what it did. The New Criticism, though it was embraced by many of us in the sixties as a method of liberating students from the domination of specialized knowledge, a way to free literature from its bondage as the private possession of a small, initiated group of highly trained specialists, didn't ultimately do that at all. What it did was to change the nature of the required training and give authority to a new group of initiated and sophisticated specialists: ourselves.

Again, let me come back to reading Swift here to make a little clearer what I mean. What happened was that a new way to read the book was substituted for the old one. The new one asked us to be aware of irony and paradox and ambiguity rather than to know or learn about historical background, and it thus asked a reader to make a quite different set of connections among elements of the text. Instead of asking students to connect Flimnap with Jonathan Swift's specific political and social context with Robert Walpole we asked them to connect him with the narrator's and the ironist's views, with Reldresal and the king and with other elements within the book. (At the same time, it was at least in part the specialist knowledge of Walpole and of Swift's social context that made it possible for us to see what kinds of connections were likely to be fruitful, although most of us were not aware of it.)

As a teacher, I found this New Critical stance a lot more comfortable, but I have never seen any convincing evidence that my students thought it was such a wonderful advance, or that they were more likely to leave my classes convinced that Swift and the other eighteenth-century writers spoke to them as well as to the ages.

I thought they enjoyed the classes a little more, but they didn't seem to enjoy Swift more. I met, ten years later, one of the brightest students I'd had in the mid-sixties, and he told me that he'd really liked the classes and the discussions of politics and morality, but he'd hated Swift and Johnson then, hadn't looked at them since, and couldn't remember anything they'd written. If I'd known of it, of course, *Literature as Exploration* might have suggested a good deal of what was wrong but of course I did not.

Another way to say this, perhaps, is that the New Critical assault had not really touched at all the citadel of the old historicism, the ability of the reader coolly and judiciously to distance herself from the text. Our distancing strategies were different, but their effect was the same: I still didn't understand why Thackeray could have been so angry. There were a lot of other reasons why we all began to question our New Critical principles in the later sixties and seventies, and many of them didn't seem to have much to do with teaching or with Swift.

One, for example, had to do with the growing interest in different kinds of texts from those predominantly, lyric poems of the seventeenth or twentieth century with which New Criticism had seemed to work reasonably well. For longer narratives, for long poems, for the novel, for texts like *Gulliver* which, when you come right down to it, doesn't have a lot of internal coherence New Criticism didn't really get us much of anywhere. After all, Flimnap and Reldresal and the rope dancing only appear once in the text: even the notion of parliamentary democracy is a preoccupation that really only occurs in Book One, and I (and many readers) have a very difficult time connecting it with the rest of *Gulliver*. It's the same with the King of Brobdingnag and the gunpowder: Swift's skepticism about technology does come up elsewhere, but you'd hardly call it the controlling theme of the book unless, of course, you were writing an article and trying to gain tenure or promotion.

But another problem was more generally important: New Criticism had called on us to disconnect writings from their authors (we weren't to ask what the author intended, or said he intended: this was Wimsatt and Beardsley's "intentional fallacy") and from their readers (we weren't to be concerned with how real readers now actually reacted: this was their "affective fallacy").

The text was all there was, and it was our job to see the real nature of each text in and of itself, to see how it attained its own unity and coherence and balance. This New Critical disconnection of the text from writer and reader as Frank Lentricchia and Terry Eagleton, among many others, have pointed out rendered literature ideologically and practically innocuous, made it seem to have little or nothing to do with real history or the real world.

As Dowling phrases it, "The same New Critical magic that made Dryden's and Pope's poetry [and Swift's prose] universal also rendered it in a curious sense bodiless, robbed it of the rootedness in human history that allows it to speak about history in a way no literature more openly engaged with cosmic or universal issues can do". In other words, if Swift was really about politics as an abstract idea, he somehow didn't seem nearly as interesting as he would have seemed to someone a contemporary, perhaps, or a carefully and fully informed and educated modern reader who knew and cared about Walpole and parliamentary history.

He wasn't really the same Swift any more. No wonder my student hadn't been as turned on by Swift and Johnson and Pope as I was: he hadn't read the same writers. He'd read writers who were going the long way round to make abstract points about politics in general points we could have made just as well by ourselves, with current examples. Surely it would be more powerful, if you wanted to make an abstract political point, to use the examples of deputy ministers in the reader's own capital city leaping up and down from their tightropes for their jobs after an election.

It should hardly be a surprise, then, that many teachers of eighteenth-century literature (among others) began to look for new ways to help other people share their conviction that writers like Swift were worth spending some time with. In recent years, one of the most important of those new ways has arisen out of a critical movement which has come to be called the New Historicism.

For some people, this has meant going back to talking about Walpole and Bolingbroke and Queen Caroline, but for others it has offered what seems a new way to reconnect Swift's work with his and our real concerns. The new reading that such an approach would recommend asks different questions of the text.

It doesn't ask the traditional historical questions: "What do we need to know to understand this text?" or "What does this text tell us about the age?" the ones Rosenblatt made fun of in her article title: "What Facts Does This Poem Teach You?" Nor does it ask the New Critical questions: "What is this text, in and of itself? How does it work and what holds it together?" The question it asks is something more like this: "What was Swift actually *getting at*"? If, in other words, we see Swift in his historical context, can we understand what he was actually using Flimnap and Reldresal and the King of Brobdingnag *for*?

As I rethought my own teaching and understanding of Swift under the impetus of this set of ideas, a number of things seemed more important to me than they had before. One of them, for example, was the fact that Swift was an Irishman. I'd known that before, of course, but it hadn't seemed very significant. Most of Swift's major works were really written in English contexts, so they didn't tell you much about Ireland, nor did you need to know much about Ireland to identify Flimnap. And if *Gulliver* was really about abstract ideas, and if Swift's intentions were irrelevant to a reading of the text, it didn't much matter what nationality Swift was.

But, in fact, it now began to seem to me that it did make a difference. Describing that difference may illustrate some of the ways in which this new approach might make "what we do with Swift" different. Let me try to explain how much difference it made to me to read Swift in this new way. If you ask most people where Swift was born, or grew up, or where he wrote *Gulliver*, they'd probably answer, "England, of course." But, of course, it's not so. Swift was born in Ireland, spent virtually all his life there, wrote most of his masterpieces there, and died in Dublin a national hero.

To call Swift English and teach his works as masterpieces of English literature makes about as much sense as calling Nathaniel Hawthorne English because he lived for some time in London, or Joyce Carol Oates Canadian because she taught at the University of Windsor. But with the sort of natural, effortless imperialism whereby England in the nineteenth century always assumed that anything fine must really be English at bottom, Swift simply got appropriated.

He's been taken over so thoroughly that textbooks that include his work rarely make much of the fact that Swift's birth and upbringing made him something quite different from a typical Englishman of the eighteenth century or of any time, for that matter.

They don't often suggest that he might have become the greatest satirist ever to write the English language precisely because he spent his childhood in a society alienated from and colonized by England, surrounded by Irish attitudes toward life, humour, and language. They don't give you much reason to guess that a great deal of the power of his satire might come from the same springs that produced Oliver Goldsmith and George Bernard Shaw, Oscar Wilde and James Joyce and Samuel Beckett, Sean O'Casey and Brendan Behan and Flann O'Brien.

It was under the influence of such a New Historicist viewpoint that I began to understand the peculiarity of Swift's position, and that of many Irish writers. He'd been raised an

Anglican in a Catholic country; he was a member of an economically privileged colonial ruling class who, almost within living memory, had been imposed on Irish society from outside, by military conquest; he'd lived in a middle-class enclave surrounded by the most abject kind of poverty, the kind we might see now only in a particularly disadvantaged third world country. These things affected Swift and everything he wrote in profound ways.

Among other things, knowing this helped me feel the depth of Swift's contempt for that political rope dancing, or why he might have thought of having the pompous little Englishman, Gulliver, offer the King of Brobdingnag the gunpowder that would have made him absolute master of the lives, the liberties, and the fortunes of his people.

Now there may not seem to be much difference between reading Swift as an eighteenth-century Irishman and reading him as an eighteenth-century Englishman, at least in terms of the reading itself. In my view, though, the difference seemed dramatic. When the New Critics argued against the old historical approaches to literature, they did so on the grounds I thought they were correct then, and I think so still that such approaches tended to make literature into a kind of inferior history, and tended to lose track of what makes literature itself important.

In their view, what made literature so important was its form, its internal perfection, its status as a timeless achievement of permanent beauty. I'd suggest that such a New Historicist reading of Gulliver which asks, among other things, who its author was and whom he was writing to takes still another view of what makes literature so special.

I think it's saying that what makes literature worth paying attention to is that it is through literature that human beings have used the power of written language to speak to other human beings about things that genuinely mattered, to writers and to readers, and that by overhearing those frozen conversations, by thawing and participating in them, we can come to understand them, both the readers and the writers, and become ourselves better participants in that long-standing conversation which is, after all, our civilization.

To read Swift as the Irish outsider this new perspective made him seem, passionately attacking attitudes and practices whose consequences he knew and had witnessed and suffered, is, it seems to me, to participate in that conversation in a way that using him as a door to history, or as an example of delicate and perfect ironic patterns, could never do. It is to call for this kind of historically coherent understanding of the context in which Swift (and other writers) wrote that Dowling wrote the article I began by quoting.

But such a New Historicist approach is only a third way of reading Swift. I said at the beginning that I knew of at least four. My last kind of reading really depends on, or arises out of, the attempt to see Swift as a real figure, acting in a real historical situation. My involvement in empirical research on reading over the past few years has made me think that there is a kind or mode of reading regularly used by people who are attempting to engage themselves with texts like *Gulliver*, that has not been much considered by literary theorists or played much role in pedagogical thinking or practice.

As I have already noted, the very idea that there may be quite different kinds of reading, and that some are promoted by educational institutions and others ignored or marginalized, is one we owe primarily to Rosenblatt's illuminating and important distinction between *efferent* and *aesthetic* reading.

As we have tried to think through the implications of this insight my colleagues in reading research and I have come to think that you can and that many people do also read in another way, one that looks like something a little different again from either of the kinds that Rosenblatt described, although it is entirely consistent with her argument that what is central is the idea of reading as a "transaction."

You can, it seems to us, read as though your central purpose were to "make contact" with another human being (Vipond and Hunt, "Point Driven Understanding" and "Shunting Information"). This may, in fact (as Rosenblatt has suggested in a personal communication of 1985) be a subcategory of aesthetic reading; we believe, however, it's important to distinguish it from the larger category, which includes reading for the vicarious experience afforded by the text, but without attention to author, purpose, or significance ignoring, that is, what one might call the status of the language as social discourse.

In a casual conversation, the sort of contact we're talking about is made through the sharing or exchange of "evaluations." as they are defined in sociolinguistic analyses of conversational storytelling by, for example, William Labov or Livia Polanyi.

Evaluations, which can be conveyed either directly (a narrator might overtly comment, "I was never so scared in my life") or indirectly (for instance, by a striking metaphor or unexpected detail or other "departure from the local norm of the text"), seem to invite the reader to share fundamental values with the narrator, and thus allow for the narrative to be understood in such a way that it seems meaningful, significant, potentially relevant to the hearer's immediate social context.

Although all the participants in such a conversation might not agree on any given formulation of what "the point" of a successful story might be, or on what the motives or character of the teller were, they would agree that it wasn't "pointless" (this is what it means to say it was "successful"). The auditors wouldn't, in Labov's terms, be tempted to ask the teller, "So what? Why did you tell us that story?" It's important to stress that "points" aren't exactly equivalent to "meanings" or "gists" or even "purposes." Nor are they something that can be found "in" stories.

They are a function of the story's relationship to its social situation, and they are much more accurately described as a social consensus about relevance than as any set of textual features. A story in one situation might afford the creation of a quite different set of "points" than in another, and in the same situation might seem to be making different points to different readers. Often, as Polanyi has pointed out, the construction of a point or points for a story can become a social process in its own right.

Some of the readers we have studied seem to be reading in a way that is closely analogous to this way of listening; for instance, they are particularly likely to notice opportunities to construct evaluations (Hunt and Vipond, "Evaluations"). They are also more likely to make connections between their experience of reading and their own immediate situations, or to take into account peripheral information about the physical presentation of the text (Vipond, Hunt, Jewett, and Reither).

Whether a reader reads in this way (or focuses mainly on acquiring information from text, or on immersion in a vicarious fictional experience), is influenced by the reader's own experience, preferences, and expectations; by what sorts of reading the text seems to the reader to afford; and by the situation in which the reading occurs.

In other words, reading is a *transaction*. Used in this way, the term is, of course, Rosenblatt's ("Towards a Transactional Theory," "Transaction Versus Interaction," "Writing and Reading"; see also Vipond and Hunt, "Literary Processing"), and was originally drawn from Dewey and Bentley. To consider an event a transaction is to make no rigid separation of *object* (text) from *subject* (reader), but to see that the two together, each participating and each being affected, produce or, rather, are an "event" (a poem).

Perhaps even more important, the transaction as Dewey and Bentley particularly insisted does not take place in a vacuum, in some grey, bracketed-out experimental space, but rather in the world, and thus in the case of reading must seen as integrally involved with the immediate social experience readers and writers indeed, cannot be understood without taking that situation into account.

Dewey and Bentley argued in 1949 that it was already becoming clear that we cannot understand even the most classically mechanical physical processes if we abstract the process from the observer and the specific situation in which it occurs, or if try to understand the objects as they are "in themselves," outside the transaction or the situation in some unimaginable isolation. In just this way, Rosenblatt makes clear that the richer, more complex phenomenon of reading cannot be understood except as a contextualized whole. Our research has supported and perhaps extended this view.

In general, we have found that the readers who seem most engaged in, and who feel most satisfied with, their readings (of these texts, in these situations) appear to act as though the purpose predominating in their reading were to make social contact, by sharing evaluations, with a narrator or author who is assumed to be somehow "behind" or "implicit in" the text. Using Bakhtin's terminology, one might say that they are taking the text as an "utterance," with all the rich dialogic connections with preceding and succeeding and concurrent utterances that that implies.

It is of course true that traditional literary theories e.g., Wimsatt and Beardsley suggest that readers should not be doing that (or, alternatively, that they should attempting to ascertain exactly what the historical author intended, as argued by E. D. Hirsch). Still, our observation suggests that many readers often those who apparently feel most comfortable in dealing with "literary" texts do it anyway (and on the other hand show little interest in investigating the opinions or aims of the historical author).

All this work leads me back to some speculations on the reading of *Gulliver's Travels*. What might it mean to "make social contact" with the implicit author of *Gulliver's Travels*? In what ways might a reader connect *Gulliver* with the immediate social context of her reading, and with the larger society in which the reading occurs? It is tempting to suggest that such "literary" contact is exactly similar to the sorts of contact we make in conversation, but that it can potentially run much deeper and entail more complicated kinds of sharing of more sophisticated evaluations and with people like the author of *Gulliver's Travels*.

It may be important to remember here that we do not normally participate in conversations in order to produce new interpretations or to voice, like Randall Jarrell's mockingbird (see also Hunt, "Lots of Holes"), condescending and "helpful" approval of the contributions of others. Nor is it usual to "respond" to conversational story or statement by voicing, to a third party, an interpretation or explanatory restatement of what has been said.

If someone in a conversation had "made social contact" (or failed to make it) with the author of *Gulliver's Travels,* she would probably not turn to explain to someone else what he had said or to expatiate on its brilliance or, if she did, such an act would constitute changing the subject and potentially derailing the conversation. (On the other hand, it might, of course, become necessary to "negotiate" an appropriate social relevance among those readers present, the way the group in Polanyi ["So What's the Point?"] describes negotiating "a point" to help their friend save her story about "fainting on the subway.")

What we normally do, when a story or piece of discourse a conversational turn, an utterance is successful, is to express our response (e.g., by laughing) or to tell a new story that responds to the original, elaborates on it or connects with it in some way, to retell the story in a new context. Or perhaps we adopt the story's metaphor and terms to deal with our own later experiences. In general, we *use* what the story has given us.

Emerson points out that Bakhtin has made the powerful argument that it is only by assimilating the word of others "retelling" that we can originate anything, and that it is this struggle between the language of others and our need to internalize it that we "recognize as intellectual and moral growth". (It is of course, also true that we may, especially if we're professional critics, try to account for the success of the story to ourselves and to others. But we can't do that until it's *had* that success.

I would suggest that it is in order to do that sort of thing, in order to participate in such dialogue, that we read writers like Jonathan Swift. I read Swift, as I converse with a friend who's important to me, in order that he might change my life, and in order, perhaps, to internalize his story and retell it to someone else (literature teaching is one important way in which this is done). If he tries to change my life in unacceptable ways it's okay for me to be angry.

Reading Swift in such a way makes him matter. It's this that makes it potentially important to know about Swift's Irish context, but the only reason that valuable to know about is if I think Swift has the potential to change my thinking, my relationship to the world around me and other people: to change what I do.

Now, there can be many Jonathan Swifts, just as there are many individuals in each of the people we converse with every day. My Jonathan Swift, this year, in the current situation of my own life, happens to be a passionate Irishman, who has things to say to me about the current troubles in Ulster and the Irish heritage of eastern Canada, where I now live. A few years ago, however, he was a skeptical Anglican rationalist, who spoke to me about my interests in the history of the Church of England and my wife's involvement in the Canadian Anglican church.

Before that, he was a profoundly committed political and social conservative and journalist, with whom I argued about the political convictions with which I was struggling, and about which I was writing. At the very beginning, he was a childlike fantasist who (as Dr. Johnson put it) "thought of big men and little men," and spoke to my fascination with science fiction and various kinds of logical extrapolation.

In each case, though, the basis of my engagement whether I was aware of it or not was my reading Swift as though he were talking to me, as though he were trying to change my mind and my soul and I think sometimes, in spite of my training, he succeeded. He has also (more often recently) succeeded in making me angry. (I now think I understand why Thackeray could have been so indignant at Swift. He misunderstood, I think, but he and I would have agreed about one thing: Swift is for us worth caring about, worth engaging ourselves with, worth making contact with. He can make us angry, with reason.)

What all this means, I think, is that people who engage themselves with him and enjoy his work don't normally read Swift in order to produce "the truth" about his meaning, just as we don't do that with conversations. We strive for what will work for us, what we can use, about conversations and about texts, as C. S. Peirce suggested we do about the world. (The question whether there is "a truth" about text like the question about truth in general, as Richard Rorty observes is not a question about which you'd expect to find many interesting opinions. The important and interesting question is what we can do with it.)

Thus, my discovery of Swift's Irishness isn't very important in itself. For one thing, it hardly counts, in the larger arena, as a discovery at all; it's far from news to most scholars of eighteenth-century literature.

One might "discover," in this sense, lots of things about the author of *Gulliver's Travels* that might make him seem more clearly an engaged, committed, living human intelligence, and one with whom one might engage oneself the Irish Swift happens to be the one I currently create. It's that process of creating and recreating and engaging with one's own Swift in one's own world that is central and it is not a process for which there's much provision in most university English classes. If we believe with Rosenblatt that the best reading is the most richly transactional, we must ask ourselves how we can create classroom contexts in which such transactions are supported and promoted.

It seems to me that they are just as unlikely to be effectively supported by situations in which we focus entirely on meaning (even when we define that meaning as the responsibility of the reader rather than the property of the writer) as they ever were by the situations in which it was our aim to read "through" the text to the historical or biographical information lurking behind it.

It's important to insist, too, that it's a matter of *creating situations* rather than of explaining things discursively. The classroom situation that already exists, what we might call the "default context," is one which, as Derek Edwards and Neil Mercer make clear, discourse is inevitably centered on the teacher and transactions are mediated by that fact. Anne Freadman has observed that the situation of a class in French means that it is virtually impossible for a text to be seen as anything more than "an example of French"; similarly, it seems to me, literature classes render texts "examples of literature." To change this we must change the situation, not merely tell people how they ought to be reading. The processes by which people make connections with texts make them into utterances in an authentic dialogue are not so easily or consciously invoked or altered.

What, then, are my alternatives? More generally, what are the alternatives of any literature teacher? Is there a way to teach literature that promotes the kind of reading (of Swift and of other texts) that I'm arguing is appropriate, that does not compel readers to break off the potential conversation, or to change the subject?

In fact, some practical alternatives are being developed to the standard classroom pattern, the pattern whereby a fixed text is assigned, read by a group and discussed with the aim of arriving at a consensus (usually, tacitly or overtly, the "right" consensus) about its meaning. Such alternatives are appearing in locations as disparate as South Australia (Homer, Cook, and Nixon); England (Miall); and in Canada at McGill (Dias) and my own university.

To illustrate concretely one way in which the situation might be changed, let me describe briefly how my classes in eighteenth-century literature have been dealing with Swift over the past few years.

The basic pedagogical strategy, which is being worked out in collaboration with a number of colleagues in English and other disciplines, is called "collaborative investigation," and full descriptions of its rationale and procedure in this and other disciplines are available elsewhere (see, for instance, Hunt "A Decade of Change," "A Boy Named Shawn"; Hunt, Parkhill, Reither, and Vipond; Parkhill; Reither "Writing and Knowing," "Writing Student as Researcher"; Reither and Vipond).

Its basic purpose is to give students the opportunity and the responsibility to create for themselves, and to share with others, the knowledge and understanding that more traditional courses attempt to transmit. (I should make clear that this particular description is based on a two-term course in

Restoration and Eighteenth-Century Literature for undergraduate students specializing in English, and usually three weeks can be spent on Swift; parallel strategies can be used at other levels and in other disciplines. I assume here, simply for purposes of making the description concrete, a class of twenty-four; similarly, details can be altered for more or fewer students.) One result of implementing this strategy in a literature class is to give a new social status to texts and to widen the range of possible student activities in connection with them.

In such a class, when we approach Swift, there are a series of assignments, which students usually undertake in *ad hoc* groups, changed for each new task. The first sends eight groups of three to the library (usually to work during a scheduled class meeting time) to bring back written recommendations for the rest of the class about what works of Swift should be read, and why. As sources (the course has no uniform text or anthology) they use literary histories, textbook anthologies, critical and text editions of Swift, critical and historical work on Swift and the period, general literary references, and so forth.

Each group prepares a list and some preliminary written arguments explaining why they believe each work is important. Before class seven photocopies of each report are prepared, and during class each is read and considered by a newly formed group of four students. Each group comes up with a consensus about works that should be read. A representative of each group then puts its list on the blackboard, and the class as a whole decides on a final list.

The class then divides up this list of works into eight workable categories or sets of texts, which might range from a selection of poems to *The Battle of the Books*, from a selection of *Examiner* essays to the Drapier's letters, from *A Digression on Madness* to *Gulliver*.

A new set of groups is formed (again randomly) to prepare full reports and to recommend whether their texts, or some portion of them, should be read by the whole class. At the end of the class session these groups decide which sets they wish to report on, and, in a sort of auction, as each group announces its decision the item is crossed off the final list.

Over the next week, groups meet to prepare reports on their individual texts. These reports have typically included descriptions of the work, summaries, quotations of representative passages, and varying amounts of critical, bibliographical, or biographical background material. Reports are limited in length a practical limit is what can be photocopied on two or three sheets of paper (eight to twelve pages, if the photocopier uses half-size reduction and the copy is printed on both sides of the page).

These reports are prepared over a week in which there are no class meetings (I am in the library for consultation during scheduled class meeting times), and then photocopied and distributed through a "mailbox system" usually a set of large envelopes attached to the wall outside my office or the classroom which allows the reports to be exchanged and read before class.

During that next class, working in new groups, the class decides on which (or which parts) of the works the whole class should read and which should be the subject of expanded and edited reports, to be included in a permanent "course textbook," photocopied and bound at the end of the term.

Groups that recommended the texts the whole class decides to read are assigned the job of making texts available (putting them on reserve in the library, photocopying them, etc.); those that recommended the ones accepted for inclusion in the course book are given the task of editing the final reports.

Finally, class time is set aside for discussion of some of the works to be read by everyone. One common way of conducting such a discussion is for each member of the class to write a page or two of immediate response, as soon as the reading is completed (or even to keep a "reading journal" of in-process responses).

This impromptu unrevised (and often anonymous) writing is brought to class and the class begins with everyone reading the writing of at least five or six other people. As they read, they respond to each piece of writing with marks in the margin next to passages that seem to them striking or interesting, and sometimes with accumulating graffiti (those of us developing this teaching strategy call this impromptu transactional writing "inkshedding"). Often the pieces are collected and passages with the most marginal marks transcribed on a word processor printed, duplicated, and distributed at a later class session.

Occasionally the class is continued with a further cycle of writing, reading editing, and commenting; on other occasions oral discussion ensues. Occasionally, the "inksheddings" are edited for preservation in the "course textbook"; more usually, they are discarded once everyone has read them.

At least some of the potential general advantages of learning in such a way which, I think, go well beyond the usual scope of a course in literature and literary history should be clear from this very cursory description. Here, I want to focus on the ways in which such a strategy is consistent with what I am arguing about the nature of reading. Students in such a situation are not reading in order to form interpretations that they can write down for evaluation by an authority whom (rightly or wrongly) they assume already knows anything they might say.

They are reading in order to describe texts to people who need descriptions, to persuade others to read them, to share what they read with their peers to assimilate the words of others and appropriate them to their own uses, as Bakhtin might say, generating texts that are in a dialogic relationship with each other.

Their success or failure in this reading (and writing) is not a matter of judgment by an outside authority, but an immediately and socially perceptible consequence: either others are persuaded by their arguments to read the text or not; others read their description of the text with interest or they don't; others are affected and respond or they aren't and don't. What is most important for my argument here is the way in which the situation I am describing enables written texts to be taken as utterances, to serve as a basis for dialogue, to become a medium for social transactions among their readers. Because the students are involved in connecting texts to both historical and immediate social contexts for the readings, it becomes more likely that they will recognize the potential of the texts to make a difference to their own lives.

Because they are so often engaged in exchanging the texts with, and recommending them to, each other, they are more likely to create relationships between the text and their own practical and immediate concerns.

In other words, the situation is one that, more than a conventional interpretation-and teacher-centered course, affords the kind of reading I have been describing. Students are more likely to respond to anomalies, to "departures from the local norm of the text," by attempting to construct evaluations and less likely to dismiss them as meaningless "noise."

A good example, and one that is of course particularly appropriate to the reading of Swift, is the long-standing pedagogic problem of irony. That students so often "miss the point" of metaphoric or (especially) ironic passages is a problem often addressed as though it were a matter of acquiring information, but, as Chamberlain points out, it is much more a matter of attitudes or stances toward texts than of availability of information.

Indeed, there is evidence that whether a reader brings any particular information to bear on a text is in large part a matter of such attitudes, and, in turn, of the situation in which the reading occurs (Hunt, "Pragmatic Aspects"). A situation that affords the construction of evaluations is almost by definition one which rhetorical devices like irony and metaphor the "literary" embodiments of evaluations are likely to find readers appropriately engaged.

Thus, in such a situation, a reader is more likely to respond to the passages about gunpowder or rope jumping in all the four ways I have described: not only as a window on eighteenth-century politics and history, or an example of brilliant ironic text construction, or even a voice speaking out of a personal context of real social suffering and conflict but also to engage in dialogue with it, to take it into her own language and society, to respond as though it embodied a voice speaking directly to her. The reader may, that is, take the text as an utterance or, to use Rosenblatt's terminology, engage in the kind of transaction with it that is, after all, the whole point of literature.

Chapter 5

Satiric Travel Narratives in Chaucer, Swift and Nabokov

Chaucer's *The Canterbury Tales* offers an irresistible and logical beginning point for the discussion of so much that followed in English literature. This seems especially true of the satiric travel narrative, which from Chaucer's day to ours has been a vital and productive subgenre. Indeed, Chaucer's masterpiece created a template which, 600 years later, shows no signs of growing archaic.

Two of the most compelling and well-known satiric masterpieces of the English language tradition, Jonathan Swift's *Gulliver's Travels* and Vladimir Nabokov's *Lolita* derive much of their vigour from the Chaucerian tradition. Perhaps more surprisingly, and more revealingly, the Twentieth-Century work exhibits an interesting and illuminating set of rather particular correspondences with the 1726 novel.

There is both instruction and entertainment in contemplating briefly such resemblances. The possibility of direct, literary influence is always present, and in this case, is surely operative to some degree. It is very difficult to deny a strong Gulliver-esque tone to Nabokov's narrator, Humbert Humbert, and his exotic voyages.

But even in the absence of such a specific link, the observation of a strict and close relationship between two works of the imagination tells us much about the shaping consciousness of both works, and gives us a valuable signpost pointing towards major thematic structures. The satirist seeks to instruct and correct his/her society, by holding the follies thereof up to ridicule, and thus inspiring the reader(s), who, of course, do not want to be ridiculed, to eschew them. However, both Swift and Nabokov, as we shall see, are satirists on the very edge-perhaps at times, a bit over the edge-of sharpening that ridicule to vitriol.

Both move very close to satire of the Jacobean, rather than the Augustan, sort: venomous portraits of an unredeemable culture. The worlds we come to know through the crazed eyes of the two mad narrators of the two novels seem at moments closer to "The Revenger's Tragedy" than "The Rape of the Lock."

We know that Nabokov knew Swift well: *Pale Fire* is full of Swift allusions. Vanessa butterflies flutter about the story of John Shade, who is himself a scholar of eighteenth-century English poetry. Priscilla Meyer demonstrates that Swift, along with other 18th-century literary lights, "figure prominently in *Pale Fire*". In Part I, Chapter 3 of *Lolita,* Nabokov speaks of "fat, powdered Mrs. Leigh (born Vanessa van Ness)". Appel notes that Nabokov is "alluding to Jonathan Swift's 'Vanessa,' as he called the young woman whose passion he awakened". Carl Proffer in *Keys to Lolita* had also noted this Swiftian moment in *Lolita.*

There are seven citations of Swift in the "index" to Nabokov's *Eugene Onegin* (none particularly revealing, it is true). Like Swift, Nabokov was a social conservative who nevertheless distrusted many specific political institutions and leaders, and relied more on common sense than systematic abstract philosophizing.

On the other hand, the two authors are quite unlike in the degree of their engagement in the political life of their times: Swift was often overtly political in his life and work, Nabokov explicitly denied the political relevance of everything he did and wrote. Although it is clear that Nabokov considers Swift a major figure on the landscape of his adopted English culture of letters, it is to be doubted that the two energetic, irascible and idiosyncratic satirists would have cared much for each other's company. This suspicion is reinforced by Nabokov's comments upon "Stella's Birthday" in *Notes on*

Prosody which he says is "typical of the 'light verse' (a ponderous and dreary machine) of the Age of Reason" and describes as "doggerel". Interestingly, the first similarity a reader encounters between *Gulliver's Travels* and *Lolita* is *not* that both are travel narratives: rather, it is that both works begin with what purport to be "objective" editorial prefaces. Swift begins his work with an exchange between Gulliver and Richard Sympson, and a "foreword" by the latter entitled "The Publisher to the Reader."

In this prefatory statement, the unimaginative Sympson, who is, of course, wholly fictitious, seeks, in rather pedestrian fashion, to establish the value of the manuscript before him and us and to articulate the *bona fides* of its author. To Sympson, a narrative has value not in any aesthetic or "delightful" sense, but solely as utilitarian, ethical instruction.

Gulliver's story, Sympson pontificates, will be "a better Entertainment to our young Noblemen, than the common Scribbles of Politicks and Party" (xi). Lemuel Gulliver himself is praised for the proverbial repute of his veracity ("There is an Air of Truth apparent through the whole..." [xi]).

The equally fictional John Ray, Jr., Ph.D., who plays the similar role in *Lolita* also affirms the truthfulness of the novel's main narrator: he cites "a desperate honesty that throbs through his confession". Like Swift's Sympson, Nabokov's prefatory narrator is conscious of the effect of the manuscript in his hands upon gentlefolk. But, where Sympson felt Gulliver's story to be uplifting to the gentry, Ray is a bit more uncertain: Humbert Humbert is guilty of "sins of diabolical cunning.

He is abnormal. He is not a gentleman". Indeed, in a wonderful Nabokovian twist, Ray is so exercised by some aspects of Humbert's character that he maladroitly elevates him into "a shining example of moral leprosy" (5). Still, our introductory voice assures us that the manuscript we are about to peruse is, like Swift's, morally instructive and, therefore, useful:

"Lolita" should make all of us parents, social workers, educators apply ourselves with still greater vigilance and vision to the task of bringing up a better generation in a safer world.

Few have derived comfort from this affirmation....

The flat, morally utilitarian voice of the prologue in both these novels is a sharp contrast to the immediate, vivid tones of shrillness which characterize both Humbert ("Lolita, light of my life, fire of my loins. My sin, my soul...") and Gulliver ("Do these miserable Animals presume to think that I am so far degenerated as to defend my Veracity, Yahoo that I am....I was able ... to remove that infernal Habit of Lying, Shuffling, Deceiving, and Equivocating, so deeply rooted in the very Souls of all my Species especially the Europeans.").

However, in spite of (or perhaps because of) this introductory hysteria, both narrators themselves seek to establish their own credentials, on the very first pages of the novels, by giving a paternalistic biographical sketch:

I was born in 1910, in Paris. My father was a gentle, easy-going person, a salad of racial genes: a Swiss citizen, of mixed French and Austrian descent, with a dash of the Danube in his veins.

My father had a small Estate in Nottinghamshire; I was the third of five Sons. He sent me to Emanuel-College in Cambridge, at Fourteen years old, where I resided three Years. [Coincidentally, Nabokov was a graduate of Trinity College, Cambridge.]

Both Nabokov's masterwork and Swift's are accounts which describe, in minute satiric detail, multiple voyages to strange lands. This is self evident in *Gulliver's Travels,* with its perpetually fascinating descriptions of the lands of the Houyhnhnms, Lilliput, Brobdingnag, Laputa, etc. In his famous letter to Pope of 29 September 1725, Swift is uncomfortably unambiguous about the purposes to which he intended Gulliver's journeys:

I have ever hated all nations, professions and communities....Upon this great foundation of misanthropy (though not Timon's manner), the whole building of my *Travels* is erected. Swift's methodology, to which he adhered only imperfectly, appears to have been to have each locale which

Guilliver visits manifest a related set of follies. Lilliput reveals the pettiness of politics, Brobdingnag the fleshly grossness of humanity, and the like. Utilizing the exaggeration of fantasy (floating islands, talking horses, giant eagles, etc.) Swift, as the classic satirist, is able to expose those follies, cast them into very clear relief, and hold them up to ridicule.

It is not quite as obvious that *Lolita* is as much the story of a stranger in a strange land as *Gulliver's Travels*. The reader needs to be reminded fairly frequently that Humbert Humbert is as new to America as Gulliver to Lilliput. Nabokov, of course, provides those reminders, e.g., "I was angry, disappointed and bored, but being a polite European...". As a traveller to, and in, America, Humbert brings a fresh-eyed vision to the landscape which makes it seem as exotic and new, just as does Gulliver. Here, for example, Humbert casts a fresh eye on the classification of various species of American motels:

We came to know *nous connûmes*, to use a Flaubertian intonation the stone cottages under enormous Chateaubriandesque trees, the brick unit, the adobe unit, the stucco court, on what the Tour Book of the Automobile Association describes as "shaded" or "spacious" or "landscaped" grounds.

Of course, most of Part Two of *Lolita* takes place "on the road," thus affording Humbert an opportunity to see America from coast to coast, and Nabokov to identify, through the eyes of his poetic pervert narrator, examples of poshlust from West ("a winery in California, with a church built in the shape of a wine barrel"); to South (Bourbon Street [in a town named New Orleans] whose sidewalks, said the tour book, 'may [I liked the 'may'] feature entertainment by pickaninnies who will [I liked the 'will' even better] tap-dance for pennies' [what fun], while 'its numerous small and intimate night clubs are thronged with visitors' [naughty]"); to East ("What we are concerned with is the adjustment of the child to group life.

This is why we stress the four D's: Dramatics, Dance, Debating and Dating"); and North ("Another group, equally misguided, collected plankton. A third studied tuberculosis in the tundra"). In very many ways, Humbert's European vision and his pervert's imagination make of mid-Twentieth Century America a land every bit as exotic and strange as any visited by Lemuel Gulliver. Here is a Dantean description of a simple unfinished storefront display in a small town:

It was indeed a pretty sight. A dapper young fellow was vacuum-cleaning a carpet of sorts upon which stood two figures that looked as if some blast had just worked havoc with them. One figure was stark naked, wigless and armless. Its comparatively small stature and smirking pose suggested that when clothed it had represented, and would represent when clothed again, a girl-child of Lolita's size.

But in its present state it was sexless. Next to it, stood a much taller veiled bride, quite perfect and intacta except for the lack of one arm. On the floor, at the feet of these damsels, where the man crawled about laboriously with his cleaner, there lay a cluster of three slender arms, and a blond wig. Two of the arms happened to be twisted and seemed to suggest a clasping gesture of horror and supplication.

At a certain point, the amused ridicule of folly which constitutes satire can become sufficiently colored by invective and hysteria, and slide into something more sardonic. This is a point which is not infrequently reached, as the above citation might suggest, by Nabokov. Swift, too, often reaches a height of invective which transcends the satiric:

As soon as I entered the House, my Wife took me in her Arms, and kissed me; at which, having not been used to the Touch of that odious Animal for so many Years, I fell in a Swoon for almost an Hour. At the Time I am writing, it is five Years since my last Return to England: during the first year I could not endure my Wife or Children in my Presence, the very Smell of them was intolerable; much less could I suffer them to eat in the same Room.

It is difficult to find examples of Swift and Nabokov's contemporary satirists say, Pope or Updike writing at this heightened level of repulsion and emotional pitch.

In both *Lolita* and *Gulliver's Travels* the inherent fascination of the plot keeps readers tuned to the satire, and keeps them tolerant of what might seem moments of excess in tone. Both novels tell unique stories; both have demonstrated a broad and lasting interest. *Gulliver's Travels* has been a popular children's cartoon, and was recently revived as a two-part television mini-series staring "Cheers" hunk Ted Danson as a somewhat frenetic Gulliver. Probably the majority of contemporary Americans who can identify *Gulliver's Travels* at all would describe it as a child's story. *Lolita* has had a different but parallel career in popular culture. It was a celebrated movie, staring Sue Lyon as the lollipop-sucking nymphet, James Mason as Humbert Humbert and featuring Shelly Winters as a frowzy Charlotte Haze.

It has been a flop Broadway musical, and is about to be made into a second movie. Moreover, words like "nymphet" and "lolita" have become part of our language. Probably the majority of contemporary Americans who can identify Vladimir Nabokov would describe him as the author of *Lolita;* probably the majority of contemporary Americans who can identify *Lolita* would describe it as a pornographic depiction of adult/child sexual relations.

Swift and Nabokov ensured the success of their satirical novels not by the accuracy or the savagery of the mockery of folly, but by the one-of-a-kind and whopping good stories which carry the theme. As readers of "The Miller's Tale" or "The Franklin's Tale" or "The Nun's Priest's Tale" know, this was a lesson they learned from Chaucer, too.

Chapter 6

Lecture on Swift

In this lecture I wish to focus on two different things by way of an introduction to Gulliver's Travels at the end of our first two semesters of Liberal Studies. Firstly, I would like to offer something of a quick summary and synthesis of two or three of the major issues we have considered in the past year by way of highlighting the importance of the seventeenth-century literature we have been dealing with lately.

Then, secondly, I want, by way of an introduction to Swift, to adopt the approach that he is reacting against the rapidly developing modernity of much of the seventeenth-century thought his satire is a cry of protest in the name of an older tradition, one reaching back to Socrates, Plato, and St. Paul. And yet, Swift, as a product of the new forces, is aware that we cannot simply return to medieval or Greek times and pretend that Newton never existed.

In short, I want eventually to lead us to the fairly obvious point that Gulliver's Travels, one of the greatest works of protest against modernity ever written, is no exercise in nostalgia but a call to shape the rapidly growing power of European culture in accordance with some old insights.

His great fear is that, in the eagerness to follow the direction indicated by Hobbes and Descartes, among others, which begins with an energetic and optimistic debunking and rejection of tradition and the enthronement of new rationality, we may be throwing out the baby with the bathwater. At the same time, I will maintain, Swift knows deep down that his cause is lost. Fuelling the pessimism and the anger of his satire is, I think, a sense that the moral position he wishes to defend is already being overrun. Still, he's going to have his say. However, before discussing Swift, I want to offer a quick retrospective. In doing this, I'm going to be offering many very large unsubstantiated generalizations, skating often on very thin ice, but if I can keep moving quickly, the surface may sustain me, and the questions and comments at the end can point out all the flaws.

To give us a line through the retrospective and up to Swift, I wish to concentrate upon a moral issue: the question of virtue. And in order to make this issue as clear as I can, I would like to pose two central questions in order quickly to survey some of the answers to them we have considered:

- What is the good life for me?
- How can we clearly and justly settle any disputes between us?

These are the fundamental questions of personal and public morality or, in a word, of justice, and in looking at some of the ways the writers we have read have sought to deal with them, I can, I hope, achieve two things: provide a useful retrospective synthesis and offer an insight into what Gulliver's Travels is centrally about.

THE NATURE OF GREEK VIRTUE

The Greek answer to that questions I have just posed anchored itself on a very interesting, influential, and sometime puzzling concept: the idea of virtue. Questions of right and wrong in the individual and in society were to be dealt with by an appeal to the character of the individuals making the decisions. We began, way back in September, wrestling in Homer with a very Greek notion of the good life in which the concept of virtue holds a central place.

Simply put, the Greek concept of virtue maintains that the good or evil of life is bound up with a person's character and the way that character is linked to particular actions in particular situations, measured against the full potential development of one's full humanity (one's human telos). The fully virtuous character seeks above all to be excellent. His or her life is characterised by an energetic self-affirmation to be the best that one can be. And characters who achieve such excellence are recognized and accepted as the natural leaders of their society Odysseus, Oedipus, Agamemnon.

The individual and the society guided by a concept of virtue in this sense have an straightforward way to resolve their moral difficulties given a puzzling choice one looks to the way in which the fully virtuous person would act. Excellence in the actions of those recognized as the best in the society sets the moral standard for the individual and the community. So the way we resolve our difficulties is to look to the standard exemplified by the most virtuous members of the community, usually its publicly recognized leaders. Socrates and Plato are, in this respect, quite consistent with their older Greek traditions.

They give to questions of character a distinctly inward turn, but virtue for both is central to the good life for the individual and for the community. What makes Plato and Plato's Socrates revolutionary is their attempt to redefine virtue in terms of intellectual striving, to replace the multifaceted concept of virtue in, say, Homer, where excellence involved a host of different external activities supported by the traditions of the community, with the pursuit of and attainment of a particular form of inner knowledge.

I have no wish here to smooth over the obvious differences between Plato's and Homer's conceptions of virtue, but I am more interested at this point in the similarities. In both, the notion of virtue is aristocratic and exclusive relatively few people in the community are capable of attaining full virtue.

There are many possible degrees of excellence. But the responsibility for educating us in virtue and adjudicating our differences lies squarely with the most virtuous. Therefore, it is appropriate in the best-functioning community that the most excellent have the power and the glory and the less excellent obey. For this concept of virtue also involves the ability to recognize those more excellent than ourselves and to adjust our behaviour willingly in accordance with those differences. Aristotle offers essentially the same vision apparently much less rigorous than the vision in Plato's Republic but still based on a hierarchy of excellence. The community is held together by the constant striving for the excellence natural to human beings and by its attainment in those who become the leaders. Since they are virtuous, they will have the characters suited to lead their intelligence, emotions, motives, and physical attributes, summed up in the concept of practical wisdom (phronesis), will have been properly socialized into the best behaviour at all times in many complex different situations.

VIRTUE IN THE OLD AND NEW TESTAMENTS

In the selections of the Old Testament we met apparently quite a different conception of the moral life, one guided above all by clear rules handed down by God and guarded as the authority on all moral questions, individual and communal. Here virtue (in the Greek sense) is not the operative principle; rather faith and obedience are. We resolve our disputes by an appeal to the rules and to the interpretation of the rules, which are binding on all. There is no hierarchy of excellence here only two classes of people the faithful and obedient, on the one hand, and the sinners and pagans on the other.

To be a member of the faithful, among God's chosen people, is to be equally blessed along with everyone else. At the heart of the OT conception of the good life for the individual and the community is a radical equality of all believers. The leaders are those who have a direct insight into God's rules either because they have a prophetic connection to God and have seen Him face to face or because they are specially chosen for reasons known only to God to interpret the will of God.

Their own particular virtue (in the Greek sense) is not the issue. They have been specially chosen for reasons which have nothing in particular to do with their virtue (in the Greek sense): the act of being chosen confers virtue upon them. And in the New Testament, this same radically egalitarian element is strong. To be a good Christian requires very little in the way of traditional Greek virtue (either Homeric or Socratic). The tax gatherer, the prostitute, the Centurion, the wealthy landowner, the widow, and the fisherman are all equally members of Christ's community of believers, provided only that they take up the challenge and follow Christ's message. From one perspective this, too, is a defence of the life anchored on virtue: human beings have a characteristic function to fulfil in order to attain the good life, and central to that function is the education of the character in the truths embodied in the nature of things and summed up by the three Cardinal Virtues, faith, hope, and charity, and exemplified in the highest role model: the life of Jesus Christ.

The most influential modern philosopher defending the concept of virtue as a guide to the moral life has summed up an important linking similarity between the Greek and the Biblical tradition as follows:

The NT's account of the virtues, even if it differs as much as it does in content from Aristotle's Aristotle would certainly not have admired Jesus Christ and he would have been horrified by Saint Paul does have the same logical and conceptual structure as Aristotle's account. A virtue is, as with Aristotle, a quality the exercise of which leads to the achievement of the human telos.

The good for man is of course a supernatural and not only a natural good, but supernature redeems and completes nature. Moreover the relationship of virtues as means to the end which is human incorporation in the divine kingdom of the age to come is internal and not external, just as it is in Aristotle. (MacIntyre, After Virtue)

THE MEDIEVAL CHRISTIAN TRADITION

The early Christian tradition, as it developed in the first five centuries after the death of Jesus was, from one perspective, an fruitful and sometimes very uneasy synthesis of these two traditions. Given the similarities MacIntyre mentions above, it is easy to see why the synthesis could be made but there were tensions within the merging of Greek thinking and Biblical creeds in early Christian thinking. One aspect of this tension came out in the debates about what exactly Christianity should be, and what sort of demands it should make on the virtue of the believer.

The Early Christian community, especially once the persecutions started, was faced with an urgent problem on this question of Christian virtue: the Greek or the Biblical tradition. Simply put, it focused on the question whether the Christian community should be, as the Biblical tradition in many eyes appeared to demand, a spiritual all star team a radically equal band of true believers, with no admittance for those whose faith had wavered, or should the Christian community be a spiritual hospital, with room for all grades of Christian virtue from saint to repentant sinner and with a hierarchy of virtue within the Christian world and authority given to those of specially demonstrated virtue to educate, cure, exhort, provide role models, and, if necessary, to punish.

We see the ambiguity of this inheritance manifesting itself in the writings of St. Paul, who can, on the one hand, urge the Romans, as a community of Christian equals, to work out their problems together and communally and, on the other hand, invoke his own special virtue, qualitatively better than theirs because of his conversion experience, as a reason why they should follow his advice and example, and see in him an authority figure.

This ambiguity, it is interesting to note, may be one of the main reasons why St. Paul is a constant reference point for those who wish to insist upon the authority of the Church (like St. Augustine) and for those who wish to challenge the authority of the Church (like Martin Luther).

The resolution of the questions arising from the Greek and Biblical traditions of virtue was not easy, and it took the lifework and genius of St. Augustine, among others, to sort out the answer. But essentially, as the Church developed into a powerful social institution, the Christian view of the good life for the individual and the community fused the two traditions.

On the one hand, all Christians were spiritually equal, equally bound to the seven Christian virtues (the three Theological Virtues of faith, hope, and charity, and the Four Cardinal Virtues of prudence, temperance, fortitude, and justice), and equally subject to God's judgement. On the other hand, the Church existed as a complex hierarchy of spiritual authority, with those at the top responsible for guiding the spiritual life of those beneath. Doctrinally Christians might be equal, but ecclesiastically there were clear differences between the parson, the bishop, the devout farmer, and the king. Salvation was an equal concern for everyone; but extra ecclesia nulla salvatio (no salvation outside the Church).

The central issue for the Christian was still, however, virtue. When we read Hildegard's poetry, we saw how she looks at nature as a constant manifestation of the work of God and, therefore, as a constant reminder to all believers of their central purpose on earth. Her poems are not simply a celebration of God's handiwork; they are also, and more importantly, a call to virtue.

And the duality in the Christian view of virtue is evident in Chaucer and Dante. From one point of view, Chaucer's Ploughman and Parson, although very humble on the social scale, are ideal Christians their virtue is independent of their station in life, their physical appearance, their worldly goods, and their fame.

The are ideal figures, on par with the socially far more important knight, and what Chaucer celebrates in each one of them is the full attainment of Christian virtue. Christian Saints, after all could come from any station in life. On the other hand, in Dante's Christian vision, there is a clear hierarchy of virtue: the more important the ecclesiastical officer, the more serious the offence and the punishment and the greater the spiritual glory for full virtue.

This combination of the Greek and the Biblical views of virtue proved to be immensely useful and effective. For it linked all members of the Christian community as spiritual equals in a manner distinctly egalitarian, while at the same time authorizing a strictly organized hierarchy within the Church and thus justifying a structure of authority in spiritual matters and in the host of secular concerns which arose from them.

Note the central metaphor of the guests arriving at the Great Supper (in Luke 14: Then the master of the house, being angry said to his servant, Go out quickly into the streets and lanes of the city, and bring in hither the poor, and the maimed, and the halt, and the blind. And the servant said, Lord, it is done as thou hast commanded, and yet there is room. And the lord said unto the servant, Go out into the highways and hedges, and compel them to come in, that my house may be filled. As guests all ranks were all equal, but there were people with authority to compel those to come in.

Outside the equal feast there was no salvation. Thus, the member of the Christian community was bound together with those authorities over him, recognizing that the same spiritual rules applied to all of them (including those in authority), while at the same time the leaders had a clear mandate to carry out all the tasks necessary for the complex organization of social life.

The union was not, however, without its strains. And throughout the Middle Ages there were sporadic but very serious challenges, often in the name of a more spiritually pure and committed sense of Christian virtue. In other words, the radically egalitarian nature of Biblical Christianity (the moral all star team) kept reasserting itself in the face of an increasingly powerful and influential Church establishment.

Sometimes the Church could respond to the challenge by incorporating it (e.g., the mendicant orders); at other times the Church responded with force. So by and large the union of the Greek tradition and the Biblical tradition held. And Aristotle's Ethics could remain a popular handbook for virtue among people who considered themselves thoroughly Christian.

THE USES AND ABUSES OF THE MEDIEVAL VIEW OF VIRTUE

After reading Machiavelli and Hobbes, it's easy to be somewhat cynical about this view of individual and communal virtue the notion that the natural purpose of human life is to strive for a standard of spiritual excellence given what they say about the innately corrupt nature of human beings. And there is no shortage of examples of corrupt popes, bishops, and prelates to gratify the cynic. But, in fact, the Medieval concept of virtue, for all the lapses, worked remarkably well for hundreds of years.

For many popes and bishops and Catholic kings took their Christian responsibilities very seriously indeed and for a believer the stakes were very high the fate of one's eternal soul hung in the balance: one's virtue was up for judgement. So the notion of justice as a matter of virtue in the characters of those in authority was by no means ineffective.

This was, it needs to be stressed, not simply a narrow matter of personal morality. The concept of virtue required just decisions in a host of economic and judicial matters. Bishops, cardinals, popes, and kings had to deliberate about the just price and the fair wage, the appropriateness of interest, the proper division of territories, and a host of secular matters. In all of these among the true Christians, the central issue was this: What was the appropriately Christian way to behave? What behaviour was compatible with the highest standards of Christian virtue?

By way of impressing this point upon you that the Medieval Christian notion of virtue was indeed a serious principle and not, as Machiavelli suggests, always simply a convenient cover I'd like briefly to mention one of the most extraordinary events in the history of Western expansion, an event little known nowadays perhaps, but one which had important effects lasting right down to the present day.

The example concerns the decision of Charles V of Spain, at the time Europe's most powerful and wealthiest monarch, who was becoming fabulously rich with all the gold being shipped home from the New World, to call a halt to all Spanish expansion until such time as the philosophers and theologians could determine "the manner in which conquests should be carried on justly and with security of conscience," that is, whether his permission and encouragement of such expansion was compatible with his Christian virtue.

There is no reason here to question Charles's sincerity. He was an intensely devout man, concerned about the state of his own virtue, and he was profoundly disturbed by what was going on in the name of the Spanish monarch in the New World. So he summoned from all over Europe the best scholars and held a long debate on the question. In that debate in August 1550, Bartolome de Las Casas presented a case on behalf of the natives of South America, 550 pages of closely argued Latin prose, taking five days out in the hot sun to present his case that the Spanish had no right to take anything from the natives.

As a result of that debate, a significant attempt was made to guide the Spanish treatment of the New World inhabitants in accordance with moral principles, a process which, however questionable we may now find them and however ineffective they might have been in many instances, did, in fact, help to preserve some of the essential features of the Amerindian cultures (the language, for instance), in a way that never happened in North America, where venture capitalists, as products of the new age, had considerably less interest in their own virtue than did Charles V.

I mention this example simply to stress that, whatever we may think about it, the curious combination of Aristotle's Ethics, the New Testament, and a derivative neo-Platonic notion of virtue did provide for hundreds of years a workable framework for dealing with the two questions I raised at the start of this lecture. Of course, as we all know, eventually that workable synthesis came apart. I referred briefly to this in the lecture on Hobbes I gave a couple of weeks ago.

And the major cause of that is clear enough: there was not enough virtue on display. In other words, those in authority became much less concerned about their consciences than Charles V was, and like King Lear lost the sense of their own personal responsibility as excellent people to carry out just actions.

There seems little doubt that the great source of the dissolution of traditional virtue was money: once Europe started, during the Renaissance, to become rich from eastern trade and New World gold, the concept of virtue in the ruler as the mainstay of Church authority began to crumble. We can already see in Chaucer and Dante the emphatic links between money and sin. And when we read Machiavelli we come to understand just where an enormous amount of this new money was going: into mercenary armies to conquer adjacent territories. Machiavelli, as we argued about, recommended that the ruler thus junk the traditional concept of virtue (except as a convenient PR facade) and concentrate on power at all costs.

In virtue there is no virtue. Whether one agrees or not that Machiavelli's advice is useful or disastrous, his call for an end to the traditional concept of virtue (and his numerous examples of what many of the rulers in Italy were, in fact, doing) is an eloquent reminder of just how that Medieval Christian ideal was falling apart.

(In Hobbes, of course, the notion of virtue has almost disappeared completely. The Commonwealth he sets up does not require its citizens to be virtuous in any traditional manner, so long as they are obedient to the will of the sovereign: one's character was essentially irrelevant; what matters is obedience to the law)

THE NEED FOR A NEW ORDER

I have already referred, in the earlier lecture on Hobbes, to the ways in which the destruction of the traditional medieval community was linked to the final split of Catholic Europe into a number of rival doctrinal camps. And it's clear that one major victim of this loss of a commonly held spiritual authority was the concept of virtue. With competing role models, no agreed upon interpretative authority, a babble of conflicting voices, and clashing of competing armies, the community stability essential to the notion of virtue disappeared.

Thus, the old idea of human life having a traditional spiritual purpose in accordance with which we could organize our understanding of ourselves and our moral duties began gradually to lose its grip. For the shared agreement about what that goal might be and how best we might reach it was gone. And with it went very slowly but inexorably the most important way human beings had organized their moral understanding of themselves and their communities for over a thousand years: the idea of virtue. It's difficult for us to understand just how seriously dislocating this experience was one of the most profound spiritual and social crises in the history of Western Europe.

All of a sudden there were competing authorities, each one announcing a different agenda, commanding a different allegiance, redefining or urging us to abandon virtue. The conflicts separated communities, families, couples and the stakes were the highest possible: the future of one's immortal soul. Of course, the conflict had important political, economic, and national dimensions, and it is important to acknowledge these, but one should never merely subsume the conflict under one of these rubrics the spiritual conflict was also very real.

No longer was there any certain assurance about what defined the good life for me or about what were the appropriate ways to sort out our difficulties doctrinal, economic, social, and personal. So profound was the distress, that there was a widespread feeling at the start of the seventeenth century that the world must be coming to an end. In this context we can understand something of the moral imperative under the interest in the new science as a source of order.

The situation is not unlike that we discussed when we came to Plato's writings right after dealing with the horrifying vision of Euripides's Bacchae. And it is no accident that many of the seventeenth-century thinkers and their eighteenth-century followers (like Hobbes and Rousseau) saw themselves as the spiritual heirs of Plato, seeking a new certainty in the realm of mathematics to deal with the rampant scepticism, atheism, and power grabbing all around them.

But this comparison with Plato needs to be treated with great care. It is true that, in some respects, the rise of seventeenth-century science marks the first beginnings of an energetic revival of Plato's project the quest for certainty through mathematics and through a repudiation of traditional authorities. But we need to be careful here for a number of reasons:

a. Plato's concern, at least in the early dialogues

(including the Republic) is directed first and foremost by a moral concern a need to know about the Good. A certain form of education will foster that, but turning our attention to the study and mastery of nature is emphatically not part of the project. Socrates is quite firm on this point: education for virtue is the plan, with contemplation of the ideal as the goal. He is not interested in applying dialectic to a study of the natural world for the sake of power.

b. Stated another way, Plato's main interest is on what Aristotle later calls final causes moral questions about the Good. What is true virtue, how do we come to understand it, how do we encourage virtue in the citizens and the rulers? The seventeenth-century scientist-philosophers were overwhelmingly concerned, as their first priority, with efficient causes. Let us study the mechanism, find out how it works, how to control and manipulate it. It's true that many of them, especially in England, hoped that through the study of efficient causes we would finally come to understand moral questions. As Bacon expressed it, the chain of efficient causes would eventually lead us to the throne of God. And Newton also emphatically states that the modern science will provide insight into final causes (as did Boyle).

Descartes, of course, was not convinced on this point. There was no way in which human rationality and experimentation were ever going to reach an understanding of God's purposes. On the other hand, Descartes's firm optimism about the powers of the enquiring mind held open the hope that we could achieve some certainty on moral questions, without direct recourse to the Divine Will.

What's important to get out of this brief consideration of the new science is its extraordinarily optimistic and confident agenda: there could, indeed, be a basis for a new shared understanding of all questions of immediate importance. All we needed to do was apply the human intellect to the natural world in a manner available to anyone and with a proper method and accurate experiments; we could find the appropriate answers to our two questions.

In the literature of seventeenth century, there is no shortage of statements about this optimistic project. But for me the key one has always been what Galileo says in a brief exchange between Simplicio (the spokesman for the orthodox traditionalists) and Salvati (the spokesman for Galileo) in the Dialogues Concerning the Two World Systems: Simp. But if Aristotle is to be abandoned, whom shall we have for a guide in philosophy?

Suppose you name some author. Salv. We need guides in forests and in unknown lands, but on plains and in open places only the blind need guides. It is better for such people to stay at home, but anyone with eyes in his head and his wits about him could serve as a guide for them.

The unabashed confidence that all is available to us if we will but look about us, together with the peremptory dismissal of that very important question, indicates as well as anything else the vigorous optimism that human beings will be more than equal to the task of applying mathematics to the world, if they will just set aside their respect for a tradition which is holding them back and get on with the job.

Besides, they knew, as did everyone else, that there was no turning back. They were onto something; they saw it as a rich alternative to a tradition which had failed them; and, with the publication of Newton's Principia in 1667, almost universally accepted as the definitive answer to a question no one had been able to resolve before, they had the proof that they were on the right track.

THE GREAT TORY SATIRISTS: POPE, SWIFT, JOHNSON

But this quickly rising faith in a new science did not go unopposed and not simply by Church authorities worried about their own power or the literal truth of scripture (although they did voice vigorous objections). The new science raised serious doubts in the minds of those moralists who did not share the optimistic assumptions of the new natural scientists, because for them it threatened the key concept of virtue. And so there was a Conservative reaction. In England this reaction is linked to three of the greatest writers in English literature: Alexander Pope, a Roman Catholic, Samuel Johnson, an orthodox Anglican, and by Jonathan Swift, an Anglican cleric.

In addition to their religious beliefs, all three were very well versed in the classics, and derived much of their inspiration from classical Roman (especially Stoic) traditions. In a word, they were great Christian humanists. These three, among others, set their sights against the modern trends. Their favourite weapon was satire, and their mood generally pessimistic.

What were they objecting to? And what did they want? Simply put, they did not buy into the great hopes of the new theoretical science and rational philosophy, that it would contribute to the moral improvement of human beings. On the contrary, they saw it as a very dangerous reassertion of pride a perilous confidence in the powers of human reasoning, which quite undermined the single most important point of traditional faith, the strong sense of human beings as limited fallen creatures, mired in ignorance.

So they saw the surge in confidence at the start of the eighteenth century the increasing wealth, the energetic trade and colonization, the amazing scientific discoveries, the proliferation of capitalist projects, this enormously exuberant and to them largely secular preoccupation as taking people's minds away from the most important moral imperative: their own virtue. At the same time, these Tory satirists were no advocates of a return to sixteenth-century religion.

For they were as aware as anyone of what goes on in a religious civil war. So they direct their satires also at those who are urging a more "irrational" approach to religion: the enthusiastic preachers (like the Methodists, the Baptists, and other non-conforming protestants). They want, in other words, to carve a course between what they say as the extreme irrationality of the new religions and the excessive rationality of the new natural philosophy. And thus, to simply matters considerably, the Tory moralists set their sights primarily on three main targets:

- Those who in a passionate zeal for their version of the truth of religion based their message on an appeal to people's feelings (especially the "enthusiastic" protestants);
- The growing commercialism of life, with its emphasis on fashion, leisure, money, licentiousness, greed; increasingly this money was not dependent upon land or the community it was a speculative wealth of the urban middle class, the product of venture capitalism, which they saw as corrupting;

c. the new rationalism in philosophy and natural philosophy, especially the fierce logic of someone like Descartes, divorcing his intellectual explorations from traditions and experience and setting up the authority of his own rational enquiries over everything else, insisting that the world answer his mathematically based understanding of it; they distrusted, too, its enormously optimistic confidence that human problems were capable of human solutions through the application of appropriate methods.

Thus they were openly hostile to the growing hopes of theoretical and experimental science. What these added up to was a fierce hostility to a changing attitude toward the nature of human beings the growing notion that human beings could "progress," could become different by overcoming all problems, including those inherent in their own natures, and could eventually become "happy."

They were deeply suspicious of any philosophy which made easy generalizations about the nature of human beings and which then constructed a theory of knowledge or of society on such a rational understanding. For them human beings were much more enigmatic and ultimately dangerous than such easy rational generalizations suggested. Human life, they argued, should be lived on the basis of one's personal interactions and on the accumulated experience of such interactions, not in service to some idealized theoretical picture of human beings.

For these Tory satirists the new natural philosophy was a dangerous assertion of human pride an illusion based upon the rejection of the traditional wisdom and to them a naive faith in the possibilities of acquiring metaphysical certainty. This for them was a recipe for disaster. Human beings were not on this earth to be knowledgeable, happy, and powerful, but rather to be as morally virtuous as possible: that was their central and most difficult challenge as human beings, the quest for spiritual excellence.

And the new thinking was threatening this old Socratic insight. As Monk writes (talking of Swift): Why was Swift inimical to these tendencies all of which are familiar aspects of our world today? Very simply, I think, because he was a Christian and a humanist.

As a Christian he believed that man's fallen nature could never transcend its own limitations and so fulfil the hopes of that optimistic age; as a humanist he was concerned for the preservation of those moral and spiritual qualities which distinguish men from beasts and for the health and continuity of fruitful tradition in church, state, and the sphere of the mind.

As both Christian and humanist, he knew that men must be better than they are and that, though our institutions can never be perfect, they need not be corrupt. the "savage indignation" which motivates all of Swift's satires arises from his anger at the difference between what men are and what they might be if they only would rise to the full height of their humanity.

Thus, they attacked the notions central to the modern scientific enterprise in defence of a particular vision of Christianity a moderate and reasonable faith, which held to the need for traditional authorities, an acceptance of scripture but without nitpicking doctrinal disputes, and a strong sense of the limitations of the human understanding.

They wanted, above all, that people regardless of their particular version of religion and interpretations of scripture should never forget they were fallen creatures in need of spiritual guidance and sustenance, and that the traditional virtues faith, hope, and charity and the traditional institutions whose job it was to insist upon such virtues (bishops and kings) were more important than some future discoveries or powers over nature.

Know then thyself, presume not God to scan; The proper study of mankind is Man. Placed on this isthmus of a middle state, A being darkly wise, and rudely great: With too much knowledge for the skeptic side, With too much weakness for the Stoic's pride, He hangs between; in doubt to act, or rest, In doubt to deem himself a god, or beast; In doubt his mind or body to prefer, Born but to die, and reasoning but to err; Alike in ignorance, his reason such, Whether he things too little, or too much: Chaos of thought and passion, all confused; Still by himself abused, or disabused; Created half to rise, and half to fall; Great lord of all things, yet a prey to all; Sole judge of truth, in endless error hurled" The glory, jest, an riddle of the world! (Alexander Pope, Essay on Man, II, 1-18)

To understand their position, we can consider two key terms in the arguments: nature and reason. The enthusiastic religions had no use for the second term, and they competed endlessly about the true nature of human beings. Because they were hopelessly divided over the interpretation of scripture and what that indicated about human beings, they had no shared vision of the good life for the individual or of the political and ecclesiastical consequences of that view.

The new natural philosophers had a mechanical conception of nature, and a mathematically based conception of reason. They varied considerably on their view of human nature (from the possible atheism of Hobbes, to the dualism of Descartes, to the mystical protestantism of Newton, to the more or less orthodox Anglicanism of Boyle). But the reason they appealed to was, as we have seen, in Galileo, Newton, Descartes, and Hobbes, the reasoning best exemplified in mathematics, especially geometry.

And this, they insisted, would be the best method to pursue in dealing with questions arising out of all nature, including human nature. The Tory satirists saw reason differently. For them it was more a matter of reasonableness. Human beings needed reason to control and guide and repress the passions, but the reason they adhered to was something much more like common sense prudence than deductive logic. Reason included a sturdy sense of the limits of rationality, with no false confidence, and they never tired of reminding their readers that such confidence was misplaced and that human beings and societies who placed their faith in such rationality would suffer dire moral consequences.

Hence, they were no admirers of the sort of reasoning exemplified in Descartes the intense rational speculation about ultimate questions. Nature for them revealed a natural order, which was reflected in the political and ecclesiastical structures of the state (hence their conservative political stance and their admiration for traditional literatures, traditional communal structures, especially that of Rome). As such, virtue for them was still an operative principle, and the state of one's soul the primary concern.

No enthusiastic religion or rational philosophy was going to replace the old verities. In this life, scientific projects to improve the lot of the poor were going to be no replacement for traditional charity. For the attainment of happiness was a dangerous illusion. In the words of Imlac, Johnson's Abyssinian thinker: In enumerating the particular comforts of life, we shall find many advantages on the side of the Europeans. They cure wounds and diseases with which we languish and perish. We suffer inclemencies of weather which they can obviate.

They have engines for the despatch of many laborious works, which we must perform by manual industry. There is such communication between distant places that one friend can hardly be said to be absent from another. Their policy removes all public inconveniences; they have roads cut through their mountains, and bridges laid upon their rivers. And, if we descend to the privacies of life, their habitations are more commodious, and their possessions are more secure.

The Europeans ... are less unhappy than we, but they are not happy. Human life is everywhere a state in which much is to be endured, and little to be enjoyed. The distrust of projects to improve happiness comes out particularly clearly in Book

III of Gulliver's Travels, when Swift satirizes the application of the modern project to agriculture. In many respects, Swift's satire is weakest in Book III because he is attacking the new way of thinking on its strongest territory. But he had a real cause in looking at what the scientific projectors were doing in agriculture, which was the first arena in which the new thinking was vigorously applied to the communal life.

For the application of new scientific procedures to agriculture with a view to making production more efficient was well under way in Swift's time, and the social dislocations it caused were very serious. I alluded to this in the lecture on Hobbes. Simply put, it involved something we are still wrestling with: the creation of large agricultural units in order to gain the advantages of economies of scale.

This meant driving the peasants off the common land, enclosing it, and turning the production over to more efficient private interests, now able to deal with large-scale farming. In the long run this did produce a much more efficient agriculture and England was the pioneer but the total upheaval and destruction of many traditional communities was the price (unlike France, where the enclosure movement did not have the same effect; we are still thus dealing with the problems of the small scale farmer in France).

So in the short term, the time in which Swift is writing, the social distress was acute, as thousands of subsistence-level farmers were driven off the land they needed to support themselves, in order to permit large landowners to revolutionize agricultural production in a modern scientific manner. Swift correctly saw this measure as a vital blow at the moral life, because it struck at the heart of what kept the traditional communities vital.

Like many of the new seventeenth-century thinkers, these Tory satirists were suspicious of language, especially of the extreme metaphorical uses of it to inflame opinions (as we have seen in Hobbes). But they wanted to control the excesses in the understanding of traditional ideas rather than to jettison that tradition and put language on a new footing entirely. So we see in Gulliver's Travels, one of the points about Lilliput and about the land of the horses which Gulliver most admires, is their attitude towards words and the uses of words in literature. One way to appreciate these points is to check the adjectives of commendation and approbation.

For these writers the highest praise one would render an adult would be to call him or her sensible guided by a nice appreciation for experience, adjusting their understanding of things and their feelings about things according to a robust sense of how the world actually worked according to our sense experience of it, without being taken in by delusions about religion, money, grandly rational theoretical structures, or one's own importance.

By contrast, words like imaginative, extravagant, enthusiastic, or fond indicated disapproval an excess of feeling or ideas divorced from the perceived realities of the world. When Swift, for example, says of the horses in Book IV, that they are not fond of their children, he is indicating an essential feature of their rationality they do not let excess devotion to their offspring impair their sturdy good sense about the world. AT the same time, of course, they do not let their aptitude for mathematics delude them into thinking that that form of reason is the proper basis for understanding the natural world.

GULLIVER'S TRAVELS

Swift's Gulliver's Travels is without question the most famous prose work to emerge from this Tory Satiric tradition. It is the strongest, funniest, and yet in some ways most despairing cry for a halt to the trends initiated by seventeenth-century philosophy. It is the best evidence we can read to remind us that the rise of the new rationality did not occur unopposed.

Before looking at how Swift deals with his resistance, however, I want to talk a bit about the basic techniques Swift uses to structure his satire. For Gulliver's Travels is not just a great work of moral argument; it is also a wonderful satire, and whatever one thinks of Swift's moral position, it is generally difficulty not to acknowledge his supreme skill as a satirist.

SOME OBSERVATIONS ON SWIFT'S SATIRIC TECHNIQUE

If the main purpose of any satire is to invite the reader to laugh at a particular human vice or folly, in order to invite us to consider an important moral alternative, then the chief task facing the satirist is to present the target in such a way that we find constant delight in the wit, humour, and surprises awaiting us.

So to appreciate just why some satires work and others do not, one should look carefully at how the satirist sets up the target and delivers his judgement upon it in such a way as to sustain our interest. In other words, the essence of good satire is not the complexity in the moral message coming across, but in the skilful style with which the writer seeks to demolish his target.

When we discussed Aristophanes, I suggested there that one main ingredient in satire is distortion or exaggeration an invitation to see something very familiar, perhaps even something we ourselves do in such a way that it becomes simultaneously ridiculous (or even disgusting) and yet funny, comical something no reasonable person would engage in. Now, the first important question to ask of any satirist is how he or she achieves the necessary comic distortion which transforms the familiar into the ridiculous.

And Swift's main technique for achieving this and a wonderful technique for satire is the basic plot of science fiction: the voyage by an average civilized human being into unknown territory and his return back home. This apparently simple plot immediately opens up all sorts of satiric possibilities, because it enables the writer constantly to play off three different perspectives in order give the reader a comic sense of what is very familiar. It can do this in the following ways:

- If the strange new country is recognizably similar to the reader's own culture, then comic distortions in the new world enable the writer to satirize the familiar in a host of different ways, providing, in effect, a cartoon style view of the reader's own world.

- If the strange new country is some sort of utopia a perfectly realized vision of the ideals often proclaimed but generally violated in the reader's own world then the satirist can manipulate the discrepancy between the ideal new world of the fiction and the corrupt world of the reader to illustrate repeatedly just how empty the pretensions to goodness really are in the reader's world. c. But the key to this technique is generally the use of the traveller, the figure who is, in effect, the reader's contemporary and fellow countryman.

How that figure reacts to the New World can be a constant source of amusement and pointed satiric comment, because, in effect, this figure represents the contact between the normal world of the reader and the strange New World of either caricatured ridiculousness or utopian perfection.

We can see Swift moving back and forth between the first two techniques, and this can create some confusion. For example, in much of Book I, Lilliput is clearly a comic distortion of life in Europe. The sections on the public rewards of leaping and creeping or the endless disputes about whether one should eat one's eggs by breaking them at the bigger or the smaller end or the absurdity of the royal proclamations are obvious and funny distortions of the court life, the pompous pretentiousness of officials, and the religious disputes familiar to Swift's readers.

At the same time, however, there are passages where he holds up the laws of Lilliput as some form of utopian ideal, in order to demonstrate just how much better they understand true reasonableness than do the Europeans. In Book II he does the same: for most of the time the people of Brobdingnag are again caricatured distorted Europeans, but clearly the King of Brobdingnag is an ideal figure. This shift in perspective on the New World is at times confusing.

Swift is, in effect, manipulating the fictional world to suit his immediate satirical purposes. It's easy enough to see what he's doing, but it does, in some sense, violate our built-up expectations. Just how are we supposed to take Lilliput and

Brobdingnag as a distorted Europe or as a utopia or what? This lack of a consistent independent reality to the fictional world which he has created is one of the main reasons why Gulliver's Travels is not considered a one of the first novels (since one of the requirements of a novel, it is maintained, is a consistent attitude towards the fictional reality one has created: one cannot simply manipulate it at will to prove a didactic point). In Book IV, Swift deals more consistently with this ambiguity in the New World by dividing it into two groups: the satirized Europeans, the Yahoos, and the ideally reasonable creatures, the horses.

So here there is less of a sense of shifting purpose at work. That may help to account, in part, for the great power of the Fourth Voyage. Now, the genius of Swift's satire in Gulliver's Travels realizes itself in a second feature the way he organizes the New World in order to make it a constantly fertile source of satiric humour. His main insight, in the first two books, has the simplicity of genius. He simply changes the perspective on human conduct: in Book I Gulliver is a normal human being visiting a recognizably European society, but he is twelve times bigger than anyone else.

In the second the technique is the same, but now he is twelve times smaller. With this altered perspective, Swift can now manipulate Gulliver's reactions to the changing circumstances in order to underscore his satiric points in a very humorous way.For instance, it's clear that the main satiric target in Book I is the pride Europeans take in public ceremonies, titles, court preferment, and all sorts of celebrations of their power and magnificence. So there's an obvious silliness to the obsession with these matters when the figures are only six inches high. But what makes this preoccupation with ceremony all the sillier is Gulliver's reaction to it. He, as a good European, takes it quite seriously.

He's truly impressed with the king's magnificence, with his proclamation that he's the most powerful monarch in the world, and he takes great delight in being given the title of a Nardac. The satiric point here, of course, is not on the Lilliputians (although they are obviously caricatured

Europeans) but on Gulliver's enthusiastic participation in their silliness.

For example, when he's accused of having an affair with the cabinet minister's wife, he does not scoff at the biological ridiculousness of that accusation; he defends himself with his new title: I couldn't have done that; after all, I'm a Nardac. Similarly in Book II, in which the main target shifts to the Europeans' preoccupation with physical beauty, the chief sources of satiric humour are the gross exaggerations of the human body seen magnified twelve times but also Gulliver's reactions to it.

THE CHARACTER OF GULLIVER

And this brings me to a key point in following Gulliver's Travels, namely the importance of Gulliver himself. He is our contact throughout the four voyages, and at the end he is completely different from the person he was at the start. So it's particularly important that we get a handle on who he is, what happens to him, why it happens, and how we are supposed to understand that. The single most important thing Swift has to say in Gulliver's Travels concerns the changes which take place in the narrator.

Now, to get the satiric point of the changes in Gulliver across, Swift has to be careful not to give the reader an easy escape, for Swift understood very well that readers who see themselves satirized will always look for some way of neutralizing or deflecting the satire away from them.

Satire, Swift observed, is a mirror in which people see everyone else's face but their own. So it's important for us to take careful stock of Gulliver, to assess just how reliable a person he is, so that we can fully understand the nature of his transformation. At the start of the first voyage, Swift takes a few pages to establish for us that Gulliver is, in some ways, a very typical European.

He is middle aged, well educated, sensible (in the best sense of the term), with no extravagantly romantic notions. He is a careful observer, scrupulous about looking after his family, and fully conversant with the importance of conducting his affairs prudently. There is nothing extraordinary about him. He's been around, and he's not a person to be easily rattled. This is important to grasp, because in effect Swift is removing from us any possibility of ascribing the transformation which takes place in Gulliver to any quirks of his character. He is not an unbalanced, erratic, private, or imaginative person.

On the contrary, he is about as typically sensible and reasonable a narrator as one could wish. And he fully supports the culture which has produced him. That's why, in the first two books, we can see why he would naturally fall in with the Europeanness of the new world.

He has never reflected at all on the rightness or wrongness of the given order of things, so he naturally supports the authority of the king, the ceremonies of the court, and the "fairness" of the justice system. Only when he himself is sentenced to be blinded do we begin to sense that Gulliver is learning something.

Circumstances are forcing him to think about, not just his own safety, but something much bigger: the justice of the proceedings. He is, in other words, beginning to develop a critical awareness of the limitations of the values of Lilliput and, beyond that, of the way in which the Europeans reflect those same values.

These initial critical insights are temporary only, and when he returns, he is quickly reconciled to European life. But in the second voyage the critical awareness returns, especially in relation to the physical grossness of the giant Brobdingnagians. The altered perspective leads him to reflect upon the way in which Europeans have become obsessed with physical beauty, especially with the feminine body, when, from a different perspective, it is comically gross and even nauseating.

However, this growing sense of a critical awareness in Book II does not lead Gulliver seriously to question his European values, and so he is prepared to defend the sorry history of Europe in the face of the King of Brobdingnag's scorn.... I cannot but conclude the bulk of your native to be the most pernicious race of little odious vermin that nature ever suffered to crawl upon the surface of the earth.

But that powerful indictment of European life which is so close to the conclusion of Book IV Gulliver is not yet ready for. His typical European consciousness is still too full of complacent self congratulation to accept this form of criticism, so he dismisses it with a snide remark about the limited understanding of the King of Brobdingnag (reinforced by his rejection of the use of gunpowder). Yet, it's clear that something is happening to Gulliver, because upon his return home after the second voyage, it takes him some time to readjust to European life.

This is quite comical, but the point is important: in his strange new land, his perceptions are changing. At this point it is simply a matter of the physical proportions of the people, but Swift is setting up the reader for the conclusions of the book, when the transformation of Gulliver is going to involve a total alternative of his moral perspectives, so that he is no longer able to return to the calm, unreflective, typical European that he was when he started.

THE FOURTH VOYAGE

I'm moving directly to the fourth voyage, because in a sense it is the logical continuation of the Second Voyage (the Third Voyage was written later), and most of the serious arguments about Swift's satire focus on this part of the book. In the fourth voyage, Gulliver's transformation becomes complete, and when he returns he can no longer participate in European society not even with his friends and family as he could before.

It's as if Swift is saying that Gulliver has discovered something that makes social life in the normal sense insupportable, so that he would sooner construct his own life among his domestic horses than return to a normal family life.

And the key interpretative questions thus arises: How are we to deal with this conclusion to the story? On the face of it, the conclusion seems an unacceptably harsh condemnation of European humanity. Their Yahoo-like nature makes dealing with them impossible, and thus the reasonable thing to do is to turn away from them. Is this not ultimately a violently misanthropic gesture, and therefore something we must turn away from? Dealing with this question is one of the great battle grounds in the interpretation of English literature (like dealing with Hamlet or Paradise Lost).

In order to clarify the issues, I'd like to review some of the positions and then suggest some of the things we need to consider in charting a way through the difficulties. I should add that I do have my own view of what is the most comprehensible interpretation (and I will add that), but I don't want anyone to think that this is not fiercely contested interpretative territory. a. The first reaction to the end of the Fourth Voyage is to acknowledge that Swift indeed wants us to understand and sympathize with Gulliver's actions.

The main satiric point of Gulliver's final actions was to ridicule the Europeans' pretensions to rationality; Gulliver's response is an exaggerated but still understandable way of underlining the point that, if we could come to understand true rationality, as Gulliver has done through his experience with the horses, and if we could have our eyes opened as to what we are really like underneath all our fine illusions about ourselves, as Gulliver's eyes have been opened by his experience of the Yahoos, then we, too, would turn away, and, rather like the person who has finally made it out of Plato's cave, want to spend our time in contemplation of the beauty and truth of reason and not be distracted by the foolish pride of those gazing at the cave wall.

This interpretation was common among Swift's contemporaries and in the nineteenth century. However, many who saw this in the satire simply dismissed it as a harsh but finally erroneous vision; they believed that the promises of the new science were, in fact, being realized, that progress was possible, and that Swift was simply wrong, out of touch with the perfectibility of human nature and human social institutions, that he was simply a grumpy, pessimistic, conservative Christian.

Thus, the book was simply a conservative complaining

about an emerging new truth. In addition, of course, the book had too many naughty words, and therefore should not be read by people concerned for politeness in literature. So those who wanted to believe in a less fiercely limited view of human nature had an easy excuse to denigrate Swift as a writer worth reading. Progress is on schedule for all Swift's negative vision.

Now this reaction is interesting because it does at least acknowledge that Swift had a serious purpose and that in the transformation of Gulliver he made that purpose explicit. Gulliver is, indeed, Swift's spokesman until the very end. The dismissal of the book, therefore, does not involve a denial of the full satiric intention. It does acknowledge the point of what Swift is doing. However, it claims that that is the wrong point. Swift's satire is clear, but his understanding of human nature and morality is wrong. A second reaction is to equate Swift with Gulliver to claim, as with the first reaction, that Swift intends us to take Gulliver's transformation seriously.

Swift, however, is mad, mentally unbalanced, notoriously neurotic, and therefore we do not need to attend seriously to the ending of the book, unless we happen to be interested in clinical manifestations in literature of various mental aberrations. Enter, from stage left, the psychoanalytic view of Swift, which quite neutralizes the satire by an appeal to various disorders. Here's a sample: Ferenczi (1926): "From the psychoanalytic standpoint one would describe [Swift's] neurotic behaviour as an inhibition of normal potency, with a lack of courage in relation to women of good character and perhaps with a lasting aggressive tendency towards women of a lower type.

This insight into Swift's life surely justifies us who come after him in treating the phantasies in Gulliver's Travels exactly as we do the free associations of neurotic patients in analysis, especially when interpreting their dreams." Karpman (1942): "It is submitted on the basis of such a study of Gulliver's Travels that Swift was a neurotic who exhibited psychosexual infantilism, with a particular showing of coprophilia, associated with misogeny, misanthropy, mysophilia, and mysophobia."

Greenacre (1955): "One gets the impression that the anal fixation was intense and binding, and the genital demands so impaired or limited at best that there was total retreat from genital sexuality in his early adult life, probably beginning with the unhappy relationship with Jane Waring, the first of the goddesses.

The common symbolism of the man in the boat as the clitoris suggests the identification with the female phallus though to be characteristic of the male transvestite. Swift showed marked anal characteristics [his extreme immaculateness, secretiveness, intense ambition, pleasure in less obvious dirt (e.g., satire), stubborn vengefulness in righteous causes] which indicate clearly that early control of the excretory function was achieved under great stress and perhaps too early." And so on and so on.

One is tempted to have some fun with this line of criticism (e.g., What about Two Years Before the Mast, Moby Dick, Three Men in a Boat, Captain Hornblower), but what such an approach does to Gulliver's Travels is important. It replaces the moral seriousness of the satiric message with a clinical study of the deranged author.

Thus, we do not have to attend seriously to any moral position at stake here. A third reaction, common in the twentieth century, quite rehabilitates Swift from this sort of criticism by claiming that, at the end of the Fourth Voyage, we are not meant to see Gulliver's actions as the natural rational outcome of what he has been through, because Gulliver himself has here become the target of the satire. Gulliver, in other words, no longer speaks for the author. What he does is, in effect, an overreaction, and Swift wants us to understand that as such.

His treatment of the Portuguese captain and his family are clear indications that Gulliver has gone overboard in his admiration for the horses and his dislike of the Yahoos, and that we are to see in his conduct a warning of sorts. This approach to the Fourth Voyage, one should note, helps to maintain the claim that Swift was an intelligent writer, fully in command of his medium, and that we do not have to deal with the disturbing effects of the satire by writing them off as the ravings of an anally maladjusted neurotic, obsessed with the cramping in his sphincter.

We simply have to understand that Swift's satiric intentions at the end of the Fourth Voyage are not as harsh as they appear to be. What this approach does to the power of Swift's satire, however, is a question that needs to be carefully considered. How consistent is this view of the ending with the general tenor of the rest of the satire in Book IV and in the other Books?

Now debating these options might be an interesting seminar exercise. But however they are resolved, I would like to offer some things that one should bear in mind. The transformation of Gulliver starts, as I observed, in Book I and becomes considerably stronger in Book II. That transformation involves a growing critical awareness of the extent to which pride rules human actions. At the start Gulliver gives no sign of ever having thought about such matters. He's a patriotic, unreflective European professional.

The insights come intermittently and do not last. But to some extent, the transformation of Gulliver at the end of the fourth voyage can be seen as a logical outcome of the trend that has started before. So, however we evaluate the end of the fourth voyage, we need to measure that interpretation against the rest of the book.

This might be connected with the growing seriousness of the initial situation that gets Gulliver into the New World: in Book I it's a shipwreck; in Book II, he's abandoned; in Book III, it's pirates; and in Book IV, it's a mutiny (and we all remember from reading Dante that a mutiny, a revolt against established authority, is the greatest crime).

Gulliver's transformation in Book IV has two motives: his sudden awareness of the Yahoo-like nature of European human beings, including himself, and, equally important, his sudden discovery about what true reasonableness really means (in the lives of the horses). So in estimating how one should assess his final state, one needs to bear in mind that it's not just a turning away from European family and social life; it is also a turning towards what he is now fully in love with, a contemplation of the truth. One's judgement on what Gulliver has gone through does not depend upon our having to decide whether it would be rational or not for us to follow suit, abandon our families, and set up home in the nearest stable.

That is not what Swift is saying. He's offering us a vision a comic and satiric but nonetheless morally serious vision of what would happen to a typical European (like us) if we had, like Gulliver, come to a full understanding through experience both of ourselves and of true reasonableness (which we like to think we possess).

The basic idea here is derived, quite clearly, from Plato's Allegory of the Cave. Gulliver has made it out of the cave, and having seen the sun, he's not about to pretend that looking at shadows on the wall is the right way to live. What is happening to him is, in fact, just what Plato says will happen to the person who returns: he is treated as insane because normal people (that's us) simply cannot grasp what he now understands.

(It's interesting, incidentally, to note just how popular this sort of ending is in satiric stories with a similar intent: the endings of, for example, Heart of Darkness and Catch 22, are remarkably similar.

The central character, once a recognizably typical representative of his culture, has gone through a transformation which leads him to reject that culture in a way that his contemporaries do not understand: Marlow takes to the sea for the rest of his life; Yossarian sets out in a rubber raft for Scandinavia).

One needs also to recognize that it's no serious criticism of Swift's moral position to observe that the life of the horses is not all that attractive, that to us it seems boring. That's part of Swift's point.

We, as readers, are Yahoos, irrational creatures and, beyond that, incapable for the most part of even understanding and responding to the attractions of such reasonable behaviour. For Swift's major point here is not that we should try to emulate the horses, for that's impossible, but rather that we should stop pretending that we are equivalent to them. We are not by nature reasonable creatures, and it is the height of folly and pride to assert that we are.

We have to start our moral awareness with the acceptance of that truth, and our dissatisfaction with the life of the horses is not an indication that they are wrong so much as that we are unreasonable. We describe ourselves in terms appropriate to the horses, but we characteristically behave more like Yahoos.

That is the source of the pride which Swift wishes to attack. Finally, it's important to recognize that our last contact with Gulliver indicates quite clearly that what bothers him about human beings is not what they are but what they pretend to be.

He would be much happier about living among human beings again, and is starting to do so, but everything would be much easier for him if their characteristic pride did not always get in the way: My reconcilement to the Yahoo kind in general might not be so difficult, if they would be content with those vices and follies only which nature hath entitled them to.

I am not in the least provoked by the sight of a lawyer, a pickpocket, a colonel, a fool, a lord, a gamester, a politician, a whoremonger, a physician, an evidence, a suborner, an attorney, a traitor, or the like: this is all according to the due course of things. But when I behold a lump of deformity, and diseases both in body and mind, smitten with pride, it immediately breaks all the measures of my patience; neither shall I be ever able to comprehend how such an animal and such a vice could tally together.

The wise and virtuous Houyhnhnms, who abound in all excellencies that can adorn a rational creature, have no name for this vice in their language, which hath no terms to express anything that is evil, except those whereby they describe the detestable qualities of their Yahoos, among which they were not able to distinguish this of pride, for want of thoroughly understanding human nature, as it showeth itself in other countries, where that animal presides.

But I, who had more experience, could plainly observe some rudiments of it in the Yahoos. The point I want to stress here is that, however one determines to navigate the interpretative waters of the ending of Gulliver's Travels, it is important to reconcile your view of Gulliver's behaviour with what he actually says and with the satiric momentum of the last book, as it arises out of the earlier voyages.

My own view (not shared by all members of the team) is that Swift does want us to take Gulliver seriously right up to the end, that we are to understand his reaction as the natural consequence of a man who has made it out of the cave, and who now is not willing to go back to what he once was. The fact that we find this odd is a reminder to us of just how much we are the product of years of watching shadows on the cave wall.

Yes, the Portuguese captain is a good person, and, yes, Gulliver's wife and family are neglected, but when you've come to see, as Gulliver has, just what true reasonableness involves, then a normal life and normal good people are not enough.

The point, to repeat myself, is not that we should try to emulate Gulliver, but that we should try to understand him and if we do that, we may come to recognize the illusory pride which makes us claim to be rational creatures.

Of course, I have to admit that the extreme anger Gulliver displays at the end (like his extreme nausea at the human Body in Book II) does invite someone to wonder about the extent to which the satiric purpose might be being subverted by an excessively strong imaginative distaste for certain elements of human life.

The borderline between very strong satire and a questionable wallowing about in ugliness or pornography for its own sake is not always clearly discernible and different readers have different reactions.

To that extent, I would admit that there is ground in Swift's style for certain questions to arise. However, I do not believe myself that such questions cannot be answered within the framework of the interpretation I have just outlined.

A FINAL COMMENT

For me Swift's language, though strong, is still in control. The vision is harsh, the anger extreme, but that's a sign of the intense moral indignation Swift feels at the transformation of life around him in ways that are leading, he thinks, to moral disaster.

The central Christian and Socratic emphasis on virtue is losing ground to something he sees as a facile illusion that reason, wealth, money, and power could somehow do the job for us which had been traditionally placed upon our moral characters. In the new world, faith, hope, and charity, Swift sees, are going to be irrelevant, because the rational organization of human experience and the application of the new reasoning to all aspects of human life are going to tempt human beings with a rich lure: the promise of happiness.

Under the banner of the new rationality, the traditional notions of virtue will become irrelevant, as human beings substitute for excellence of character the development of the individual human life according to some telos, some spiritual goal the idea that properly organized rules, structures of authority, rational enquiry into efficient causes, profitable commercial ventures, and laws will provide the sure guide, because, after all, human beings are rational creatures.

Book IV of Gulliver's Travels is the most famous and most eloquent protest against this modern project. The severity of his indignation and anger is, I think, a symptom of the extent to which he realized the battle was already being lost. To us, however, over two hundred years later, Swift's point is perhaps more vividly relevant than to many of his contemporaries. After all, we have witnessed the triumphant unrolling of the scientific project, the extension of Descartes's rationality into all aspects of our lives.

And yet we might want to ask ourselves whether the cheque which Descarttes wrote out for us is negotiable, whether his promise has, in fact, made us morally better creatures, more able to live the good life, more charitable to our neighbours, with a greater faith in the excellences life does make possible, better able to work out our differences justly, and more able to achieve true happiness. Or, on the contrary, has giving the enormous power of the new science to the Yahoos not created some of the those very dangers which Swift is so concerned to warn us about will happen? The yahoos now posses the secrets of atomic energy and genetic engineering; their commercial zest is punching holes in the ozone and deforesting the planet.

Meanwhile, in Moscow and Washington, DC, the life expectancy of adult males is plummeting. Has all this increase in knowledge and power made us any more just towards each other? Has it clarified the good life for me and a means of settling justly our disputes? The jury is, one might argue, still out.

Chapter 7

Nabokov and Swift, Achilles and the Tortoise

The vogue which the Zeno's famous paradox enjoys in poststructuralist theory is not surprising. It is this paradox which provides a point of convergence between the main strands associated with the illustrious names of Deleuze, Lacan and Derrida as well as between the crucial issues of poststructuralist project-those of difference/alterity, identity construction and the "bar games" with the referent (Genosko 1994: 7, 41)-furnishing the framework for the allegedly non-logocentric redefinition of the status of the work of art and aesthetic activity in general.

However, as the attempts to attain a critical distance from what has already become a poststructuralist orthodoxy gain in strength and scope, the reasons that of yore have pushed our paradox to the fore become obscured if not obfuscated. This paradoxical fate of Zeno's paradox deserves most minute attention.

If the efforts to carve the path beyond deconstruction have thus far so obviously failed to produce anything worthwhile, then precisely because the paradoxicality just mentioned points to the very heart of the problem with which theorists unsuccessfully grapple for the last thirty or so.

In most general terms the problem in question is the undoubdtfully honorouble task of surpassing logocentric tradition in all its forms and disguises, the task for which the name of Derrida has become totemic. And yet the very mood characteristic of the current theoretical scene-that of melancholic scepticism-seems to suggest that the deconstructive project, by and large, has fizzled out. Fortunately, as we shall see, the funeral is not fatal, for the deceased has been buried alive. Put otherwise, it is not so easy to kill the mocking-bird of deconstruction, this Phoenix of sorts.

Exemplary of the strategy deployed by Derrida's critics 1 are the numerous articles by Irene Harvey focusing on the issue of exemplarity (Harvey 1988, 1992). Basically, Harvey reproduces the charge made by B.Johnson according to whom Derrida reproduces precisely that which he wishes to deconstruct (Johnson 1977; Harvey 1992: 199). However, over the years the general tone has shifted from benevolence to suspicion prompting Harvey to identify the mentioned reproduction with the "return ... to classical metaphysics", with the inability to deconstruct it.

If, for Johnson and those who remain faithful to the banner of the old school (cf.Sallis 1992), there is an uncanny coincidence between deconstructive strategy and the strategy of Lacan as an alleged representative/example of logocentric tradition, now this complicity is traced back to the origins of the tradition itself (Plato, Rousseau, Hegel, Kant), so that Derridaean strategy becomes a (privileged) example of the tradition to be deconstructed by it.

The paradox with which this train of critical thought pushed by Harvey to its logical end leaves us with remains unnoticed. In effect, even if Harvey is correct in her surmise that Derrida has failed to theoretically justify an example as something which subversively escapes the laws of logocentric economy, it is still possible to argue that he has succeeded at least practically, for in Harvey's account Derridaean discourse becomes precisely the impossible exemplary non-example. Of what? the reader is allowed to inquire mimicking our critic who cannot help obsessively reiterating the whats and whys without providing a distinct answer. Since our solution is bound to be disconcerting to an average reader infected as s/he is with theoretical commonplaces it will be wise not to put it before the cart of the evidence.

To assert that a given discourse can at one and the same time fall under the dominance of a law and subvert the latter does not necessarily mean to adopt the Derridaean theory of the two laws on which deconstruction hinges. Harvey is quite correct in conceding, however implicitly, that it is precisely this theory and the undecidabilty foregrounded thereby which is responsible for the metaphysical entrapment of deconstruction. What our suggestion boils down to is the necessity to radically reconsider the logic of this conspicuous coincidence. The paradox is that only thus we can provoke a coincidence between the best intuitions of Derrida and his critics, the coincidence which will be fruitful in its uncanniness.

The value of Harvey's analysis stems from the fact that up to this date she remains the only one to unequivocally charge Derrida with the inability to discursively situate himself beyond logocentrism. The irony of her discussion stems from her own inability to maintain this charge, to wit, from the reluctance to trace the true logic of exemplarity. And this precisely because from the vantage chosen by our critic one can only show that there is no actual coincidence between deconstruction and traditional hermeneutics. In other words, although "one could argue that Derrida's work has from its inception never been concerned with anything other than exemplarity"(193; italics mine), it is advisable to think twice before taking this bait

Unfortunately our critic is only all too hasty to violate this sound rule of commonsense. Whence her wonder that "in his readings" Derrida "never asks ...: why exemplarity itself?" If Derrida was actually interested in exemplarity per se then it would have been surprising that Harvey is compelled to leave the question unanswered, or, to be more precise, to provide an answer in the manner described by Freud in The Psychopathology of Everyday Life.

Put differently, Harvey cannot help to unwittingly mimic Derridaean strategy and in so doing to bare the text she is reading. Since according to Derrida such is the function of example and its subversive force, whereas according to Harvey we have here the first instance of his metaphysical entrapment,

Harvey's discourse is immediately transformed into an example of deconstructive exegesis and added to the infinite series of examples which is the logocentric tradition itself.

But by the same token it becomes impossible to maintain that the deconstructive discourse and the one to be deconstructed coincide as a fact, for the mechanism through which this coincidence is brought about is that of device-baring that, in the wake of Russian Formalists, is conceived of as the production of the gap, recently thematized as the non-logocentric différance.

In Harvey's words, "the space is kept open for the truly non-exemplary example". However, as she argues in respect to Derrida and uncannily shows in her own practice, this space is non-logocentric only at the face of it: the dialectizing movement remains possible, and, I would add, inevitable-so long as one hesitates to conceive otherwise of the principal terms of our discussion.

The first to be reconsidered among those is the concept of device-baring which, underpinning the mechanism of exemplarity, represents a more adequate but not yet the proper name of the logic that interests us here. To bare the device means to introduce the disparity, unequality between the two discourses-the one which is subject to deconstructive deciphering and the deconstructing one.

According to Harvey, this is precisely what Derrida has performed in his reading of Kant: "the list of examples (given by Kant at least) can be shown to be a hierarchical stacking of far from equal or substitu-table cases. Some cases (examples) are thus more equal than others 2. Though significant and revealing, this analysis again reaffirms the traditional view that examples are examples insofar and only insofar as they are examples of a law".

The subversion of the latter is concomitant with pondering over the problem "What else is taking place in these relations between example-text-example such that ... they can always-even after Derrida-be read otherwise ... Derrida's analysis here, as elsewhere on this issue, seems to stop short-on the brink-and turns back to feigning metaphysical forms, laws, and machinations at the very moment when some other articulation-not mimetic, not doubling, not castrating or circumcizing becomes possible"(197; last italics are mine). Why, then, not rush to seize this possibility to articulate-at long last!-the strategy of surpassing logocentrism? Precisely because the latter has been equated with non-mimetic discursive relationship which was previously equated with the discursive inequality as a hierarchizing/dialecticizing logocentric movement.

It follows that, strictly speaking, there was no baring of depth structures-neither of those of tradition in the work of Derrida, nor of those of Derrida in the analysis of Harvey. Instead, "the concealment of the problematics of exemplarity" for which Harvey takes Derrida to task is furthered by her own critique. Nevertheless, a certain baring takes place, and, what is more, takes place in perfect accordance with the general rules of discursive (self)deconstruction established by Derrida. However, to conclude that Derrida overtakes his critics would mean precisely to seize the bait which one should avoid taking.

For the coincidence in question, apparent as it is, is not the one we are after. In fact, exactly this coincidence lays lame every deconstructive effort undertaken thus far. To claim with Derrida that deconstruction is, actually, a self-deconstruction means to associate logocentric discursive mastery with the self-presence of intention in the consciousness of an author. Something always escapes the intention of the subject who cannot master her/his own discourse exposing thus his/her rear to plucking by a newcomer who suffers the same fate-and this ad infinitum. It is this process which at first sight is unwittingly bared but actually barred by Harvey. Witness the following passage:

> *"There we have it: there is no law, but, then again this law, that of the example of Rousseau, is now an example of another law. The law of the law here is therefore that abssolute laws of inauguration cannot be found, named, articulated, thematized or presented. Why not?... Why has Derrida incessantly to do the impossible in all of the above? Why does*

he now insist that this impossibility is itself a law, and thus he obeys it and manifests it, and, therefore, finally, can justify his choice of example as unjustifiable justifiably"(214; italics mine)

Since the quoted passage, exemplary as it is for strategy of Derrida's critics 3, is itself an example of the general laws of deconstruction as described above, the reader may wonder what can justify our attempt to see in such a plain affair an example of device-baring? what can be bared thereby? However, the italicized sentences should give us pose. For, especially the last one, points to the very heart of the problem which we attempt to circumscribe.

What justifies our interest in this sentence is the fact that it represents a version of the paradox of the Cretan Lier which itself is a version of another paradox which the stoic semiosis boils down to. I mean the paradox of Achilles and the tortoise. These paradoxes underpin all the elaborations of structuralism and its successor barring the break with logocentrism, and this already by virtue of their filiative interdependence.

In effect, Derrida's view of deconstruction reenacts the Achilles/tortoise paradox and therefore corresponds neatly to the notion of (literary) history as indirect filiation propounded by Russian Formalists-indisputable precursors of structuralism. According to the pregnant formulation of Victor Shklovsky, it is not the father to whom the son is (intertextually) indebted but the uncle.

In terms of the theory of genres, this view of the transmission of tradition boils down to the ressurection of the marginal genres of the day before yesterday with the (provisional) exclusion of the yesterday's ones. The result is the reversal of generations, the deconstructive version of which provides the celebrated discussion of the Socrates-Plato relation (Derrida 1980).

Derrida's hope is to undermine tradition by showing that the author never controls his/her text/utterance being always already before or behind it. Whence the celebrated undecidability on which the whole postructuralist project stands or falls. However, the gist of the matter is that, according to Derrida, in order to be complete deconstruction must show that the author is not simply ahead or behind the text but is this at one and the same time. Otherwise undecidability will concern only the outcome of the race but not the identities of the participants. But there's the rub! For, as Harvey has convincingly argued, the "and" of deconstruction is in fact the "or" The irony of the matter stems from the fact the same applies to the paradox of the Cretan Lier which structures Harvey's discourse.

The conclusion which suggests itself may well make a panic-monger of a hard-boiled poststructuralist who is bound to pay for intellectual astuteness with an emotional stress. Fortunately, what seems to come very close to a death-sentence on deconstruction for the first time clears the way for the deconstruction worth its name, for the deconstruction of the second degree. In fact, the strategy of Derrida's critics doubles his own in the dimunitive manner in which the Achilles/tortoise paradox relates to that of the Cretan Lier. Which means at one and the same time the (logocentric) hierarchization of both discourses and their non-mimetic intertextual/dialogical correspondence?

It follows, that the deployment of deconstruction, promoting as it does the possibility of reading as reading otherwise, is the deployment of the mechanism of the transmission of logocentric tradition astutely divulged by Harvey. So long as thus far nobody has suggested how to deploy deconstruction otherwise, it follows that it is impossible to deploy it at all. Which explains why, despite the conspicuous strategical coincidence(s) Harvey is at pains to stress that what she is doing "is not a deconstruction of Derrida"? And, paradoxically, she is quite correct at that.

This self-dimunition is what allows us in the first instance to speak about the paradoxical fate of Zeno's paradox in poststructuralist theory. For the unavoidable corollary of the deconstructive self-dimunition is the uncanny return of the referent which, as is generally believed, has been annihilated once and for all. My contention is, however, that only this return can help deconstruction to do what it strives for. Another (overtaking) baring of postructuralist project takes place in the writings of C.S.Peirce who with increasing persisitence is boosted as a true precursor of poststructuralism, as a thinker who has precipitatingly solved the quandaries encountered by contemporary theorists, as a figure to replace Saussure in theoretical worship. Therefore one should not be surprised to find that our paradox plays a prominent role in Peircean ruminations. Equally, thanks to our exploration, the reader will not be surprised at the form in which Peirce came to grapple with Zeno's paradox.

In effect, our analysis for the first time allows to divulge why in order to safeguard dialogicity and a-refentiality of his semiotics Peirce had to prove that Achilles will overtake the tortoise, or, as a contemporary commentator puts it, that "he will have (always, already) overtaken the tortoise" (Weber 1987: 16; italics added).

Only this overtaking, by virtue of pointing "both toward the past and toward the future" can guarantee the diachronicity of semiotical process (which, allegedly absent from saussurean structuralism, is said to account for the logocentric alliances of the latter), to wit, its dialogicity as a possibility of reading otherwise implicit in Peircean definition of the sign which maintains the relation of partial equivalence to its object/refernt, albeit the final logical interpretant (Achilles's final overtaking) on which the diachronical dialogicity hinges does not itself have an object.

However, half-heartedly and obscurely, Weber cannot help acknowledging that this model is "self-defeating". I hope that the preceeding part of our analysis has already satisfied an astute reader as to the logic of this self-defeat. Which is not to say that there are no more surprises laying in stake.

However, to continue in the same wain we have to take recourse to textual reality which, placing the post-structuralist theorizing in an uncanny light, will make of our analysis something more nourishing than a mere rereading of rereadings. That the poststructuralists one and all are inveterate fans of Achilles is quite logical, since only his victory in the race can secure the belated priority of the deconstructingly interpretive discourse situating it both ahead and behind of the discourse to be deconstructed. In Derridaean terms, this means to encircle the discourse supposedly guilty of logocentrism with the parergonal frame (1987: 96-101 et passim).

The result is the non-mimetic mergence between the two. Deconstruction is not the discourse of its perpetrator, but the effect of the mentioned operation, that is, a process. Now it is precisely "the process by which /the deconstructive/ Achilles will overtake the tortoise /of logocentrism/" (Weber 1987: 13) for which Peicean semiotics "fails to account".

As we have seen, this failure stems from the inability to substitute the allegedly non-logocentric "and" for the supposedly logocentric "or". What accounts for the trouble is the reluctance to discern in the uncannily familiar concepts as deployed in the traditional texts a potential more subversive than the new sense with which these concepts are endowed in the deconstructive practice. Paradoxically, this applies primarily to the concepts on which Derrida's attention has been so long focused. I mean the notions of "mimesis" and "writing".

According to one of Derridaean seminal postulates, the gist of the matter is not to restore to writing its dignity, that is, not to simply reverse the old hierarchy, but to radically reevaluate the notion of writing in order to make it include the notion of speech. Which means to show that the new notion of writing which apparently overtakes the traditional one has been always already operating in the traditional formulations and therefore is at the same time behind the latter?

This explains why the theory of mimesis becomes the priviliged object of deconstruction, for the very existence of the latter hinges on the non-mimetic character of every mimetic doubling. The paradox of the matter is that if Derrida is correct in his assumptions, then it becomes impossible to deconstruct prima facie the theory of mimesis.

For, on Derrida's own terms, to strive for truth/referent by deploying the mechanism of mimesis-and this is what, says

Derrida, the Western hermeneuts have been always already doing-means to endlessly post-pone the advent of it. Although this endless postponement obviously cannot help but imlicitly make of the "truth" a simulacrum of sorts, it is the postponement itself which deconstruction boils down to 9.

This reduces the difference (i.e. non-mimetic coincidence) between the two strategies to the opposition conscious vs. unconscious, intentional vs.unintentional and thereby re-introduces the framework of logocentric binarism.

However, to rest satisfied with this conclusion would not only mean to treat deconstruction all too leniently but in so doing to futher the obfuscation of logocentrism along with the best intuitions of its critics which uncannily remain in abeyance.

Put bluntly, our conclusion-and up today nobody commenting on the work of Derrida has managed to propound anything else-is nott up to the point at all, for it happens to be invalidated by the dialectics of blindness and insight which seems to establish precisely the structure of "at one and the same time" as the royal way of deconstruction.

Ironically, precisely this structure turns out to be the very mechanism of transmission of traditional values. What deManian dialectics aims at is primarily the undermining of the notion of self-presence equated in poststructuralist theory with that of truth.

That nobody can claim to be exempt from this dialectics means the non-mimetic mergence between the two discourses, to wit, the uncertainty/undecidability as regards the identities of the participants in Zeno's hermeneutic race. The result is the certainty that someone's rear is always already in the process of being plucked.

The paradox of our paradox is that the conclusion just reached, far from promoting paradoxicality in the Cretan way, explains why deconstruction is such a sublime affair. Unfortunately, in the literal sense of unavoidable evaporation.

The reasons are twofold and interrelated. As we have seen, the difference between deconstructive and traditional strategies is not the one between conscious and unconscious deployment of the same strategy, for both are subject to the same dialectics. Which means that deconstruction in actual fact has always already been there, for every reading/interpretation as such, no matter what overt strategy it deploys, cannot be anything else than a deconstruction. By definition-and in strictly Derridaean sense.

Exactly for this reason there can be no talk of deconstruction at all, so long as we con-ceive of it along the Derridaean lines, i. e. as a sub-version of logocentric tradition by means of the reformulated concept of writing. For the latter does not need the slightest alteration to satisfy Derridaean demands.

In effect, in Derrida's view there is deconstruction only insofar as it can be conceived as a process without begginning or end, that is, as perpetuum mobile of sorts. Which makes of the practice of writing the mechanism of interpretive transmission just described?

However, this mechanism can function only by diminishing every new interpretation in respect to the preceeding one. This is not to say that Achilles will not overtake the tortoise, but that in order to win he has to non-mimetically identify with the tortoise, i.e. to reverse the quantitative priorities, to (self-deconstructively) diminish himself.

Put otherwise, the postsructuralist belief that the deconstruction is the baring of the unthought and excluded elements of the traditional discourse compels the adept to descend into the hole and to have a drop (always already too much) of the beverage which has made the innocent Alice grow smaller.

The irony of the matter is that this practice of writing has been always already thematized in the texts which recently have come under the fire of deconstructive critique as patent examples of logocentric values, mastery being the first of them.

To cite only two instances: the dimunition inherent in writing conceived intertextually as the production of new interpretations is foregrounded in such a work as Gulliver's Travels which can be conveniently viewed as the encyclopedia of patriarchal prejudices, as an avatar of colonial fiction(s). However, the narrator-and Gulliver is obviously a self-conscious one just as a typical postmodern narrator is apt to be-is fully conscious that the price to be paid for (ethnocentric) dimunition of the Other is the dimunition of one's own representation, i.e. a certain linkage, aphanisis of rhetorical force.

Another example of the same dimunitive practice firnishes H.James's tale In The Cage: the movement described as the Achilles's dimuninitive identification with the tortoise is the very movement of emplotment in James's narrative: in order to understand-and it is worthwhile to note that this understanding is a process of a certain non-mimetic coincidence between fiction and reality-the heroine has to abase herself, which takes the form of the process of the realization of metaphor, i.e. of device-baring/making-strange.

Although the poststructuralist theorists have never addressed themselves to the process under discussion, let alone recognized in it the very (de)structurizing movement of Derridaean writing, our sketch seems to corroborate the current stance to treat James as a promoter of discursive mastery under the guise of the commitment to aesthetism which, according to the general view, is far from being innocent (cf. Norris 1988; Przybylowicz 1986).

For to diminish discursively means to make characters manipulable. As we have already become tired of hearing, this patently logocentric way to deal with the Other is especially notorious in case of women and children. According to Rose, the drive for mastery-epistemic, sexual etc.-explains why in Barrie's narrative Peter Pan is not allowed to grow up.

However, this strategy can only be aggravated by the poststructuralist stance to blur the border between fictional and explicitly referential narratives. In due time we shall take issue with this stance adopted by Rose in order to show that the genuinely innovative rereading of children's fiction is impossible on these premises which lead to the drastic simplification of the textual reality along with the obfuscation of the subversive power of texts-traditional as well as recent ones 15. James's tale is a good intermediary stage of our discussion, for it alerts us to the fact that matters are far more intricate and intriguing than the recent theorizing would allow us to believe. And this because dimunition is uncannily interrelated with intertextuality-this postsructuralist sesam par excellence.

That the perpetuum-mobile of Derridaean writing is intertextuality in etat pur is obvious enough: there is neither beginning of nor foreseeable end to the text's simultaneous reference to itself and to other texts. The paradoxical consequence of this fundamental rule of deconstruction is that it leads to the sublime evaporation of the deconstructive project.

For the infiniteness of the intertextual interpretation conceived as the practice of deconstructive writing cannot help but end with the dimunition of deconstruction which becomes invisible to the eye as a virtual entity and thereby proves to be an exact counterpart of the notion of an "aesthetic object"- perhaps the most troubling one among the concepts of Bakhtin whose legacy has been all too hastily appropriated by poststructu-ralism along the dialogical/intertextual lines.

As we have shown elsewhere 16, the virtuality of an "aesthetic object" stems from its being a product of an interpreter /reader who represents for Bakhtin a fictitious other. Since the latter performs all the functions with which the Other has been endowed in poststructuralism, one is justified to conclude that the true otherness is a subversion of logocentrism precisely by virtue of being a subversion of dialogism, that is, has to be located beyond the opposition of dialogism vs. monologism exposed as a logocentric affair.

In order to fully appreciate the subversiveness of Bakhtin's theory we have to attend more closely to the mechanisms which structure the textual reality by barring the actualization of the virtual aesthetic object. In so doing we shall not only provide a more adequate picture of literary tradition but also pinpoint the actual meeting-place of Bakhtin and Derrida, the place which thus far remains a blank on the maps of poststructuralist (mis)reading(s).

The sublime fate of the deconstructive writing is the paradox of Zeno's paradox the consequences of which remain to be spelled out. What has promoted it to its status of the depth-structure of poststructuralist theorizing is the hope to annihilate once and for all referentiality as such. Whence the vogue currently enjoyed by the theory of the sublime in the version given to it by Kant. In effect, the basic feature of the Kantian sublime is its a-referentiality which has a necessary corollary in the communicability of the sublime feeling.

Part of the value of our analysis stems from the fact that for the first time it makes explicit the necessary character of the mentioned connection which has not been spelled out by Kant, whereas contemporary commentators, for reasons that an astute reader need not be promted to guess, have said and done all to slyly obfuscate it. The reasons for this obfuscation are just as simple as they are compelling, for the thematization of the sublime within the poststructuralist framework cannot help but bring about exactly what should have been precluded by deconstructive machinations, to wit, the uncanny return of the referent.

This return, unavoidable on the premises of the third Critique, accounts for the generally acknowledged iadequateness of Kantian theory, for its openness to deconstructive re-readings. However, the latter can be dubbed deconstructive only in the sense suggested above. Significantly, it is the most sustained effort to deconstruct Kant-the one undertaken by Derrida-which proves the validity of our reasoning and in so doing paves the way to the theory of discursive innocence which is nothing else than deconstruction of the second degree.

At first glance, it appears surprising that precisely the uncanny return of the referent in Kant's theory of the sublime, the return which cries for deconstruction is carefully avoided in the allegedly deconstructive reading supplied by Derrida. Unfortunately for the poststructuralist project our surprise is not justified. For Derrida cannot help referring, however unwillingly and briefly, to the main contradiction of Kant's treatise and in so doing to radically undermine his own claims as regards the always open possibility to read otherwise, that is, to stage the reading on the grave of an author without taking recourse to his/her intentions. Derrida's reference comes at the very end of his attempt to substitute logocentric ergon with non-logocentric parergon and deserves to be cited in full:

"Why can magnitude, which is not a quantity, and not a comparable quantity in the order of phenomena, let itself be represented under the category of quantity rather than some other category?

Why this reference, still, to a cise in space?

Then, another question, still the same, if phenomenalization is to be admitted, why should the sublime be the absolutely large and not the absolutely small?... Why this valorization of the large which thus still intervenes in a comparison between incomparables?... An object, even if it were indifferent to us in its existence, still pleases us by its mere largeness ... and this feeling is universally communicable ... Kant does not ask himself why this should go without saying, naturally toward the largest and the highest ... what decides that, in this quantum, the more is worth more than the less, and the large more or better than the small?

The agency of decision or 'preference' can as such be neither phenomenal nor noumenal, neither sensible nor intelligible. The question comes back to the origin of presentation. Why does the large absolute (the sublime), which is not a quantum since it exceeds all comparison, let itself be presented by a quantum which does not manage to present it? And why does this essentially inadequate quantum present it all the 'better' for being larger?... Kant has introduced comparison where he says it should have no place. He introduces it ... in an apparently very subtle manner ... by comparing the comparable with the incomparable"(1987: 136-137)

Derrida's manner of handling deconstruction equals Kantian strategy in subtlety which in both cases happens to be ostensible. Already the purely quantitative excess of questions over the answers, especially if compared with the discourse of his critics which winds up with the same correlation, should alert the most lazy reader to recognize here the strategy of Achilles-becoming-the-tortoise described above. What distinguishes our own discourse radically from the critical strategy beyond which thus far nobody has managed to move, is that we can easily avoid lingering on this formal coincidence which, as an instance of Cretan discursivity, can only make a tortoise of ourselves. Our abstinence from falling over the logocentric bait offered by Derrida will immediately be rewarded.

To succumb to the mentioned temptation means to maintain that Derrida's questions strikingly miss the point. This would certainly explain their quantitative excess but by the same token promote the interpretive transmission the mechanism of which we are at pains to divulge. Fortunately for our enterprise the outcome of the hermeneutic race hinders the deployment of the blindness/insight dialectics to which, as might appear at this point, we are bound to fall prey. The sleight of Derrida's hand is to make us believe that the question of the absolute large emerges in Kant's discourse as a Freudian Abkommling of the concern with the problematics of referentiality qua truth which stamps the theory of the sublime as a logocentric affair. The paradox of the matter is that to grant him this point means to assume that Kant's most implicit intention is to secure precisely the interpretative transmission which hinges on the success of Achilles's slyness.

Which means to exhaust the paradoxicality of our paradox, to wit, to bring about the interpretive aphanisis as a sublime evaporation of deconstruction? And this because the result of Derrida's reading is the baring of the mechanism that can produce simulacra only by promoting referentiality.

However radical Kant's intentions as regards referentiality may be, runs Derridaean argument in the cited passage, within the logocentric framework they can be realized only by an omnipotent subject as a locus of self-presennce qua truth. The same argument has been turned against Derrida himself by Harvey, and, as we have seen, can be turned against herself. Ad infinitum? That is the question ... to which precisely the work of Derrida provides a negative answer.

If we are to understand why Kant has equated the sublime with the absolute large, we have, according to Derrida, displace the question in order to see in it an issue of preference, i.e. of purely deliberate choice. Derrida is the first to acknowledge that this answer is a displacement, that is, a misreading. As everybody believes, the reading by definition cannot be anything else. Derrida's slyness is to (mis)present what actually is a faithful reading as a misinterpretation.

The sheer quantitative force of Derrida's rhetoric cannot fail to produce an overwhelmingly sublime effect upon the reader versed in Derridaean writings prompting her/him to conclude that the message of logocentrism (sublime as the absolute large) becomes the medium of deconstructive attack. However, this conclusion-with which Derrida's critics habitually wind up-immediately undermines itself, for it implies that the coincidence between the two discourses is not perfect which means to keep deconstruction on the run. Unfortunately, just the opposite seems to be true. That is we have to account for the mimetic relation not only between the participants in the hermeneutic race but also between the message and its medium in their discourses.

At first glance, our passage boils down to the suggestion that in order to clear the theory of the sublime of logocentrism it is sufficient to equate the sublime with the absolute small. Further it might appear that this message is quantitatively at odds with its medium as just another reiteration of Derrida's why the absolute large and not the small? However, this disparity turns out to be ostensible, for the effect of reiteration is to make the issue of seize appear indifferent. It follows that Kant's equation of the sublime with the absolute large does not make any difference or différance.

The disappearence of the quantitative issue is precisely what enables Achilles to overtake the tortoise in the hermeneutic race by means of (non-mimetic) identification. However, the same outcome has the foregrounding of our issue in Kantian discourse. In effect, according to Kant, the sublime pertains to the aesthetic domain only insofar as it shares a-refentiality with the feeling provoked by the beautiful.

On the other hand, Kant would like to maintain that the sublime feeling is far more adequately experienced before the objects of nature, i.e. before referents in etat brute. Now it is precisely this contradiction which the equation of the sublime with the absolute large allows to solve. At least at first sight.

In effect, the only way to retain the phenomenological purity of the sublime feeling and at the same time to claim for it the aesthetic character is to assume that in producing the art object an artist is deploying the Achilles-becoming-the-tortoise strategy. For the self-dimunition implied in the latter suggests that the art object overtakes its natural referent which by definition is the absolute large by making it disappear from eye-sight and by the same token by disappearing itself.

Hence the issue of seize becomes irrelevant/undecidable but only insofar as we assume that the referent is the absolute large, for otherwise the referentiality of the latter would make the question of the sublime disappear as such. Paradoxically this does not mean to do away with referentiality but to reinforce it.

For, according to the Achilles-becoming-the-tortoise logic which guides this train of reasoning, the disappearance of the art object can mean nothing else than its becoming the referent. Taken at face value, the result is precisely the one divulged by Derridaean deconstruction. As postructuralism would have it, striving to bring about the revelation (of truth) as the disappearance of the sign(ification) logocentrism makes the issue of thruth undecidable: the sublime evaporation (aphanisis) of the signifying matter is said to have a corrosive effect on the order of referents/signifieds transforming the latter into simulacra.

Whence the notion of the sign as pharmakon as well as the view of deconstruction as self-deconstruction. The reader tolerably versed in Freudian theory would not be surprised at the uncanny effect of these reassuring views.

According to Derrida, an attempt to naturalize the sign is a logocentric demarche par excellence. According to Bakhtin, the naturalization of the work of art is what makes the Formalist poetics founder transforming the latter into a version of gedonistic (i.e. logocentric) aesthetics and thereby limiting it to the domain of an isolated (i.e. logocentric) consciousness (Medvedev 1993a: 117-160). Along these lines Bakhtin can unambiguously be dubbed an avatar of poststructuralism. However, to regard this issue as settled would mean only to promote the logocentric tradition.

So long as the movement of naturalization strengthens the position of the logocentric omnipotent subject and by the same token fosters monologism generally viewed as a main feature of Western tradition, it seems natural to conclude that the dialigic option can be considered as a valid alternative only if it will undermine the very foundation of logocentrism. However, the means deployed to this end cannot help but have an uncanny effect.

To undermine the (epistemic) omnipotence of the logocentric subject means to drive him out of his mono-logic seclusion into the polyphonic field of intertextual forces. This is the task of Bakhtin's critique of Saussure as well as of Derrida's reading of Husserl (1967), both of them striving to bare those ele-ments of discirsivity which the tradition has failed to accommodate.

The emerging models cannot fail to closely resemble each other and in so doing to evoke Peircean semiotics as a poststructuralist alternative to the structuralist Saussurean stance dismissed as logocentric. It is precisely the retroactively baring recourse to Peirce which accounts for the sublime fate of poststructuralist theorizing.

The discursive elements on which Bakhtin and Derrida place the stakes of their intertextuality are identical. According to Bakhtin, what makes a discourse social are the elements which the tradition has always treated as marginal, paralinguistic. According to Derrida, exactly the privilege given to meaningful signs over indicative signs, to expression over indication stamps Husserlian theory as logocentric (1967: 37 et passim).

In order not to weary the reader who is supposed to be tolerably versed in these matters, suffice it to say that Bakhtin and Derrida's elaborations can be summed by the Husserlian dictum read in self-dimunitive reverse: for both theorists, "facial expressions and gestures /the list can be enlarged/ that /in/voluntary accompany speech with/out/ communicative intent"(1968 ii/1: 31) become the object of primal interest. At the same time, it is on this point, indicated by the parenthetical insertions, that the paths of Bakhtin and Derrida seem to part. The uncanniness of our story is that this divergence is only provisional, so that the ultimate coincidence boils down to the contradiction with which every version of inter-textuality is bound to end.

In effect, the gist of Bakhtin'a argument, as it is habitually read (e.g.Stewart 1986), is that the elements dubbed paralinguistic accompany speech voluntary and with a communicative intent. It is the involuntary introduction of the notion of intent which threatens to make of his theory an easy prey for the logocentric appropriation and at the same time for the deconstructive critique along the lines of the dialectics of blindness/insight. Significantly, Bakhtin is fully conscious of this threat. Whence his critique of Freudian unconscious and the notion of the social evaluation: both allow to avoid attributing the communicative intent to the subject, i.e. to regard a given utterance as involuntary.

The intertex-tual model grounded in the concept of the collective unconscious works fine-but only in the absence of the referent, for example, of the textual reality for the explanation of which it was primarily designed. By now the reader need not be prompted to recognize what kind of effect these ruminations are bound to have, for s/he has already discerned in the disappearance of the referent-both in and of-Bakhtin's theory the fate of the art object in the Kantian theory of the sublime.

However, in Bakhtin's case the conclusion is more disastrous since his intertextuality hinges on the celebrated assumption the a (literary) text is never written in a dead language, i.e. should never become naturalized. Ironically, Bakhtin's students deem themselves sufficiently equiped to meet our argument. I say ironically, for the supposed refutation is advanced as a departure from the (dead) letter of Bakhtinian legacy in order to adjust the latter to the demands of the day (Hirschkop 1989), whereas in actual fact it remains quite faithful in the most conventional sense of the term. Nei-ther monologism nor dialogism, runs the mentioned objec-tion, is the property of the text itself, but the way of how it is read under current social circumstances, that is, of how it is contextualized.

Unfortunately, on these premises we have either to see a contradiction between Bakhtin's critique of Formalist aesthetics where the charge hinges on the refutation of the materiality of the art object and his attack on formalist linguistics refuted for the disregard to the materiality, to wit, sociality of the signifying process 19,-or else to concede that Bakhtin is saying exactly what his legataries say.

That the latter are at pains to deny this in-debtedness is quite understandable, for to acknowledge it would mean to sign a death-sentence on dialogism/inter-textuality as a theory of unrestricted debt on which poststructuralism has placed its stakes.

In order to see why this is so, let us cast a brief look at the path stroken by Derrida from the point where we have left him. That the parenthetical modification of Husserl's quote, necessary in case of Bakhtin, would misrepresent Derrida's position is sufficiently explained by the apparent dissent of our theorists on the issue of psychoanalysis and the notion of context. So long as our analysis has already successfully stomached the apparently indigestible first apple of dissent, we are justified not to pay much heed to the second.

Derrida's (evaluating, i.e. a not too tight one) cuddle of the Husserl's quote is a direct consequence of his equation of contextuality with a successful (truth-revealing) communication (cf. 1982: 307-330). Whence the role of iterability in his theory: to launch deconstruction in the first head it is necessary to prove that the sign can be reiterated in the absence of an author, without recourse to his/her intention(s).

Put otherwise, signification, for Derrida, is essentially an involuntary process without communicative intent. On the other hand, this very process is said to be triggered by différance. Whence the return of/to contextuality as an attempt to solve the contradiction. What makes this return uncanny is the perfect coincidence between contextuality thus introduced and the notion of context as deployed by Bakhtin.

Despite (or thanks to) the proliferation of the Bakhtinian studies, the utlization of his concepts remains amateurish so long as their function, to wit, genesis remains undivulged. Witness the notion of context. Thus far nobody has described the paradoxical logic of its apperance in Bakhtin's work which makes of it another instance of Zeno's paradox.

In effect, the notion of contextuality emerges as a result of the transfer of materiality from the object of art to the product of interpretation. The imperative to which Bakhtin thus succumbs is the same which triggers non-mimetic self-dimunitive identification of Achilles with the tortoise. The social evaluation can take place only by means of the contextualization which is the always open possibility of reading otherwise.

The privileged instance of this practice is, according to Bakhtin, intonation that should secure iterability and at the same time non-coincidence of the utterance with itself and its referent. This assigns to intonation the same fundamental role in Bakhtinian theory that the notion of différance has for Derrida: in fact, both concepts are synonyms. The striking difference in their fate, i.e. the marked reluctance of Bakhtinians to recognize in intonation a concept, let alone to thematize it, is not surprising, for Bakhtin's intonation turns out to be an innocently profane version and, by the same token, a mimetic baring of the Derridaean différance.

On the one hand, intonation throws light on the most clandestine issue with which poststructuralism has placed its stakes, substantiating the charge for repe-tition with difference. It appears that to achieve an (intertextual) splitting it is not necessary to materially alter anything in the utterance but only to differently intone it. On the other hand, Bakhtin is candid enough to acknowledge that this practice, which, once again, should testify to the materiality of the signifying process, to wit, to its intertextuality and poliphony (social and otherwise) does not leave any material traces, or, to be more correct, these inter-textual traces are subject to inevitable evaporation. However, only the most crude among the literal-minded readers will be surprised at that.

Irony stems from the fact that to save Bakhtinian intertextuality a poststructuralist reader, this inveterate adversary of any kind of literality qua referentiality, has to argue for the literal understanding of Bakhtin's theory, i.e. to stipulate that materiality on which our problem hinges is used by Bakhtin in the metaphorical sense. To make matters worse the second part of the argument does not follow from the first. And this precisely because Derrida's writing is a neat counterpart of the Bakhtinian intonation.

What the former is at its straightforwardest, shows Derrida's Glas. Derrida's own discourse inserted between the quotations from the works of Hegel and Genet, far from functioning as an interpretive go-between, is bent upon maintaing its independence, which makes of it a quotation of sorts, i.e. a reiteration. Consequently, the text as it stands is an instance of pure iterability, repition without différance. The latter, synonymous with contextualization/intertextualization and deconstruction, can be brought about only by deploying intonation, i.e. for the time being remains in abeyance. Intonation will certainly intertextually juxtoppose what as a fact is simply opposed. Whence the mechanical character of both operations, to wit, their materiality-and non-coincidence.

However, to make deconstruction of the metaphysics of presence dependent on the presence of the reader, in itself, does not undermine poststructuralist claims. Paradoxically, to criticize Derrida solely on these grounds is the surest way to bar the way for deconstruction worth its name. What signs the fate of deconstruction is not the return of the sovereign reading subject on whose deliberate option everything seems to hang, but the uncanny return of the referentiality and the inability to recognize in it the possibilty of the genuine subversion.

To surmise that Derrida remains prey to metaphysical

assumptions as regards omnipotent subjectivity-and up this date nobody has managed to think of anything better by way of critical reading of his work-means to do him an injury and thereby to misrepresent the so-called metaphysical assumptions themselves. What Derrida's readings of the classical texts suggest is that there cannot be any omnipotent subjectivity-neither in his discourse nor in the traditional one. And this is what makes of the current version of deconstruction as self-deconstruction, or, in terms of our present discussion, as a deployment of Achilles-becoming-the-tortoise-strategy, i.e. of Cretan discursivity, a sublimly futile affair.

The same would apply to the Kantian theory of the sublime so long as we see in it primarily an attempt to secure the interpretive transmission which is obviously the tradition itself. As we have seen, the Achilles's strategy, underpinning the Kantian account, serves pre-cisely this end. However, the self-dimunition implied in it radically undercuts the subject's claims to omnipotence. Whence the coincidence, i.e. absence of deconstruction, between Kant and Derrida's discourses.

It follows, that the main argument of Derrida's critics who limit his complicity with tradition to the issue of the metaphysics of subjectivity is more than shaky. Not only because it is always possible to counter-act it by claiming that the presence of the reader is always virtual, i.e., is in fact an absence.

But precisely because this counter-argument bares the literality on which Derridaean project uncannily hinges. Paradoxically, the first-intertextual-effect of this literality is to abolish the apparent contradiction between Derrida and Bakhtin, whose theories, as it seems, are doomed to remain at odds by virtue of different valorization of the writing and voice respectively. However, to maintain this contradiction one has to treat both notions literalily and thereby to ascribe metaphoricity to the much hailed materiality of the signifying process of which Bakhtin remains an avatar.

Unfortunately, writing is material to the same extent and in the same sense as Bakhtin's speech/intonation was shown to be. Ironically, only by acquiescing to see matters from our standpoint one can explain the fate of the Derridaen letter/ signifier which is said to be always in danger of getting lost. To assert that this danger belongs to the structure of every writing means to give it up to the same doom to which Bakhtinian intonation is subject. Appearances notwithstan-ding, this is not to say that Derrida's writing fails-as a fact-to rewrite the logocentric structure of the voice.

To the contrary. Witness his strange reluctance-for once and precisely in case of the signature (1984)-to take recourse to undecidability (i.e. to the immaterial mate-riality of the naturalized sign interpreted as the phar-makonization of the order of referents which it joins) which boils down to an implicit acknowledgement of the disappearance of the deconstructive writing and by the same token of the Bakhtinian intonation conceived of as interpretive strategies of intertextual contextualizati-on.

Instead, Derrida is bent upon retaining the factual materiality at all costs and in so doing cannot fail to fall prey to what was identified in the Bakhtin critique of Formalism as the main fallacy of the latter, to wit, to the materiality of the art object conceived in the most crude literal sense of the term.

It remains to show that this recourse, inevitable as it is within the frame-work of Zeno's semiotics, was not avoided by Bakhtin himself. Fortunately, this return to/of the referentiality has nothing to do with the dialectics of blindness/ in-sight, for it clears the path for the deconstruction of the second degree.

It is here that Derridaean ruminations on the structural effect of signature come into play. At first glance, these boil down to a transfer of material responsibility from the author/ text to the reader/interpretation along Bakhtinian lines: now it is the reader who signs. Nevertheless, the signature remains for Derrida primarily that of an author. And it is by virtue of this fact that the whole problem takes a new and promising turn allowing for the juncture between Derridaean and Bakhtinian intuitions-nourishingly enriched and delishiously flavored with tho-se of Kant, Freud and Heidegger-beyond the monologism /dialogism opposition which underpins the metaphysic of subjectivity. Our discussion draws part of its value from the fact that the alternative just evoked, at first sight, seems no alternative at all. The reader may be inclined to accuse us with leaving him/her with an uneasy choice between the disappearance of the art object in the Kantian theory of the sublime and the same fate of the pro-duct of interpretation in poststructuralism.

To make matters worse, at second glance, it appears that the choice itself is ostensible: however brief, our inquiry into Kant's Third Critique following in the steps of Derrida's reading has proved that in both cases what is bound to disappear is the hermeneutic attitude, to wit, the double bind on which poststructuralism stands or falls. Far from calling for radical means, the double bind can be untied, and quite easily at that. What distinguishes it from the Gordean knot, is the impossibility to tye it properly. Which explains why the untying operation has nothing to do with the return to logocentrism.

In order to function, the interpretive machine has to do what the production of the art object supposedly cannot achieve, to wit, to extinguish the referential traces. Which means to dimunitively identify with the artist and in so doing to overtake him/her. This is why interpretation cannot be anything else than the deployment of the Achilles-becoming-the-tortoise strategy. By definition.

It follows that interpretation hinges vitally on the non-coincidence. As Lacan puts it, "... what Zeno has not noticed is that the tortoise is not exempted from the fatality to which Achilles is subject-his every step becomes more and more small ... And this is why he cannot help but overtake the tortoise, but he cannot join it". Whence the foregrounding of the double bind as a general rule of interpretation, for the double bind is nothing else than the most radical version of the non-coincidence, non-mimesis. As was already hinted above, the paradox of the double bind is the impossibility to tie it.

According to the device-baring logic of the Achilles's strategy divulged by our analysis, interpretation is bound to evaporate and thereby to bare the referentiality which it has to abolish. Irony stems from the fact that what at first glance seems to represent a perfect case of the blindness/insight dialectic actually subverts the very premises for its deployment, for as a last hope an interpreter has to thematize referentiality, i.e. to quite consciously take the prohibited step. And this is why the uncanny outcome is the very opposite of the Cretan discursivity. Witness Derrida's thematization of the effect of signature.

Taken at face value, the signature as Derrida conceives of it is a step back in respect to Bakhtin's critique of Formalism that is a return from the materiality of interpretation to that of an object of art. For once the appearances are not misleading. And this is exactly why Derrida's theory cannot fail but bring about the coincidence between Bakhtin's and the Formalist theories, which, to believe certain Bakhtinians are destined to remain forever at variance.

As we have already had ample occasion to ascertain ourselves, to subscribe to the view just mentioned would mean to see in Bakhtin's critique an instance of Achilles's strategy, i.e. to wind up with the conclusion that the radical deconstruction of the hermeneutic tradition is impossible. For what we have been ramming into the heads of our readers is precisely that on these premises deconstruction becomes interpretation and shares the sublime fate of every interpretation. By introducing the notion of signature Derrida directly thematizes the hermeneutic aphanisis and in so doing brings about the coincidence between textual reality and the reading of it, the coincidence which precludes the tying of the double bind that makes of the unreadability an issue of restricted economy.

For Bakhtin, the materiality of interpretation, to wit, its con/intertextuality, hangs on the notion of intonation which, as we have just seen, corresponds neatly to the Derridaen writing. So long as signature is the deployment of writing, it is not surprising that Derrida thematizes signature in just the same terms which were introduced by Bakhtin in his thematization of intonation.

Theoretically, the result should be the intratextual

grounding of intertextuality, i.e. the promotion of exegesis along the lines of repetition with difference. Disturbingly for a poststructuralist reader, his/her expectations are radically subverted by the textual practice of an author who is constantly called upon as a reliable witness for the persecution. In effect, it is nobody else than Vladimir Nabokov whose uncanny intervention into the hermeneutic race we are discussing helps to rectify a number of commonplaces which enjoy so much vogue. Nabokov's short-story "The Potato Elf" is an excellent litmus-paper for testing the effects of Derri-daean signature. For Nabokov's narrative is another mi-seen scene of the Zeno's paradox-however, on a more appropriate Schauplatz.

In order to non-mimetically merge with the text our prefatory lines (i.e. an outwork of sorts) should be read literally, since the setting of our story is a theatrical one: what comes to be narrated is a life of a dwarf Frederick Dobson whose successful circus-career has been by the libidinal complications. The latter reinforce the grotesque implied in the set-up and thereby seem to make of a story a hermeneutic double-bind tied in accordance with Bakhtin's instructions to be found in his theory of the carnivalesque ambivalence.

The paradox which underpins the plot is an hermeneutical one. In its turn, it is doubled by the paradox of the story. Whence the temptation to identify the structure as that of Derrida's square that boils down to the non-mimetic self-dimunitive identification of Achilles with tortoise and thereby to baringly equate the effect of Achilles's strategy with the effect of Derridaean signature. As we have seen, the Achilles-becoming-the-tortoise strategy which should ensure interpretation by abolishing referentiality as a fact makes the interpretation dependent on the referent.

It follows that the (im)possibility to maintain the (de)naturalized status of the referent becomes an issue on which poststructuralism stands or falls. Whence an interest of Nabokov's intervention into the controversy. What forces the Potato Elf to give up the circus career and, ultimately, life is the love-affair with the spouse of his one-time partner, the juggler Schock. After a libidinal bliss, he assumes that Nora will follow the conventional path and elope with him. Instead she leaves with her husband for America where the latter has found an engagement. Betrayed by the partner and paramour Dobson gives up the scene and goes to live in seclusion. The monotony (iterability) of his existence occupied solely by avid reading, is interrupted by Nora's sudden reappearance. Her purpose is to inform him that he has a son.

The surprise makes him mute. Upon regaining his wits he remembers that he had forgotten to ask an address and rushes after Nora in hope to overtake her on her way to the station. He succeeds but dies of heart-failure unaccustomed as he is to physical exertion. Nora remains quite callous. Her answer to the besieging spectators is that she has lost her son. With this phrase the story ends.

To surmise that at the level of story the crucial junctures boil down to the issue of overtaking means to commit oneself to a literal reading-in the non-evaluative sense of the forced proximity to the textual reality. The subversive force of "The Potato Elf" stems precisely from this mimetic constraints which bring about the aphanisis of the interpretive attitude. And this due to the uncanny dependence of hermeneutic overtaking on the referent.

The first narrative juncture is Dobson's love-affair with Nora. Ultimately, his aim is as immaterial as an hermeneutic aim could be. To physically overtake his partner means to assert his discursive equality with the "giants". According to the poststructuralist doctrine, this equality is synonymous with dialogical deconstruction of monologism, to wit, with con/intertextualization grounded in the misreading as the self-dimunitive over-taking which keeps open the possibility of reading other-wise.

Whence the (possible, undecidable) misreading of Nora's intentions by our hero who is bent upon acting as if the sexual reunion has actually taken place. In order not to diverge from the paradoxical manner of presentation, we can say that the Potato Elf has to take as a fact, i.e.literally/referentially what others (may be inclined to) take metaphorically.

What seems to exhaust the paradox is that intertexuality

thus established cannot help turning out to be of a mimetical order 34: at this point the narrative is threatened with a dead-end which would leave the reader with a trite version of adultery. Which explains why the intertextual iterability should be revitalizingly doubled by an intratextual différance. Every narrative, claims Derrida, is its own explicator, to wit, its own best deconstructor. In our case this can only mean the furthering of the hermeneutic paradoxicality.

At first glance, Nora's appearance in Dobson's (intertextual) seclusion amounts to an attempt to revitalize the conventions of the adultery genre by deploying the baring device of making strange. Shortly, we shall restore to its rights the subversive power of this concept neglected by Bakhtin. In accordance with the Formalist and contrary to the poststructuralist theory the price to be paid for discursive revitalization is the return to the actual/ literal/referential substance of the narrative. In our case this means that the appearance of Nora immediately abolishes the undecidability in which intertextuality was grounded. It becomes clear that there was a sexual union.

This amounts to an hermeneutic coincidence between the expectations of Achilles disguised as tortoise and the tortoise feigning to be Achilles. If the text is to remain interpretable, the hermeneutic race should continue. Whence a new-and the last-attempt to tie the double bind-in hope to prevent both ends from meeting. Ironically, it is precisely an effort to deploy the Achilles's strategy in a radically poststructuralist way which brings about the exhaustion of its hermeneutic potential.

In poststructuralist doctrine, the repetition with difference boils down to an intratextual grounding of intertextuality. The result of this grounding, which is believed to prevent a text's coincidence with itself, is the undecidability located, primarily, at the stylistical level. The poststructuralist theorists are so certain of their success that they deem that thereby they have exhausted the textual reality. Instead, they have freezed the latter, to wit, taken it literally and by the same token made of a skating contest a turn of figure skating.

As an attempt to intratextually revitalize the arid

intertextuality, Nora's appearance should make the mea-ning of "The Potato Elf" undecidable. Witness her announcement- "I had a son from you..."-which immedia-tely awakens Dobson to his Achillean destiny giving a new impetus to the hermeneutic race. On the other hand, her final phrase: "I have lost a son" seems to make of the race an infinite marathon, prompting the reader to take the place of the unlucky participant, that is, to non-mimetically identify with Dobson. However, on more close inspection it proves that our conclusion has been drawn all too hastily. For the price to be paid for Achilles's victory makes of it a Pyrhean one.

In fact, undecidability comes to be dependent on referential structure in its most brute form. For only Dobson's death can prolong the hermeneutic race to infinity by soliciting Nora's remark which splits the grammatical certainty of her first statement. Whence the apparent possibility of two readings-the one supposedly literal, the other-allegedly metaphorical. Forsooth, Nabokov's textual strategy makes the distinction hard to maintain-but not in the sense preferred by Derrida.

Paradoxically, it is the literal reading which utilizes the Derridaean supplementarity (there is no contradiction between Nora's having a son from Dobson and her having lost him). To make matters worse, the much hailed discursive equality turns out to have a refential structure that it should abolish (this reading would imply that Nora takes Dobson seriously: as an equal).

Paradoxically, a reading deemed metaphorical-Nora has been always treating the dwarf as a son-hangs on the same referential structure, for her last phrase inevitably refers to Dobson's corpse. So long as it is only this reading which can secure intertextuality by furnishing it with the intratextual foundation, it follows that what we are dealing with is not a double bind but the double baring of intertextuality as an inevitably hierar-chizing device and of referentiality as a true subversion of logocentric interpretive transmission.

At this point the only possibility left to a stubborn postructuralist is to take back all the claims as regards the current version of deconstruction and to argue that our text will retain all its aesthetic force without any recourse to the problem of meaning. To elicit precisely this admission is what our discussion was striving for. As we shall shortly see, the restoration of the notion of aesthetism to honour denied to it by poststructuralism can clear the path for a genuine deconstruction of the hermeneutic tradition.

The vicissitudes of the notion of aesthetism in recent theory is another baring of deconstructive project. Paradoxically, the main argument against deconstruction which thus far nobody has attempted let alone succeeded refuting is too weak: it is not true that deconstruction needs a structure produced by the (logocentric) Other to come into being, but that this structure is produced by deconstruction itself.

In other words, this means that it was necessary at first to make a bogey of aesthetism, then to equate it with the omnipotent subjectivity in order to be able to speak of logocentrism at all. Which is not to say that the latter should be exempted from deconstruction but that deconstruction itself cannot help promoting tradition precisely by virtue of furthering the interpretive race?

What logocentrism is primarily concerned with, is the safeguarding of conditions of its own possibility. The accomplishment of this task falls to the part of deconstruction. Whence the radicalization of the Achilles-becoming-the-tortoise strategy which is the structure of interpretation itself. The inevitable corollary is the drastic misrepresentation of tradition. In short, it is intertextuality/dialogism which is the true essence of logocentrism, whereas the notion of the omnipotent subjectivity should be neither defended nor deconstructed, but rejected tout court as making no sense at all.

It follows that the beyond of the hermeneutic tradition is the baring of the potential of mimesis an access to which has been barred from Plato to his poststructuralist ancestors. And yet it would be too spendthrift not to set Derrida aside from the latter. For it is nobody else than Derrida who corroborates our postulate. Witness his interest in the effects of signature which, forcing the reader to give up the Achilles's strategy, elicit the conclusion mentioned afore. Now it is up to us to spell out the consequences of the latter.

What allows us to treat Derridaean signature as a synonym of Bakhtin's intonation, is the fact that to sign and to intone means one and the same thing: to read. Whence the intertextual appropriation of both practices: intertextuality as repetition with difference receives a firm foundation, since the signing (or intoning) of a given text by its author, by definition, can never coincide with how the text comes to be signed/ intoned by the reader.

Whence the celebrated undecidability that, in actual fact, is only the reader's uncertainty as regards the extent to which his/her signing/intoning coincides with that of an author. However, this self-dimunition is underpinned by another one, i.e. by an a priori surmise that it is possible to qualitatively (intratextually) equate the intentions of the author and the reader and consequently to conceive of non-coincidence as a quantitative (intertextual) affair.

One need not be a gourmet to reject this dish of poststructuralist cousine for its logocentric taste-and this precisely because one ingredient supposedly essential to logocentrism is lacking from the receipt. My contention is exactly that by ommitting the notion of intention the plain dish has been made more digestible, the text more readable. For it is the author's intention which makes of a reading a futile enterprise.

In order to clear this statement of all ambiguities, let me render it thus: it is an author's intention to make a text unreadable, unassimilable by hermeneutic tradition. Which explains why the signature remains for Derrida primarily that of an author, but does not as yet explain how the appropriation takes place? However crucial, this question has not been even posed by the assailants of the logocentric edifice-with the exeption of Derrida himself.

Unfortunately his remarks remain brief and superficial, so that it would be fair to say that he takes the appropriation as a fact rather than trying to examine its mechanism. This reluctance, which in itself is another point in favour of our argument, will ultimately clear our analysis of deliberate twisting things around in order to state matters in the chosen fashion, for it proves that the deconstruction of the second degree is ultimately Derrida's deconstruction put for the first time to practical use.

Derridaean theory of the signature is the best example for the workings of the mechanism of appropriation which is set in motion the moment we identify an intention as aimed at the revelation of truth/final meaning instead of seeing its aim in establishing the possibility of reading (in case of an hermeneut) and the strategy of the subversion of this possibility (in case of an author).

To succumb to the first view, accidentally being the current one, and at the same time to remain coherent can only mean to recognize in intertextuality what it has always already has been, to wit, a logocentric affair. Significantly, the recognition will fall especially easy for a psychoanalytically informed reader.

To be sure, poststructuralism is only all too ready to dwell on the psychoanalytic underpinnings of our problematics. The subversion of logocentrism cannot be regarded complete without the subversion of such a no-torious version of it as the Freudian orthodoxy hanging as it does on the notion of castration. In accordance with the basic deconstructive rule of pharmakonization of the discourse subjected to deconstruction, the castration complex is not rejected but turned against itself.

As a result, another Father Figure claiming absolute knowledge/unambiguous meaning is exposed to be castrated. Which explains why the readings claiming fictionality of Freud's case histories are so fashionable? At this point even the most patient part of our auditorium will be tempted to mimic the diagnosis recurring throughout this paper. If we have already exhausted the patience of our readership, only now we are about to exhaust the referntial uncaninness of the effects of Achilles's self-dimunitive strategy.

As an intertextual device, Derrida's signature, just as Bakhtin's intonation, splits and scatters, to wit, castrates the signing/intoning subject barring him/her from the full meaning. The paradox of Zeno's paradox is that precisely the impossibility to ever attain an unambiguous meaning turns out to be the very possibility of reading as such, i.e. of transmission of the hermeneutic heritage. Which explains why the Achilles-becoming-the-tortoise strategy has been always already used in the most orthodoxical psychoanalytic applications of the castration complex to the texts of creative writers as well as to those of neurotics?

Witness S.Ferenczi's paper on "Gulliver Phantasies" where the dreams of the neurotics as well as an account of Gulliver's travels are referred to the same source, i.e. to the castration complex as an interminable vascillation (whence the interminability of analysis qua interpretation of which Lacan makes so much hail) between penis as dwarf (i.e. referent, material object) and phallus as giant (i.e. immaterial sign), the vascillation which, in Lacanian terms, should allow Achilles to overcome, but never to join his partner in an hermeneutical/ sexual race.

Whence two fundamental postulates of Lacanian hermeneutics: sexual relation never takes place but never stops to write itself. The constant possibility to overtake/interpret grounded in the impossibility to coincide coincides perfectly with the constant errancy as non-arrival of the letter/writing posited by Derrida. Whence the impossibility to take the much-hailed break of poststructuralism with psychoanalytic orthodoxy seriously, that is, literally.

Not so much because, for strategical reasons, Lacan was the first to concede that the hermeneutic sublimation of penis into phallus along the lines of the Kantian theory of the sublime was launched by Freud himself, but owing to the familiar attempt at de-refenrentialization of the castration complex instead of taking it literally/materially, the attempt which underpins the whole affair. Whence the line of divide between Freud and his immediate followers, primarily, E.Jones-and the poststructuralist appropriation of his legacy, to wit, the separation between libidinal/hermeneutic aphanisis and the castration anxiety which is nothing else than the interpretation of the castration complex, i.e. an aesthetic object in Bakhtinian sense.

Whence the uncanny (referential) coincidence between Lacan's stress on the indivisability of phallus qua signifier and Derrida's insisitence that just the opposite is true. Which explains why the double bind of the celebrated controversy is ostensible just as it is in case of "The Potato Elf". The result is the same: the withdrawal of the issue of undecidability from the foreground of the debate. However our analysis of Nabokovian textual strategy can only gain by referring to the familiar theoretical issues.

The as yet unappreciated lesson of Derrida-Lacan controversy is the conclusion an astute reader cannot fail to draw from Derrida's critique, namely that the notion of truth/full meaning has nothing to do with real concerns of logocentrism that boil down to a radical warding off the letter's ever arriving at its destination. This explains why Derridaean stance to see in the non-arrival a possibility justifies our use of culinary allusion to dubb the difference between tradition and its deconstruction as that between plain and more refined cousine, i.e. to trace it to the material problem of digestibility of certain dishes in certain historical circumstances.

The Achillean framework of Lacanian hermeneutics subjects it to the same sublime evaporation to which Derridaean and Bakhtinian exegetical models were shown to fall prey. The result of the aphanisis of interpretive matter is the brute materiliazation of the object of art. Owing to the self-dimunitive interpretive strategy grounded in the qualitative identification between author's and the reader's intentions the object of art comes to be regarded by our trio as fundamentally mutilated, i.e. castrated.

In other words, an art object that most fully corresponds to the demands of poststructuralist theorists is the mutilated statue of the Milos Venus which, at the same time, has always already been an ideal object of logocentric aesthetics. And hardly surprising, for the Venus statue is simultaneously the law and example of an attempt to make virtue of necessity to which logocentric as well as Derridaean theorizing boils down.

What makes of the Venus statue a sublime object, to wit, an ideal object of interpretation in the Kantian and poststructuralist sense is the uncanny impossibility to settle an issue of premeditation/unpremeditation, of intention and the lack of it. This undecidability as a constant vascillation between two participants in Zeno's hermeneutic race is the same which emerges from Derridaean interpretation of Socrates-becoming-Plato movement (1980) boosted as an instance of deconstruction at its best. If the notion of an (omnipotent) author is equally repugnant to the tradition and its deconstruction, then precisely because of the uncanny return of referentiality with which an interpretation cannot adequately cope.

In effect, the issue of undecidability, however crucial for hermeneutic race, has to be withdrawn according to the logic which "The Potato Elf" has allowed us to divulge. The Venus statue amplifies our preceding discussion by showing that this withdrawal happens for hermeneutic reasons in order to avoid literality of interpretation, to wit, its materiality. Whence the paradox of Zeno's paradox: in order to function interpretation has to substitute its own materiality for the materiality of the art object but in so doing cannot help but trigger the return of the referent which leaves a reader with an uncanny choice between the literality of interpretation (in fact, its evaporating coincidence /mimesis with the textual strategy of an author) and the dematerialization of interpretation (in fact, its annihilation, since a new reading as a differential

repetition/con/intertextualization of a given text has to be material in order to be anything at all). And this clears our analysis of a rebuke for twisting things around to state matters in Zenonian fashion: far from being another metalanguage (i.e. an instance of Cretan discursivity), the Achilles-becoming-the-tortoise strategy is the language of interpretation as such.

It is this paradox as the impossibility to ever tie the interpretive double bind which makes of an hermeneutic race a cold war against the notion of truth/full meaning. The reasons are as obvious as they are compelling. The case of Venus statue lays bare the referential structure of interpretive a-referentiality and thereby provides an ample description of the mechanism of tradition transmission, i.e. of the (im)possibility of appropriation.

In order to cope with materiality of an art object, interpretation has to make virtue of necessity, to wit, to direct its force against every attempt to amplify/finilize the mutilated text, i.e. to take castration literally. Put in more familiar terms, the parts which have been cut off should never be restored: the letter /writing should never arrive at its destination. But by the same token Lacan's persistence on the arrival bares his project as a subversive enterprise alligning it to the most radical avantegarde attempts at amplification of the mutilated texts.

Since it is precisely finalization which is the true enemy of hermeneutic tradition (from Socrates to Derrida and beyond), it is only logical that the latter, in actual fact, depends on the furthering of mutilation, for this process allows to hope that the dematerialization of an object of art will be brought about naturally.

Whence an infantile character of interpretation (to be understood literally and metaphorically): an interpreter is frozen in the situation of a boy, who on seeing that the girl is lacking a penis decides that it is only too small and decides to wait, but this waiting can only end with the full-scope castration complex as a radical abolishing of the penis. However, even this hope to secure interpretation is doomed to fail, for the hope itself has a referential structure: to surmise that the immaterial object is synonymous with the sublimated one means to take immateriality itself materially.

Obviously, it is this purely logocentric concern which underpins Derrida's interest in negative theology (1989; 1995). It follows that Derrida was correct to say that the aim of logocentrism is a book as an immaterial object (1981a: 53, 185). But the paradox is that, far from threatening logocentrism, the multiplication of copies is the only conceivable way to attain logocentric aims. Especially in the age of technical reproduction the law of which is the Achillean interplay between production and consumption-without restance. According to the laws of the Derridaean unrestricted economy, which is also the one of hermeneutic tradition?

And herewith the description of the mechanism of appropriation may be regarded complete. Unfortunately, it resembles the prepetuum mobile not in the poststructura-list sense of perpetuation of the interpretive transmission, but in the crudely material sense of an impossible, unreal device. For what radically resists con/intertextual appropriation is the referential structure of the art object, its materiality, which subverts all attempts to dematerialize it by dematerializing the interpretation. It remains to see what insights this assessment can buy and whether they should still be paid for by blindness.

Ironically, among the problems with which post-structuralism is unsuccessfully grappling the most notorious one is that of history/change. Irony stems from the fact that the relation between poststructuralism and its predecessor is generally thematized precisely along historical lines: as a shift from synchrony to diachrony. At first glance, this description might appear sly and unjust, for all the structuralist concepts can easily be shown to rely on the concept of literary history as indirect filiation propounded by Russian Formalists.

However, economically speaking, the model in question is not rentable: the mechanism of interpretive transmission comes to be described and secured, but only by making of the whole affair a matter of natural history, i.e. of an all too smooth functioning which leaves no place for accidents, that is, for the influence of social context. Whence the current discontent with structuralist historicity and an attempt to improve the strategy in which our reader has already recognized the Achillean one.

As our analysis of Nabokov's short-story has shown, this improvement boils down to the intratextual and at the same time intertextual deployment of interpretive self-dimunition, since the separate deployment of intra-and itertextuality cannot do away with referntial structure as the hermeneutic obstacle par excellence. The improvement may indeed appear perfect, especially since it removes the main charge against deconstruction said to be dependent on pre-existing structures:

"... in its very relevance this objection /mentioned above/ cannot be sustained ... except by referring to extra-literary and even extra-linguistic juridical norms. The objection appeals to law and calls to mind the fact that the subversion of La Folie du jour needs the law in order to take place.

Whereby the objection reproduces and accomplishes its staging within La Folie du jour: the account, mandated and prescribed by law but also ... commanding, requiring, and producing law in turn. In short, the whole critical scene of competence in which we are engaged is party to and part of La Folie du jour, in whole and in part, the whole is a part"(1980b: 219;)

In order not to limit deconstruction to a Foucauldian model of trangression of a pre-given law one has to thematize exactly the extra-literary and even extra-linguistic elements, to wit, to textualize them. Whence Derridaean dictum about limitless textuality. Unfortunately this dictum looses all its subversive force the moment it comes to be pronounced.

Put otherwise, the true paradoxicality of deconstruction stems not from the celebrated (and readily embraced) difficulties with articulating its fundamental notion of the différance but from the trite impossibility to articulate the prefix "de-". Which explains why the succinct description of the invaginating, abyssal structure just cited turns out to be a perfect example of the famous Kettle-logic read in reverse, i.e. bared as another version of the Achillean self-dimunition.

If the abyssal intertextuality founders, then not so much due to the fact that its articulation requires a number of denials/ restrictions but primarily because the final articulation, however mutilated, makes of de-construction a perfect mimesis of the construction of tradition: what the invaginating stricture (the text's dependence on the pre-existing structure which is produced by the textual movement itself) boils down to is the unrestricted accumulation, to wit, the radical impossibi-lity for anything to get lost: everything is bound to arrive at its destination: in Formalist terms, everything can be revitalized, or, as Bakhtin would state it, "every sense will have its day of ressurection".

Which means that the two fundamental postulates of poststructuralism-the one about the influence of the social context as determinant to the act of interpretation, and another concerning the act of exclusion constitutive of the logocentric identity-happen to be at odds, for an act of exclusion can be conceived only as an accident, and therefore as a con/intertualizing affair.

Morally speaking, this means to wash logocentrism of all guilt, to claim for the hermeneutic tradition innocence and in doing so to load guilt on literary texts and their authors exposed as unremittable debtors. Therefore it is only logical that the most advanced versions of intertextuality are phrased in overtly moral terms of guilt/debt.

Fortunately, to counter this tendency all one has to do is to take recourse to psychoanalysis. What sharpens the paradoxicality of the proposed move is that it requires the mediation of a theorist whose current vogue stems from the belated overtaking of poststructuralism. The man in question is Mikhail Bakhtin.

If one pays too much heed to the current appropriation of his legacy, the role we are about to make him play is bound to appear paradoxical, and this not at the least because, as every-body knows, he was the first to see in Freudianism the logocentric (monological) bogey which now haunts theory. The true nature of the Freud-Bakhtin connection, which cannot be divulged from the poststructuralist standpoint, is another issue that will be added to the list of questions clarified in the course of our discussion.

Fortunately, the psychoanalytic framework itself seems to need no justistification since the notion of the unconscious is implied in every attack on the logocentric subjectivity, whereas Freud's complicity with the latter is believed to stem from the fact that his unconscious is not unconscious enough, to wit, remains immaterial and conscious. This charge on which Bakhtinian critique of Freudianism hangs is unwittingly furthered by poststructuralism. Whence another quandary:

how to re-marry the legacies of both men? The solutions propounded thus far are invalidated by virtue of their perfect coincidence.

For, appearances notwithstanding, to bridge the gap hermeneutically mean to foreground the ethics of subject creation and vice versa. What comes to be barred thereby is the possibility to divulge the intuitions which make the names of Bakhtin and Freud allies in the deconstruction of tradition. Elsewhere we have already bared the sublime fate of the unconscious in the two dominant versions of postst-ructuralist theory, to wit, the impossibility to maintain this notion on Derridaean as well as Lacanian terms-precisely because these terms are hermeneutuc ones.

It is nobody else than Bakhtin, an alleged avatar of this stance, who highlights how to preclude the evaporation. What corroborates the view of Freudianism as an hermeneutic abridgement of psychoanalysis is an apparent absence of our notion from Bakhtin's major works. Hence, just as in case of Heidegger, it seems necessary first of all to find a place where unconscious may appear in Bakhtinian theory (cf. Richardson 1965). Those who are bent upon remaining blind to the most promising intuitions of both our thinkers are free to exercise their wits in the boy-scoutian manner.

To put it in plain language, the notion of the unconscious underpins the earliest works penned at the moment when Bakhtin, more likely than not, was as yet anaware of Freudian theory. Despite (or perhaps thanks to) this innocence, Bakhtin's early view of aesthetic activity deploys our notion in the way which allows us to treat an essay on "The Author and Hero in Aesthetic Activity" as a model of applied psychoanalysis at its best. Whereas his major works can be regarded as extended explorations of the (im)possibilities to retain the Freudian concept within the framework belatedly dubbed poststructuralist. Which explains why the genuine return to Freud can only be a return to early Bakhtin?

An optimal way to prove our point would be to mimic Derridaean mimicing of the itinerary of Bakhtin's letter and select one of the mature works. An essay "Discourse in Life and Discourse in Poetry" signed by Voloshinov suggests itself as a succinct summary of the accepted ideas of the Bakhtin Circle.

Therefore it is not surprising that the best summary of these ideas is provided by our last quotation from Derrida. It remains to see whether the difference produced by (this) mutual baring is the repetitive/interpretive one. At first glance, the argument of our essay proceeds along quite familiar, i.e. patently poststructuralist lines: The signifying process is fundamentally a social, to wit, intertextual affair.

The gist of the matter is to prove that this applies equally to a given text as well as to its interpretation. Which means the (inter)textualization of the extra-literary and even pre-linguistic discursive elements, i.e. an inscription of the reader in the text. The result of this Achillean invaginating intratextualization of intertex-tuality is, once again, the limitless textuality which finds its limit in the dependence on the referential structure. The threat posed by this dependence explains why it was intonation which was foregrounded by Bakhtin as an hermeneutic/intertextual device par excellence. In effect, the promise of this notion is to suspend the issue of referentiality as undecidable.

And yet the promise is bound to remain unfulfilled-due to the same necessity which in case of Nabokov's "The Potato Elf" has forced our reader to relinquish the same argument. The resoluteness of Bakhtin's representative to persevere up to the last helps us to exhaust the uncanny logic of Zenonian discursivity.

At this point we may already flatter ourselves to have sufficiently explained why con/intertextualization should be equated with intonation or signature. Achilles's strategy as the mechanism of interpretive transmission hinges upon a certain amount of self-dimunitive hermeneutic exhaustion: a given interpretation has to invaginate the possibility of aphanisis in order to allow for a substitution by a new one.

Whence the necessity to preserve traces or ashes. But by the same reasoning, the problem on which poststructuralism stands or falls turns out to be not that of conservation as such but of conservation as revitalization. Whence the trouble with the notion of unconscious as adopted by the psychoanalytic establishment. It is this trouble as well as the way to solve it which is disclosed by Voloshinov.

Within the psychoanalytic framework the postructuralist complicity with tradition becomes even more evident, for the result of the deconstructive engagement with Freudian legacy aimed at baring the multiple forms which the logocentric alliance has in psychoanalysis is the unequivocal equation of Freud's Copernican revolution with the theory of children's sexuality, which is said to radically do away with the logocentric attitude to child-hood as an age of innocence (e.g. Rose 1984: 12-42).

The paradox is that precisely the denial of this innocence is a necessary corollory of the logocentric stance which is essentially an hermeneutic, i.e. a moral one. Witness the psychoanalytic narrative on the emergence of the castration complex-discarded by poststructuralism as a patently logocentric fiction-which is possible only on the a priori denial of innocence. If it were otherwise, it would have been impossible to claim the childish character of the unconscious and its essential lack of innocence.

However, to rest satisfied with the conclusion that it is its own innocence which logocentrism is concerned with would mean to drastically simplify the problem. For the hermeneutic innocence presupposes the textual victimization, the current form of which is the intertextuality of all stripes. It was up to Bakhtin, by mimicking overtaking of poststructuralism to remove the obstacle which barres way to the most fruitful Freudian intuitions as regards unconscious as well as childhood that can be alligned not along the hermeneutically-moral lines but along aesthetic ones. Before we pick our discu-ssion where we have left it, the reader should be reminded that a self-sacrificial act is the very opposite of a self-dimunitive one.

Significantly, precisely the point in the conventi-onal theory of the unconscious where logocentric (Kanti-an) underpinnings of it are at the foremost is explicitly carefully avoided and implicitly strengthened by poststructuralist theorizing. I mean an attempt to define the unconscious processes by their indifference to contradictions-a feature which the unconscious is said to share with savage and/or child's thought.

It is this reasoning which triggers the hermeneutic evaporation/dematerialization of our notion, to wit, the transformation of the material unconscious into the (immaterial) consciousness. Fortunately, to bar this sublimation it is sufficient to radically change the framework of theorizing-psychoanalytic and otherwise: rather than that of Hegel, we should place ourselves in the shadow of Kant. This suggestion is another point where Derridaean and Bakhtinian intuitions fruitfully converge.

The disregard to contraditions attributed to the unconscious makes of the theory of the latter a psycho-analytic transcription of the Kantian theory of the sublime. Derrida's reading of Kant has pinpointed the unlawful deployment of mimesis in order to downplay the contradiction (impossibility to compare) between qualitatively incomparable entities as the essence of logocentric stance. Understandably, nobody has bothered to draw the only possible conclusion, namely, that the non-perfect, impure mimesis (Achilles's non-mimetic identification with tortoise) is the aim which the hermeneutic tradition has always already been after.

To refute this conclusion as a familiar argument of Derrida's ill-wishers would mean to argue that deconstruction draws its strength from the weakness of its adversary and thereby to take recourse to the Cretan dis-cursivity in its blindness/insight version, that is, to not simply reintroduce the conscious vs unconscious opposition but to do this to the detriment of the second term. The sublime fate of Bakhtin's intonation cannot fail to defamiliriaze this whole passage.

As a theorist, Bakhtin is quite notorious for constantly contradicting himself. Significant for our discussion is that Bakhtin himself has been more than conscious of this apparent weakness of which his students can make neither head nor tail representing it as an instance of faithfullness to the polyphonic/intertextual messiness of everyday life, i.e. to the discursive materiality. However, contrary to his students bent upon understanding this "messiness" metaphorically, he took it literally. And this difference makes all the différance in the world. At first glance, to dub Bakhtin's thematization of intonation contradictory would mean to treat it too leniently. Paradoxically, this is precisely how it should be treated from the morally-hermeneutic, i.e. poststructura-list point of view.

For the paradox is that on more close inspection it turns out not only that seemingly contradictory remarks can be reconciled without recourse to any elaborate contrivances but that they are subject to a strictly logical necessity. Witness the evaporation of what may appear as the main aporia of Bakhtinian theory of intonation pushed to the fore in Voloshinov's essay. According to Bakhtin, intonation is a primal bearer of social evalution as a movement of con/intertextualization.

Somewhere above we have already referred to the fact that Bakhtin makes no secret of a precarious fate of intonation, i.e. its disappearance, to wit, materialization which seemingly compels the reader to give up every hope of dialogizing retrieval. The only possibility left is to give the problem an hermeneutical/moral turn and thereby to radically annihilate a text. This is precisely what will happen with Bakhtin's text if we succumb to the aporetical solution, i.e. to seeing here an unparalled example of candidness. Voloshinov spells out all the consequences of adoption of this stance.

Within the poststructuralist framework to hold to the suggested solution means to immediately become one's own undertaker. Precisely because the last chance to se-cure intertextualization is to thematize the very frailty of its bearer. The materiality of a text fostered thereby impaires interpretation, makes it impure. However, this impurity as the self-dimunitive triumph of aporetical Cretan discursivity is precisely what the hermeneut has always already been after. The paradox of Zeno's paradox as elucidated by Bakhtin's disciple stems from the impossibility to claim for the referential structure the simulacroid character. Which boils down to the impossibility to say one thing and to do another? "A healthy social evaluation remains in life and from there organises the very form of utterance and its intonation, although it never strives to find an adequate representation in the content of utterance. When the evaluation regresses from form to content, this is a sure sigh that the re-evaluation is underway".

The provisional death of intertextuality is a necessary moment of interpretive transmission. An utterance should die, to wit, wash off the traces of previous interpretations, in order to allow for a revitalization. A Derridaean term for this moment is "blanc" or "khora"-a scanssion which punctuates the interpretive chain. It remains to see whether this punctuation does not accidentally preclude the very possibility of the desired revitalization.

Certainly, the Cretan discursivity allows to deny our surmise. But the paradox is that in so doing its adept would have not only to attribute logocentrism to the main proponents of the attack on the tradition and thereby to accomplish the work of mourning-a monological enterprise fostering mastery-but that even this sacrifice-the only hope to preclude coincidence-would end in the total mimesis of the textual strategy. Since the full impact of the latter can be appreciated by recourse to psychoanalysis let us follow the poststructuralist appropriation of Bakhtin and Derrida to its logical end.

The moment of khora remains an hermeneutic moment par excellence only insofar as the disappearance of the utterance/text/art object marked by it remains provisional. Which explains the necessity of the postructuralist rendering of this traditional goal of Western hermeneutics, to wit, of limitless textuality, to wit, of the intratextualization of intertextuality as the inscription of the reader and his/her intonation/signature in the text?

Further, we see why it is necessary to conceive of intertextuality as discursive equality, that is, to ground it in the blindness/insight dialectics which, in its turn, becomes the final proof of the subversion of logocentric hierarchies to be achieved by means of intertextuality. It is the strength of our analysis that instead of dwelling on the apparent coincidence of the deconstructive double-bind and the traditional hermeneutic circle we see the point of complicity in the impossibility to tie the former and to close the latter, to wit, the impossibility to utilize Derrida's signature and Bakhtin's intonation as means to poststructuralist ends.

Within the dialogical framework the disappearance of a text as its discursive dematerialization means that the intertextualizing device, inscribed in the text, suffers the same fate. Whence the necessity of the uncanny choice between discursive equality as intertextuality and intertextuality as the discursive revitalization. To make matters worth both options boil down to one and the same thing.

The discursive equality precludes the possibility of discursive revitalization by making the text immortal. For to become material in the discursive sense, in case of the device(s) of intertextualization, means exactly to save the text from the moment of khora. This is precisely what Voloshinov is saying.

Whence the necessity to read his statement literally in order to impute a contradiction, to wit, a point of logocentric blindness. In other words, one has to equate "the living intonation" which, according to Voloshinov, "leads the word beyond its discursive boundaries" with a patently logocentric notion of self-presence, whereas in actual fact, as was mentioned above, it is a patently poststructuralist claim for the materiality of interpretation.

It would have been a fortunate accident if we were to succeed in proving that this attempt to deploy the Achilles-becoming-the-tortoise strategy boils down to a self-deconstruction of deconstruction. Unfortunately, in trying to limit the whole affair to the dialectic of blindness/insight poststructuralism cannot help making an accident of itself.

On poststructuralist terms, the failure to achieve a textual coma is synonymous with the reinforcement of traditional notions of truth/full meaning. Since this reinforcement is a corollary of an attempt to pursue a poststructuralist aim of materializing interpretation, it follows that the last hope to save the whole affair is to give up precisely this aim.

Which means to treat the intertextualizing devices-be it

Derridaean signature or Bakhtin's intonation-literally, i.e. in a radically non-discursive sense? Since it is this suggestion with which Voloshinov leaves us, one has to try to counter it by suggesting that thereby Voloshinov contradicts himself as well as another Bakhtin's dummy-Pavel Medvedev whose critique of Freudianizm has been readily embraced by poststructuralism.

As everybody knows, an apple of dissent between Freud and the Bakhtin's Circle is the notion of the unconscious which, according to Medvedev and Voloshinov, puts psychoanalysis into a logocentric corner by virtue of being a consciousness in disguise, to wit, an anti-social, monologic, and therefore immaterial affair. Whence an apparent impossibility to reconcile this attempt to put Freud to a dialogical school and the Programme of the latter elaborated by way of rectifying the Formalist aesthetics.

According to Bakhtin's dummies, what delineates the dialogical imagination from the monological one is the way of inscription of the reader in the text. The proper dialogical manner of textualization of the hermeneutic attitude is to assume that the social evaluation saturates a text/utterance unconsciously. Within the framework of the Bakhtinian critique of psychoanalysis this is an apparent contradiction-but a salutary. For the Cretan discursivity would have been saved were we allowed to rest satisfied with the conclusion that Bakhtin's disciples say one thing and do another (or vice versa). Uncannily, such is not the case.

As we have seen, the trouble with intertextuality is that its mechanism functions all too perfectly, to wit, do not function at all: an essential moment of khora cannot be produced so long as interpretation claims materiality/ intertextuality. This is precisely what Voloshinov means by dubbing an intertextual inscription un-conscious, i.e. a-social, monological.

Whence the necessity of an intratextual grounding, for the moment of khora, of provisional death of intertextuality cannot be produced otherwise than by intrinsic/innocent means of a given discourse. Which explains why an ostensibly dialogical/

unconscious inscription of the reader is immediately opposed by Voloshinov to the "conscious taking into account of readership"? It remains to see whether the addition of this ingredient would not make the dish indegistible for the dialogical stomach.

Certainly, a poststructuralist can always reject to even partake of the meal but in so doing should be prepared to starving to death. For compared with our dish a Cretan one resembles a hunger ration, if not a hunger hallucination. To return to plain language, one has to make virtue of necessity and to sacrifice the very framework of all poststructuralist machinations by making of the avatar(s) of the latter the epigons of logocentrism.

In effect, the Voloshinov's essay we are examining seems to re-introduce the logocentric binary (conscious vs. unconscious) to deconstructively undermine which was the aim of the Bakhtinian appropriating critique of the psychoanalytic notion of the unconscious substituted by an exproppriatingly extended consciousness.

However, on more close inspection, it turns out that Voloshinov has remained faithful to the aims of his group and in so doing has baringly barred the poststructuralist project. Witness his discursive strategy which is nothing else than a holier-than-Thou version of the Achillean self-dimunition practiced by poststructuralism.

Whence the uncanny overtaking. In effect, the whole affair boils down to a certain conceptual rechartering: it leaps to the eye that Voloshinov readily appropriates the terms of the Freudian theory of the Ego/consciousness to describe intertextual inscriptions.

Which makes of the extended consciousness a neat counterpart of Derridaean writing, that is, another generalized notion which includes what traditionally has been splitted as writing and speech? Theoretically, what should have been produced by this expropriating doubling of the appropriating double is a destructure as a beyond of logocentric theorizing aimed at the production of the subject of knowledge. Whence the vogue enjoyed by the psychoanalytic theory of mourning and melancholia with which psychoanalytically informed deconstruction as well as deconstructively informed psychoanalysis have placed their stakes.

At first glance, the melancholic set-up seems to answer perfectly all poststructuralist needs without contradicting common-sense. To equate the textual production with the work of mourning is an obvious move, whereas the product itself can be said to bear witness to the inability to accomplish this work, the inability stemming from the human reluctance to give up libidinal ties. It follows that the impossibility of mastery is natural to human species, to wit, that logocentrism is a violation of nature itself. But as a result deconstruction appears as another attempt to return to origins or at least to the things themselves.

The paradox is that this conclusion which at first glance seems to sign the death-sentence actually would only foster the Phoenix-discursivity and Cretan textuality. For what it implies is that the impossibility of deconstruction is the impossibility of this return, to wit its possibility, since the return to the things is the return of the things, i.e. an instance of repetition automatism. It is this movement, an hermeneutic movement par excellence which is put in question by Freud's ruminations on mourning as well as by Bakhtin's theory of aesthetic activity. Whence their coincidence at the point which precludes the very possibility of Cretan misrecognition.

At the face of it, the work of mourning as described by Freud is a perfect instance of self-deconstruction. Irony stems from the fact that the law remains with-out example whatsoever, for Freud's account cannot be advanced as an example of the general rule. What the poststructuralist appropriation of our theory has bared is the notorious impossibility of the work of mourning to ever be accomplished.

In fact, the very success of this process, envisaged by Freud as an exception, is the impossibility of the success. And this precisely because the giving up of the object/referent is its inscription within the intrapsychic/intratextextual household, naturally disruptive of every economy. The result is that the object becomes a ghost/signifier and comes to haunt the ego. However, it would be an easy sailing to conclude that thereby the desired intertextuality has been securely established.

At the face of it the latter has indeed received an intratextual grounding. And yet precisely this grounding happens to disrupt the whole machine: instead of flaunting the artifice, it bares the referential structure. Which explains why Freud's conclusion is basically the same with which Voloshinov's essay has left us with: the point which the theory of mourning just sketched cannot cope with is mania, to wit, repetition compulsion, to wit, intertextuality itself.

At first glance this outcome is not so much paradoxical, as unexplainable. In effect, the hermeneutic potential of mourning /melancholia stems precisely from a radical a priori bracketing of the object/referent, the bracketing which seems to preclude the problem from ever arising at all.

The premise of mourning is precisely the disappearance of the object, the disappearance with which a mourner/ hermeneut has nothing to do at all. On the contrary, the success or failure of mourning is bound up with the giving up/ preserving of the signifier and/or signified and not with the referent which has always already disappeared-by itself, to wit, by natural means. Put differently, the work of mourning can be launched only after the work of nature has been accomplished.

The disappearance we are speaking about is the premise of the mourning/interpretation-but not an un-acknowledged one. To the contrary. Witness Lacan's objet petit a which grounds discursivity precisely by virtue of its radically non-discursive nature. It is this grounding which an intratextual one has to non-mimetically mime but in so doing cannot help evaporating.

The result is the baring of the unconscious an anccess to which should have been barred by intratextual invagination of intertextuality, to wit, by the work of mourning as a psychoanalytic version of production of Cretan discursivity. Whence the splitting of the hermeneutic model: it seems that hermeneutics as (the semiotics of) unconscious and unconscious as (the semiotics of) mourning are at odds. And once again the splitting is only an ostensible one.

The self-defeating, i.e. hermeneutic status of mourning stems from the fact that the withdrawal of the libido from the outer world does not lead to the enrichment of the ego but to its impoverishment. To explain this paradox one has to take recourse to Zeno's paradox and this exactly what Freud does. Thus we come to hear that it is the Super-ego and not the Ego onto which libido flaws back.

Whence the necessity for the Ego to practice adultery of sorts, i.e. to try to seduce the Super-ego to fall in love with it-which can be achieved only by practicing self-dimunition. Whence the impossibility to identify the participants of the work of mourning, for what this view boils down to is another generalized concept-now of the intrapsychic economy which comes to resemble the Derridaean notion of writing. Therefore it is not surprising that Freud's troubles are the same which we have encountered above.

In effect, the Freudian machine functions all too perfectly by virtue of intratextual flaws. Once again the gist of the matter is to introduce the provisional death, the essential khora. However, the mourner is a sleepless creature (Freud 1916: 439), to wit, a dialogical one (434-435). Whence the problem how to put the patient and a text to sleep? The first question is no question at all: forsooth nature will do her task and the analyst his/hers.

This is possible because clinically melancholia relies on the actual/factual disappearance of the object. Significantly, precisely clinically/literally the disappearance is perfectly Derridaean, for its first effect is to blur the distinction between natural and accidental. And this is why melancholia can be cured-as a fact. But by the same token it becomes impossible to cure/interpret a text.

The paradox is that this impossibility is exactly the very possibility of deconstruction of which Derrida speaks (e.g. 1995: 43 et passim). What invalidates the way deconstruction is currently handled is not the fact that the Cretan discursivity cannot cope with referentiality and therefore blinds itself to its reliance on the referential structure, but that it copes with it all too perfectly and in so doing puts itself into a corner from which there is no Cretan escape.

What sets Freud's account of melancholia aside from the poststructuralist culmination of the hermeneutic tradition is its rootedness in clinic which allows him to divulge that it is neither the failure which makes interpretation nor the success which promotes mastery. If the possibility to cure melancholia is the impossibility to use the work of mourning hermeneutically, then precisely because an analyst's success is bound up with the disappearance of the referent brought about naturally, to wit, accidentally.

It follows that in order to apply the melancholic set up to hermeneutic ends one has to claim exactly the opposite, that is, to take success literally-as an exercise of mastery. Which explains why precisely Freud's theory of melancholia is used by poststructuralism as a main evidence of Freud's logocentric blindness? The Cretan discursivity would have been saved if the poststructuralist handling of Freudian and other texts could have been shown to deploy the self-same strategy denounced for its logocentric implications.

Unfortunately such is not the case. The (im)possibility of (mis)reading is the possibility to impute to an author an excercise of mastery and to unconsciously practise the same thing. The necessity of this strategy is the necessity to ground intertextuality intratextually. However, the radical independence of referentiality thus achieved poses a supplementary problem which, in strict accordance with Derrida, turns out to be the one on which the whole enterprise hangs.

For the referential independence is synonymous with the textual immortality, with the absence of the moment of the provisional death. Logically, to wit, paradoxically, the only possibility left to introduce the moment of khora is to deploy Cretan discursivity consciously, that is, to not only accuse others of mastery but to thematize one's own exercise of it. Obviously enough, the resulting self-deconstruction could have been only embraced by poststructuralism as a radical form of discursive Creta-nism enabling Achille to win the hermeneutic race by practicing self-dimunition. The paradox of Zeno's paradox is the impossibility of the self-deconstructive non-coin-cidence. It is Achilles's ultimate joining the tortoise laid bare by Freud and Bakhtin to which Nabokov's textual strategy boils down to.

The Bakhtinian counterpart of Derrida's khora is the moment when the conscious taking in account of the actual readership gains the upper-hand. As a result "a work of art looses its artistic purity and degrades onto a lower social level"(Voloshinov 1995: 83). It is the strength of Cretan discursivity to compell a conventional ill-wisher as well as a fan to do the same thing: to lin-ger over the fact that the loss of purity essential as it is for the dialogical poetics is conceived by its avatar as an outcome of an exercise of mastery. Fortunately, the traps are there only to be avoided.

What comes to be bared in Voloshinov's essay is that the moment of khora has an invaginating structure: instead of marking a Derridaean blank and/or Lacanian scanssion in the signifying order it marks the blotting gap of referential eruption, to wit, the self-same death of the natural object on which a clinicist can safely count and which, in case of textual exegesis, can be brought about only by artificial means. However, the erupted lava tends to immediately freeze. The paradox is that an attempt to diminish the literality of this statement will not fail to make matters worse.

To be sure, one can always argue that the death of the referent is not the death of a person from the clinical picture of melancholia. What this argument implies is that in the first case there remains a possibility of ressurection, to wit, of a new interpretation. Whence the apparent complicity of intertextuality with one of the fundamental archetypes of Western culture. However, carried to its logical end this reasoning makes of an interpretation a vigil, a wake: far from always already having taken place, the interpretation sublimates itself into a hope that it will take place. Which means that once again interpretation cannot gain materiality, to wit, intratextuality? Whence the necessity to equate both deaths. And this is precisely what the textual strategy compels an interpreter to do.

Up today literary theorists have carefully avoided 56 addressing one aspect of literary history, namely, the mechanism by virtue of which from time to time certain texts come to be denigrated onto a lower social level, to wit, descend from adult literature to children's. More often than not such denigration turns out to be irrevo-cable.

Where it is not, the return is undermined by the fact that no text written for children has succeeded entering the adult literature. Far from being marginal, this process bares the general laws of interpretive transmission qua tradition/canon formation thematized by poststructuralism under the rubric of genre.

Taken at face value, the poststructuralist interest in the law(s) of the (literary) genre(s) is exempt from any laws whatsoever being purely arbitrary as an attempt to leave no territory deconstructively unploughed. What Derridaean plunderings boil down to is the same undecidability qua impurity, to wit, the pharmakonization of the notion of genre in order to make of it another generalized concept.

Whence the correspondence with Bakhtin's theory of the novel as an essentially impure genre. From our vantage the poststructuralist curiosity appears to be uncannily innocent. Consider the case of Gulliver's Travels which exemplifies the uncanny (im)possibility to revitalize a text once denigrated onto a lower social level. Satire as which Swift has originally conceived his book is one of the forms of Bakhtinian intertextuality.

Which explains why Swift's narrative is structured by the multiple hermeneutic overtakings, i.e. by the self-dimu-nitive exchange of discursive identities between the participants in Zeno's race? Therefore it seems that there should be no problems with the revitalization of a text currently read rather by children than by adults. More-over, our case seems to be a perfect example of how intertextuality is grounded intratextually.

Not only the denigration lends itself to be conceived as just another supplementary self-dimunition always already inscribed in the text, but the debasement itself seems to be a perfect khora. Whence the apparent ease of revitalization, i.e. of the reawakening of the intratextual elements to a second life, for the debasement as an exercise of mastery is a neat counterpart of satirical debasement practised by an author.

Carried to its logical end this reasoning winds up with an already familiar paradox: once again, the moment of khora becomes accidental, which means the accidentality of revitalization, to wit, of deconstruction itself, since the latter non-mimetically mimes the strategy supposed to be the authorial one. To worsen matters this result is the effect of author's signature.

It is a widely acknowledged fact that Swift's narrative is marked by an increase of satirical elements (cf. papers in Browning 1983). Whence the suggestiveness of the pyramidal structure. As Derridaean deconstruction of Hegel's semiotics is at pains to stress, the pyramid-and this applies to every hierarchy-is bound to collapse into a pit. At face value, Swift's text corroborates Derridaean assumptions.

In effect, the satirical culmination in the fourth part is precipitantingly, i.e. self-dimunitevely envisaged in the preface, where the author acknowledges his self-defeat. Swift is quite conscious that a hope to gain mastery very society, to change it, by means of satire is bound to be of no avail, has to be given up.

This act implies the recognition of a death of intertextual elements. Whence the necessity, amply used by post-structuralism, to denigrate satire as an impure form of dialogism, to wit, as an all too logocentric one, for only thus it becomes possible to sustain the notion of deconstruction as a self-deconstruction of a given discourse. In short, one has to prove that Swift does the opposite of what he is saying, i.e. that an act of giving up intertextual mastery boils down to an attempt to save mastery on the intratextual level, as mastery over his own text. Unluckily, there is a perfect mimesis not only between Swift's sayings and doings but, paradoxically, between his strategy and the poststructuralist one. One of the leitmotives which intratextually structures Gulliver's Travels is that of the writing 58. Its satirical acme is to be found in the third part. I mean the narrator's visit to the school of languages of the grand academy of Lagado. Of principal interest is "a scheme for entirely abolishing all words whatsoever and this was urged as a great advantage in point of health as well as brevity.

For, it is plain, that every word we speak is in some degree a dimunition of our lungs by corrosion; and consequently contributes to the shortning of our lives. An expedient was therefore offered, that since words are only names for things, it would be more convenient for all men to carry about them, such things as were necessary to express the particular business they are to discourse on"(Swift 1995: 139; first italics are mine). What this Heideggerian attempt to return to the things themselves boils down to is the Cretan self-dimunitive discursivity, which, according to the post structuralist doctrine, can function only by mal-functioning, to wit, by non-coinciding with itself.

In other words, in order to intratextually ground intertextuality and in so doing to allow for an interpretive transmission we have to be able to prove that Swift's textual strategy is at odds with our passage, to wit, that he is practicing the exact opposite of what serves as an object of his satirical attack.

That such is actually the case seems to be evidenced by the fact that we were compelled to formulate our problem the way we have done. It leaps to the eye that Swift's way of writing coincides with the one he is criticizing. Whence the transformation of the latter into an object or thing precisely in the sense suggested by our passage and the non-coincedence of the Swiftian textuality with itself. The result is the moment of khora: an intratextual death of intertextual elements, to wit, the (im)possibility to settle once and for all the question of adherence of Gulliver's Travels to the satirical genre.

For the moment it becomes possible to read our book innocently-as children do, and in so doing to make the author innocent of satirical intentions, i.e. of logocentrism in disguise. Which means to make logocentrism innocent by means of the strategy aimed at exposing its guilt? Clearly, this innocence and this paradox are not the ones we are after.

Therefore it is necessary to discard the reasoning sketched in this paragraph, for carried to its logical, to wit, paradoxical end it inevitably winds up with a Cretan proof of the impossible possibility of deconstruction. Fortunately, attended more closely, the textual reality backs us up in our decision.

What discursive Cretanism as the intratextual invagination of intertextuality boils down to is the self-dimunitive non-coincident interplay between the (deconstructive) pit and the (logocentric) pyramid, to wit, the constant reversal of generations.

In other words, the whole affair hinges on the manner of revitalization/re-contextualization of a given discourse. For obvious reasons there should be a gap between discursive death and resurrection. To resurrect Gulliver's Travels means to return the book to the adults, i.e. to once again foreground the intertextual guilt of the author, that is, his satirical intentions. Let us see how this task can be accomplished.

If the view of deconstruction as self-deconstruction is to be maintained the essentials should be provided by the text itself-in our case by the already cited account of the linguistic innovations propounded by Laputian scholars.

From the poststructuralist standpoint it is to be expected that another (logocentric) attempt to invent "an universal language to be understood in all civilised nations" should suffer a (self-deconstructive/self-diminishing) pharmakonization by an "inconvenience" to which a logocentric eye is supposedly inclined to blind itself: "... the new scheme of expressing themselves by things ... hath only this inconvenience attending it; that if a man's business be very great, and of various kinds, he must be obliged in proportion to carry a greater bundle of things upon his back, unless he can afford one or two strong servants to attend him".

What logocentrism strives for is the depharmakonized, pure intertextuality as the interpretive immortality. In order to preclude the (self)-dimunition of interpretation, its aphanisis one has to treat words as things which means an attempt to overtake a text by loosing sight of it. Poststructuralism is quite correct that an expurged pharmakon will continue to haunt the discourse till its ultimate ruination.

At first glance, this is precisely what happens to Lagadian scholars who are to dye not from the inner exhaustion but from an extrinsic one. This death would be a Cretan unconscious one-to the same extent as conscious, for logocentrism has always already conceived of death as a force coming from the outside. This fact alone should already give pause to the adept of Cretanism.

Forsooth, logocentrism cannot fail but bring about its self-deconstruction, to wit, the intratextual death of intertextuality. However, the gist of the matter is to prove that this deconstruction is a self-deconstruction, to wit, a self-dimunitive interplay between blindness and insight. Unfortunately, to pluck one's rear is far more simple than to expose one's own to the same ordeal.

Put otherwise, the problem with self-deconstruction is that it remains a natural and unconscious process. Which means that as a fact logocentrism does attain its goal: instead of being a provisional gap, an intratextual death mimes perfectly an intertextual eternal life. Swift is quite sensitive to the emerging paradox that hints at the subversive power of mimesis as a death of interpretation. Witness his account of Luggnagg which occupies a symmetrical position in respect to Lagado.

Two peculiarities of this land that strike Gulliver-the race of "Struldbruggs, or Immortals" and "the language of this country always upon the flux"-are hinted to be interdependent. The result is precisely the death of interpretation as a naturalization of an (intratextual) pharmakon: the Struldbruggs live "like foreigners in their own country". Since a visit to Luggnagg in its turn acts as an intratextual pharmakon to the intertextuality of Lagado, our conclusion applies to the whole book which tends to become a material thing.

Witness the squaring of a mimetic double Lagado-

Luggnagg by another one-Glubbdubrib-Japan which reconfirms referentiality. As we shall momentarily see, it is this reconfirmation which, subverting the poststructuralist effort to improve the interpretive machine of Cretan discursivity, highlights a genuine beyond of the Western hermeneutic tradition.

From the preceding it is clear that the issue on which poststructuralism stands or falls is the denaturalization of Cretan discursivity, to wit, the denaturalization of the moment of khora essential to the institution of interpretation. An answer, as it seems, is already inscribed in the naturalized (logocentric) version of Cretanism.

If the "artificial converse" of the La-gadan scholars cannot help fostering the interpretive aphanisis it was designed to counteract, then precisely because there is no difference between things and words: semiotically, both are subject to the same proliferation. Whence the inevitable appearance of the supplement: a Lagadian linguist will certainly dye of hernia or heart-failure, unless there be "one or two strong servants" to deliver him from the burden.

Unfortunately, this solution winds up with the same interpretive aphanisis. For to rely upon the supplement, as poststructuralism does, means to rely on the material existence at hand of a porter, i.e. on the referential structure of the supplementary interpretive discourse and in so doing to make of the deconstruction an accident and a natural process. Consequently, the last hope to do away with materiality is to stake on the perfect coincidence between words and things, that is, to try to make the former include the latter, just as in Derrida's jugglery writing includes speech. An assurance with which this solution comes to be propounded and deployed testifies not to a new blind-spot but to the fact that the Cretan discursivity has a limit.

For to take things as words means nothing less than to make of an interpretation a natural process, to wit, that of the growing-up as mastering the unconscious bent upon treating words as things, which is not the reverse of the Achillean strategy of the Ego, but its genuine subversion. Within the framework of the practice of everyday life the growing-up boils down to simply loosing sight of a set of objects. The definition of the play-thing implies the possibility of a total material aphanisis.

Which means that even if preserved and recontextualized, say, as objects of collection, they are not the same things but radically new ones? A collector does not misunderstand a toy but understands it differently, to wit, does not understand it at all but uses it-just as a child does. Which explains why a fetishistic model-another transcription of our problem-comes to be invalidated along with its semiotic predecessor-the Formalist concept of defamiliriazation as a possibility to use the same unit of signification multiply, to wit, differently?

The psychoanalytic as well as poststructuralist edifices will easily grant us that the fetishistic attitude is an hermeneutic one. However, as certain dissident wispers suggest, there is no common measure between the adult fetishism and what is conventionally termed a child's one, so that it would be more correct to not use this notion in respect to childhood at all. Corroborating this insight our examination provides a lacking explanation why it should be so. There can be no talk about childhood fetishism precisely because what is supposed to be a fetish is not understood but only used by the child.

In case of an adult fetishist matters are radically different: for the sake of discursive symmetry, it could be said that s/he does not use a fetish but constantly (re)interprets it. Whence the apparently infinite substitutability which testifies to the absence of substitution/interpretation/partial (mis)understanding. The gist of the matter is that the fetish does fit all too perfectly and therefore precludes the very possibility of interpretation. The result is best exemplified by the Venus of Milos: to substitute the lacking parts means to abolish the statue.

The preservation coincides with exhaustion: both boil down to the same hermeneutic aphanisis. In other words the very possibility to return a book to the adults is the impossibility of the Cretan attitude which is an hermeneutic one. Whence the necessity to take recourse to the rhetoric of mastery as a last resort to save the hermeneutic attitude. However, the very ease with which every attempt at mastery can be shown to be self-deconstructive suggests that poststructuralism relies upon the natural order of things.

Mastery, were it ever to be achieved, could only mean the irretrievable disappearance of the object of art qua object of interpretation, to wit, the immortality of interpretation, to wit, its naturalization. Which explains why the poststricturalist version of the Achillean strategy presupposes not the disappearance but the dimunition of a text/object-in order not to control the more effectively but to leave a chance for a text to overgrow/overtake the current interpreter?

At this point an argument in favour of indistinguishability of things and words can still be maintained. But the very logic compels to complete the argument with a supplement: with the inscription of traces. Whence Derrida's stress that the effects of signature are "ill-detachable" (1987: 59). Unluckily, this means precisely an infantilization of interpretation, to wit, the re-introduction of the whole logocentric paradigm of castration. Whence the ethical terms in which intertextuality is talked about.

In effect, a text/child should be a spoiled one, for only on these premises there remains a hope of interpretation. Which explains why the moment Swift becomes the reader of his own text he starts to treat it as spoiled by a "careless ... printer". Only a spoiled child /text can remain interpretable in its unreadability, al-lowing for a transfer of responsibility from the progenitor to the tutors. Which means that the notion of mastery is basically repugnant to interpretation, or, to be more precise, irrelevant to the hermeneutic attitude? What the latter boils down to is the self-dimunitive transfer of guilt. Which means shame on the other pole?

In other words, it is the innocence which has never been taken seriously by logocentrism. Precisely the (textual) innocence precludes the possibility to tie the her-meneutic double bind, subverting the Achillean interplay between guilt and shame, monologue and dialogue. And this explains why the conclusion can only be a psychoanalytic one. To conclude that the generalized concepts we have been examining exclude unconscious would mean to succumb to a Cretan haste. The paradox is that their over-inclusiveness has to be taken literally-in perfect accordance with the rule of appropriating disappropriation established by Derrida.

What the fate of the notion of the unconscious bares is the impossibility to deconstruct logocentrism by applying this rule, for the generalization of the unconscious cannot help disempowering it. And this precisely because the conceptual generalization is a radicalization of the Achillean strategy as an hermeneutic strategy par excellence.

In other words, the poststructuralist attempt to dislocate logocentric subjectivity inevitably winds up with transforming the unconscious into a natural phenomenon. Since nature and history continue to remain at odds, what we are left with is the uncanny impossibility to maintain that logocentrism is allergic to the notion of unconscious precisely because its aim is to achieve a hermeneutic closure as an end of history. It is this Cretan dilemma to which our investigation provides a radical solution.

In effect, all one has to do in order to historicize the unconscious is to abandon the hermeneutic stance, i.e. to conceive otherwise of consciousness itself as well as of its relationship with other intrapsychic agencies. In so doing we will only return to the quite familiar Freudian postulate that the textual reality backs psychoanalytic insights. Among these latter there is one which is particularly pertinent for our discussion. I mean Freud's contention to see in the unconscious a "living, developing" entity, instead of conceiving of it simply as a "residuum of development".

This remark seems to contradict the celebrated lines about the unconscious's disregard to contradictions and to the notion of death: since precisely these features make of the unconscious a residuum, it follows that a living unconscious is not the one which knows nothing about death and time. In other words, the paradox we come to be confronted thereby is basically identical with the one we have been examining throughout this paper.

What makes Freud's theory of the unconscious founder is the hermeneutic attitude, to wit, the impossibility to ground intertextuality (unconscious qua living entity) intratextually (unconscious qua developmental residuum). What allows us to see here an unambiguous insight is Freud's sensibility to the sublime evaporation of the unconscious along the lines of this Zenonian paradox, evidenced by the concluding statement of his "Mourning and Melancholia" referred to above.

What, finally, precludes this evaporation from actually taking place is Freud's stress that the unconscious works with object-representations (Ding-Vorstellungen) and not with word-representations (Wort-Vorstellungen). It is this stress which by making it impossible to treat unconscious hermeneutically reconciles two aspects of the unconscious beyond the inter/intratextual (monologue/dialogue) binary making of the unconscious the material object and by the same token an exact counterpart of the textual reality as we conceive of it.

To understand the literary history as the text-becoming-the-thing process means to assume that the textual reality is a mimesis of the unconscious strategies which make of this agency a Freudian thing by historizing it. Whence the subversive power of the text qua unconscious: as we have seen, the textual strategy of an author subverts the hermeneutic attitude forcing the reader to give up (to debase) a text, to wit, to treat it as a thing in the brute sense of this word. Significantly, Freud and Bakhtin are in perfect accord over this issue which bares their theoretical thrust to be a radically anti-hermeneutic, anti-dialogical one.

The clinical picture of schizophrenia, as described by Freud, is governed by the Zenonian paradoxical logic: an attempt to resurrect an object by trying to materialize word-representations is exposed as a restorative affair, to wit, an hermeneutic one. And once again the result is the dematerialization of the interpretation itself: what the schizophrenics wind up with is "treating the concrete things as if they were abstract ones". Since this strategy is said to have nothing to do with the work of repression which is the chief evidence for the existence of the unconscious, it follows that exactly the disappearance of the word, to wit, the transformation of a text into a thing is the outcome of the aesthetic activity, conceived in the Bakhtinian way as a cooperation between an author and a hero. Now it is precisely the cooperation between psychical agencies which, according to Freud, opens the unconscious towards history.

Put differently, the only way to save the unconscious from the sublime fate to which it remains subject so long as it is treated along Zenonian/hermeneutic lines, is to conceive of it as an artificial, to wit, textual product of the mimetic mergence between the Ego and the Super-Ego. This is a patently Bakhtinian way to treat the product of the aesthetic activity. In other words, it is only the mimetic dependence of the Super-Ego upon the Ego, of the author upon the hero, i.e. a conscious intention which can produce a radical form of unreadability: an unconscious qua innocent/blank text.

We could have smuggly concluded here were there no possibility left to add pungency to our analysis. This addition will exhaust the supplementarity of discursive Cretanism. As we have seen, the potential to become children's fiction is what defines literary text. The matter is that of time and genuine accidentality. Witness the case of Nabokov's Lolita. In order to be able to claim the poststructuralist unreadability which is the very possibility to read we have to show that Lolita is structured by an Achillean race, to wit, by an intratextual invagination of intertextuality. At the face of it nothing barres the possibility of this (mis)reading.

In effect, the unfolding of the narrative seems to testify to the impossibility of Achilles/Humbert to ever join his non-mimetic half. In perfect accordance with Lacan, the sexual relation takes place by not taking place-owing to the essential non-coincidence between the participants, primarily, to their literal difference in size 69 68-69.

The price to be paid for this non-coincidence is the uncanny transformation of phallus into material penis-for only on these premises Lolita would be unable to hermeneutically invaginate Humbert's limb, i.e. to (mis)read his intentions. And yet Humbert cannot help acknowledging that she understands him perfectly well, to wit, that a sexual relation does take place as a fact 70 68-69.

Whence the necessity to (mis)represent her as a spoilt child and in so doing to feign the castration anxiety, i.e. to ruminate upon the fact that the "magic nymphage" is bound to evaporate. The result of this intratextual self-dimunition is the foregrounding of intratextuality, which cannot fail but have the by now familiar effect. Lolita's becoming the text triggers the evaporation of Humbert's intertextuality, to wit, the aphanisis of the hermeneutic attitude itself. Which explains why thus far nobody has paid attention to the essentional gap in our narrative, that is, to the lack of explanation of how Lolita's elopment with Quality represented as an exercise of intertextual self-dimunition ends in a banal marriage.

Since banality, vulgarity of Lolita, to wit, her childish innocence have been from the outset foregrounded by Humbert, we are justified to conclude that this marriage was the aim of Lolita's strategy, the fulfillment of her destiny, the Bakhtinian term for which is aesthetic finalization. The paradox is that this finalization has been consciously brought about by the narrator whose aim in writing down The Confession of a White Widowed Male was to prove his own innocence before the jury.

For only hermeneutically the gap can appear as an instance of the disregard to narrative logic, whereas in actual fact it is the very logic of narrative aimed at hermeneutic aphanisis. Humbert has said everything-and therefore left nothing to be supplemented by a reader. Such should be the outcome of aesthetic activity according to Bakhtin, for this hermeneutic aphanisis is the logical consequence of Bakhtin's theory of aesthetic finalization.

It follows that the reader is forced to give up a text. Elsewhere we have already shown that precisely the act of giving up is essential for the psychoanalytic notion of sublimation. The only hope to save the hermeneutic attitude is to try to (mis)represent the giving-up as debasement. Which means to try to speak about a text in ethical terms? This is precisely what prefaces are there for, and the one to Lolita is not exempt from the Cretan rule.

The paradox is that the result of this strategy is an ultimate mimesis. For to foreground the moral value of a literary text means to acknowledge the possibility for it to become a child's toy, i.e. to get irretrivably lost, exhausted-beyond any hope of Cretan revitalization. Obviously, nothing barres the possibility of Lolita's suffering this fate, to wit, of the possibility for Nabokov's novel to become children's reading.

Chapter 8

Interzonality and The Uncertainty of Geographies

In the title essay of his book, *Imaginary Homelands*, the author Salman Rushdie recalls returning for the first time, after several years of absence, to the city of his birth, Bombay, to which he refers, almost sadly, as "my lost city." During his trip Rushdie visits the house where, in 1947, he was born, before his family moved "across the border to that unnamable country", and before he was sent away to England never to return.

He does of course return, in a manner of speaking, to a house that he imagined in monochrome, his memory formed more by an old black and white family photograph upon which he had called time and again in his expatriation and upon which he had come to rely with certainty greater than faith. He returns to the site of his childhood and discovers something he most certainly would have stumbled upon again and again as he prepared himself for his homecoming, and would have repeatedly and off-handedly swept away as we all are wont to, a source of profound trepidation, something greater than loss, namely, the fear of loss.

As he weighs the rather strange relationship between him and the city of his birth, excited yet deeply frightened and uncertain, like one about to meet a long-lost love on whom they had walked out, he is drawn to find what memories of him the old love had retained, had allowed to remain, had saved from obliteration. He turns to the telephone book to see if the city still remembered him and his family, and sure enough it did, more out of that indifference which all memorials and monuments possess, than any special concern for one, undistinguished family out of a million, and this in the most appropriate medium of all inert memories; the telephone book. While the returnee cowers in trepidation and writhes in the grips of emotion, the city betrays nothing, gives little, recalls only partially. It remains only an appeal, not a promise.

Our bond with the site of our nativity is a largely one-way affair. It is an ambivalent bond borne out of a one-sided loyalty and a proclivity to possess, a desperate striving to belong, to lay claim to something that lays no claim in return. Severed from the womb and the body that bore us and hauled into the void of life and existence, we crave to attach ourselves to something, a moment, a location, an event; we crave an anchor which we readily find in the contours of the house of our upbringing, in the streets of our childhood, in the city of our birth. But the city has a different desire and a different response, for we need the city more than the city needs us.

In his essay Rushdie quotes L. P. Hartley where he writes that the "past is a foreign country, they do things differently there.' We may in fact paraphrase Hartley and say that the past, including the city of our birth, the geographies that define our beginnings and for which, ever so often, we are called upon to die, is in a significant sense a foreign country where we never belonged. It is a place to which we are tied not by a mutual care or love but by trepidation, by a profound fear on our part of the loss of the familiar.

The idea of our city's special love is a fiction of our own making, a necessary justification for our possessive fixation on it. The conviction that we own the city, that in losing our place to others or to distance we lose that which belongs to us, that to which we have an exclusive right, derives in no small measure from the wish not to compete for the attention of something whose love we crave, but fear, even know, that it does not love us back. It is as much a craving to own as it is an appeal to be owned. And as for city, so for country. In time, this apprehension transforms into a romantic longing in the hold of which we are blinded to the specifics of our relationship. Everything takes on a different hue; the ugly turns unique, the trivial symbolic. We argue the illogical, defend the indefensible, stake out the frontiers and keep out others. We weep at the sound of the anthem and worship the flag. We descend into the habit of kissing the earth. And there is no love more blind than the love of country. We spend our lives in the shadow of the knowledge that the city may not remember us, that upon our departure the city will forget. On the tablet of the city's mind we are only a record, not a recollection.

Which is why after departure we crave, yet fear, to return? Rushdie returns to his father's former house in Bombay and finds, also, that memory is an untrustworthy friend, especially memory committed to print. Where he had been led to expect monochrome, to wish for and desire monochrome, he is met with the dazzle of colors, and his fear returns to him, coupled now with a confirmation of the loss which he had feared. Where he had expected the straight he is met with undulations, the simple replaced by the multiple, quiet displaced by life, recollection thrown into doubt. Memory had manufactured for him, in the safety of time and distance, a false vision of the familiar with which he must now be met or else is left lonely and betrayed.

In the end, excitement is dislodged by bitterness, by a certain hollowness within not unlike the god-hole Rushdie would describe years later in a different context, a touch of disappointment with ourselves but more so with the site of our pilgrimage. It is a strange, mixed feeling when we return to meet an old love. The smile is never truly free, the first handshake never firm, and the hole in the heart that we bring with us is never completely filled. Often we find there is more than time between us and the one we come to reclaim.

Yet, this encounter is the beginning of our recovery from our feeling of unbroachable tragedy. Departure, and return, is our best cures for the irresoluble attachment to the geography of our beginnings. By leaving, by venturing beyond the borders of the familiar, we put our fear, and our love, to test. We bring our attachment into crisis. An Igbo aphorism has it that the traveled youth is endowed with greater wisdom than even his gray-haired country-man father. In Jonathan Swift's 1726 classic, Gulliver's Travels, the protagonist, Lemuel Gulliver, after a shipwreck on the high seas finds himself in an epic and enriching adventure of eight years that takes him to four kingdoms and to peoples and cultures of statures and virtues never before known to his English sensibilities.

Yet it is his return to London at the end of this journey, upon which he is forcibly consigned to an asylum and made to prove his sanity and wholesomeness under the rigors of the rule of reason, that proves the most revealing and rewarding lesson of all his adventures.

Upon return Gulliver discovers the opposite of something which hitherto he was wont to take for granted, namely the right to country. Feted by the benevolent giants of Brobdingnag and tested by the philosopher horses of Houyhnhmland, Lemuel Gulliver returns to his country to find he is the stranger in a savage nation where reason is placed at the service of brutal power. He survives the dangers of a distant world and returns with the certainty to find love and unconditional acceptance in his own country. But the city of his birth and the flag for which he would die both denounce and deny him. His reward is a lesson in the profound uncertainty of all claims to geography.

Far more than endow us with wisdom, therefore, departure, and return, reveal to us also, the folly of unquestioning love of home and country, and the possessive bigotry that is bred from it. While our lives in expatriation may yet be ruled by the craving to return and reclaim, return confronts us with the loss we feared, and places us on the path to recovery, for in revealing the imaginary nature, and ultimate futility, of our claims, we are made to question the foundations of our love and loyalty, and of our tenacious defence of territory.

Distance and its negation become the cycle we must follow in order to discover an original truth, one which, though it leaves us with the sadness of unrequited love, ultimately sets us free. Rushdie refers to Bombay as "my lost city", and in this recognizes that the Bombay of his loss is a city of the imagination, an indefinable construct unto which his desires and projections are latched. He recognizes also, that bonds that are manufactured in the confines of the imagination must equally find their unraveling in the seamlessness of the imagination, outside the pressures of rhetoric and passion.

Swift's moral tale, too, is an investigation into the geographies of the imaginary where, outside the reign of reason and convention, our true migratory nature finds sanctuary. There are we able not only to play out the distortionary configurations of our fictions of peculiarity but also to supersede them. Lemuel Gulliver's fantastic journey emerges from the imagination yet simulates the disentangling powers of real distance and removal.

In the landscapes of the imaginary where our fictions of ownership are formed, there, too, are we allowed to question the certainty of our affiliations, to mine under the foundations of our convictions, and to expose ourselves if only for an intermission, to the possibility of a fundamental infidelity in the bond between us and the physical geographies that we claim for ourselves. There the monochrome of memory invites us not to latch unto and battle for the supposed truth which it decidedly betrays, but to construct a new reality, to build a new world on the uncertainties of the imagined, to realise how city and country and place are all of our own making and therefore loose without permanent anchor.

In the temporal ambiance of its appearance, Swift's interrogation of the certainties of geography was, perhaps, ahead of its time, located at the exact median between Copernicus's challenge to the dogma of our planet's peculiarity which, a century later, would bring Galileo before the Inquisition, and Rushdie's return to the lost city of his birth. In all three instances, however, what is shared is the ability of the transcendent spirit to reveal the fictiveness of our claims over territory. Corpenicus made the leap beyond the ideological restraints of a domineering faith and the physical constraints of rudimentary science, and in his moment of removal from the immediate perimeters of his location confirmed our inconsequence in the vast patterns of the universe. Through Lemuel Gulliver, Swift transported rationalist England beyond the strictures of its bondage to myopic logic to discover not only the existence of territories outside the cartographic confines of a North Sea isle, but the presence in those territories, also, of knowledges and cultures to challenge it's claims to a superior disposition. In both cases, the reaction of those not enamored of the revelatory benefits of translocation is to submit to the fear that the anchors of their faith and loyalties are about to unhinge, that ideas and delineations which they had hitherto taken for certain are under threat of exposure.

The consequence of this fear is a blind resistance, and a battle to restore the fictions of certainty. Under the guise of loyalty to city and nation, this struggle to hold unto territory and geography calls upon the instruments of power and human regulation in order to expunge the body of threat and shut the window on the world. Today we find this in the fierce struggles against digital subversion of territorial cartographs and borders and affirmation of interzonality through the thoroughfares of the information super highway.

We find it in the increasing appearance, even along those thoroughfares, of structures of regulation that negate the very idea of interzonality and instead reaffirm territorial claims. In the end our greatest hope lies, it seems, in the individual will to depart, to allow ourselves beyond the border, like Rushdie, and Gulliver before him, and upon return to discover, and acknowledge, the fictionality of assumed geographies and imagined affinities, this way opening ourselves, and the doors of our consciousness, to the bountiful revelations of a seamless world.

Chapter 9

Swift's Moral Satire in Gulliver's Travels

"In its most serious function, satire is a mediator between two perceptions-the unillusioned perception of man as he actually is, and the ideal perception, or vision, of man as he ought to be," (Bullitt, 3). Likewise, "misanthropy" can be understood as being the product of one of two world views:

1) The Pure Cynic or Misanthropist has no faith in human nature and has given up on any notion of ideals. This type lies and manipulates as a matter of course and these are the types that tend to run the world.

2) The "Burned" or Disillusioned Idealist's misanthropy arises out of disappointment in humankind. In many ways, the second type exhibits more bile as he is constantly frustrated by what men do as opposed to what they ought to do. Jonathon Swift is the second type of misanthropist and *Gulliver's Travels* is arguably his greatest satiric attempt to "shame men out of their vices" by constantly distinguishing between how man behaves and how he thinks about or justifies his Behaviour in a variety of situations.

Pride, in particular, is what enables man to "deceive himself into the belief that he is rational and virtuous when, in reality, he has not developed his reason, and his virtue is merely appearance". This satire works on so many levels that a paper such as this allows me to deal with only three elements, and in a necessarily superficial way: the ways in which the structure and choice of metaphor serve Swift's purpose, a discussion of some of his most salient attacks on politics, religion, and other elements of society, and his critique on the essence and flaws of human nature. Swift's purpose was to stir his readers to view themselves as he viewed humankind, as creatures who were not fulfilling their potential to be truly great but were simply flaunting the trappings of greatness. *Gulliver's Travels* succeeds in this goal brilliantly.

The form and structure of the whole work enhanced Swift's purpose, as did the specific metaphors in each of the four voyages. Firstly, Swift went to great pains to present *Gulliver's Travels* in the genuine, standard form of the popular travelogues of the time. Gulliver, the reader is told, was a seaman, first in the capacity of a ship's surgeon, then as the captain of several ships. Swift creates a realistic framework by incorporating nautical jargon, descriptive detail that is related in a "factual, ship's-log" style, and repeated claims by Gulliver, in his narrative, "to relate plain matter(s) of fact in the simplest manner and style."

This framework provides a sense of realism and versimilitude that contrasts sharply with the fantastic nature of the tales, and establishes the first ironic layer of *The Travels*. As Tuveson points out, "In *Gulliver's Travels* there is a constant shuttling back and forth between real and unreal, normal and absurd...until our standards of credulity are so relaxed that we are ready to buy a pig in a poke." The four books of the Travels are also presented in a parallel way so that voyages 1 and 2 focus on criticism of various aspects of English society at the time, and man within this society, while voyages 3 and 4 are more preoccupied with human nature itself, (Downie, 281).

However, all of these elements overlap, and with each voyage, Gulliver, and thus the reader, is treated not only to differing but ever deepening views of human nature that climax in Gulliver's epiphany when he identifies himself with the detestable Yahoos. As such, the overall structure also works like a spiral leading to a centre of self-realization. Or, as Tuveson puts it, Swift's satire shifts from "foreign to domestic scenes, from institutions to individuals, from mankind to man, from others to ourselves".

The choice of metaphor in each voyage serves more particularly the various points of Swift's satiric vision. "The effect of reducing the scale of life in Lilliput is to strip human affairs of their self-imposed grandeur. Rank, politics, international war, loses all of their significance. This particular idea is continued in the second voyage, not in the picture of the Brobdingnagians, but in Gulliver himself, who is now a Lilliputian,". And where the Liiliputians highlight the pettiness of human pride and pretensions, the relative size of the Brobdingnagians, who do exemplify some positive qualities, also highlights the grossness of the human form and habits, thus satirizing pride in the human form and appearance.

In the voyage to Laputa, the actual device of a floating island that drifts along above the rest of the world metaphorically represents Swift's point that an excess of speculative reasoning can also be negative by cutting one off from the practical realities of life which, in the end, doesn't serve learning or society. And in the relation of the activities of the Grand Academy of Lagado, Swift satirizes the dangers and wastefulness of pride in human reason uninformed by common sense.

The final choice of the Houyhnhnms as the representatives of perfect reason unimpeded by irrationality or excessive emotion serves a dual role for Swift's satire. The absurdity of a domestic animal exhibiting more "humanity" than humans throws light on the defects of human nature in the form of the Yahoo, who look and act like humans stripped of higher reason. Gulliver and the reader are forced to evaluate such Behaviour from a vantage point outside of man that makes it both shocking and revelatory.

The pride in human nature as superior when compared to a "bestial" nature is satirized sharply. However, the Houyhnhnms are not an ideal of human nature either. Swift uses them to show how reason uninformed by love, compassion, and empathy is also an inadequate method to deal with the myriad aspects of the human situation.

Within this framework, very little of human social Behaviour, pretensions, or societal institutions escape the deflating punctures of Swift's arrows. Ewald states that, "As a satire, the main purpose of Gulliver's Travels is to show certain shortcomings in 18th century English society...". Much of the first voyage lampoons court intrigue and the arbitrary fickleness of court favour. The rank and favour of the Lilliputian ministers being dependent on how high they can jump over a rope literally illustrates this figurative point. Gulliver himself falls out of favour because he does not pander to the King's thirst for power.

The two political parties being differentiated by the height of their heels points out how little substantive difference there was between Whig and Tory, (or today between Democrat and Republican), and similarly, the religious differences about whether the Host was flesh or symbol is reduced to the petty quarrel between the Big-Endians and the Small-Endians.

Swift also highlights the pretensions of politics by informing the reader of some of the laudable and novel ideals and practices of Lilliputian society such as rewarding those who obey the law, holding a breach of trust as the highest offense, and punishing false accusors and ingratitude, but shows that, like humans, even the Lilliputians do not live up to their own standards when they exhibit ingratitude for Gulliver's help and accuse him of high treason.

Of course, the perspective shifts in the second voyage, where Gulliver finds himself in the same relation to the Brobdingnagians as the Lilliputians were to him, which not only leads to some different kinds of satiric insights, but many which are slightly darker in tone. Most of the social and political criticism occurs in Chapters six and seven. Gulliver describes European civilization to Brobdingnag's King, including England's political and legal institutions and how they work, as well as some of the personal habits of the ruling class.

Yet, even though Gulliver subsequently confesses to the reader that he cast this information in the most favorable light, the King still deduces that every strata of society and political power is infested with rampant corruption and dismissively concludes "the bulk of your natives to be the most pernicious race of little odious vermin that nature ever suffered to crawl upon the surface of the earth." This echoes a basic message of the first voyage but the attack here is more direct and corrosive.

The relative size of the Brobdingnagians adds a physical dimension to the King's judgment and enhances its veracity. Also, "all the transactions of life, all passion, and all social amenities, which involve the body, lose their respectability in Brobdingnag", from Gulliver's description of the odious breast to his viewing of a public execution.

In contrast, Brobdingnagian society has many things to recommend it such as excellence "in morality, history, poetry, and mathematics," although Gulliver ironically laments that these are only applied to the practical aspects of life and not used for abstractions. However, much of Swift's political writings indicate that he, like the Brobdingnagians, favored a conception of government and society based on common-sense.

The supreme moment of ironical criticism of European civilization occurs in Chapter seven when, after offering the secret of gun powder to the King and his subsequent horrified refusal, Gulliver declares the King to possess "narrow principles and short views!" Of course, mankind would never be so short-sighted as to turn away from learning a new method of injuring, torturing, or killing one's fellows! Aside from this sharp comment on human nature, Swift is also alluding to the eagerness with which European nations would leap at such an offer as an aid to waging war against their neighbors.

The main focus of social criticism in the voyage to Laputa is on intellectuals, such as scholars, philosophers, and scientists, who often get lost in theoretical abstractions and conceptions to the exclusion of the more pragmatic aspects of life, in direct contrast to the practical Brobdingnagians. Many critics feel Swift was satirizing "the strange experiments of the scientists of the Royal Society," but may also have been warning his readers against "the political projectors and speculators of the time". The Laputians excel at theoretical mathematics, but they can't build houses where the walls are straight and the corners are square. Instead, they constantly worry about when the sun will burn out and whether a comet will collide with the earth. This misuse of reason is hilariously elaborated on in Chapters five and six, where the various experiments occuring at the Grand Academy of Lagado are described. Of course, the point is highlighted as Gulliver professes his sincere admiration for such projects as extracting sunbeams from cucumbers and building houses from the roof down. The satire in Voyage three attacks both the deficiency of common sense and the consequences of corrupt judgment.

Most of the criticism in the Voyage to the Houyhnhnms is directed at human nature itself, although the trend to more particular targets begun in the third voyage is continued with glancing, but increasingly direct blows to the subjects of war, (destruction clothed in the pretext of valour and patriotism), lawyers, (social parasites who measure their worth by their excellence at deception and therefore, actually inhibit justice), and money, (the greed of a few is fed by the labour and poverty of the many, as well as the relative uselessness and corruption of these priveleged few).

In addition, Swift makes some very cogent observations on imperialism in the concluding chapter which point out the arrogance and self deception of European nations when they claim to civilize, through brutality and oppression, groups of indigenous people who were often mild and harmless.

Of course, as Swift implies, the real goal of imperialism is greed. The most ironic point occurs when the author disclaims that this attack on imperialist countries does not include Britain, which history shows was equally as brutal as its European rivals and, in many cases, even more so, considering its Empire became at one time the largest of any European country. What I found most interesting was how many critics took this disclaimer seriously as an expression of the author's patriotism.

It seems obvious that Swift is making the point that Gulliver's naive patriotism, the last remnant of identification he has with his own kind, is misplaced and it is Swift's final, palpable hit. The main object of the satire in *Gulliver's Travels* is human nature itself, specifically Man's pride as it manifests in "pettiness, grossness, rational absurdity, and animality". Gulliver's character, as a satirical device, serves Swift's ends by being both a mouthpiece for some of Swift's ideals and criticisms and as an illustration of them; Thus, critiques on human nature are made through Gulliver's observations as well as through Gulliver's own transformation from a "naive individual...into a wise and skeptical misanthrope".

Chapter seven of the first Voyage, where Gulliver is informed that he is about to be indicted for high treason by the Lilliputian Court, provides the most bitter satiric attack on hypocrisy, ingratitude, and cruelty, yet Gulliver, and the reader, are able to distance themselves from these qualities by concluding that though these tiny creatures are aping human Behaviour, they are still not human.

In the second voyage, both the human pride in physical appearance is attacked through Gulliver's perspective of the Brobdingnagians, and Gulliver's own pride in himself and his country is reduced to ridiculousness as Gulliver becomes the object of comic satire. Gulliver's offer of the secret of gunpowder only underscores that he is a typical member of his race. From Gulliver's theme of the excellence of mankind, begun in Chapter six, the episode concludes "with the shocking demonstration of what man's inhumanity is capable of".

One of the most interesting comments on the human condition is the description of the immortal Struldbrugs in Voyage Three. Swift's treatment of the subject of immortality is characteristically practical and down to earth. What would it really be like to live in perpetuity? His answer: A living death. The main problem is that the human body ages and is not a fit vessel to house a perpetual consciousness.

In relating this episode, Swift affirms with cutting precision that we have much in common with the rest of earth's creatures; any superior reason we may possess, and the pride we take in it, does not exempt us from the natural laws of physical death and regeneration. In Book Three, Swift not only shows the possible perversions of reason in the doings at the Academy of Lagado, but also shows its limitations in shielding us from the natural consequences of physical life. Here, he implies the importance of a moral structure to human life; reason is not enough and immortality would only make things worse.

Yet on the surface, Book four seems to argue that reason is the one quality, when properly developed, that can elevate man to his ultimate potential. But ironically it is the horse-like Houyhnhnms that possess this perfect development of reason, whereas the Yahoos, whom Gulliver most resembles, are primitive and bestial. I agree with Ewald that Voyage four contains Swift's clearest attack on human pride.

Indeed, the quality of reason only enables humans "to aggravate their natural corruptions and to acquire new ones which Nature had not intended." Even a dispassionate view of human history would find it difficult to dispute this conclusion. Whereas the attacks on human nature in the first three Voyages deal with actions that are symptomatic of man's nature-"the corrosive satire of the last voyage is concerned with the springs and causes of action", in other words, the essence of man.

As such, the satire directed against the pretensions of court, political corruption, and the excesses of speculative reasoning may divert and disturb Gulliver, and the reader, but it is possible to distance oneself from the attacks. But the object of the satiric attack in the last voyage is man himself: it is Gulliver and the reader. Here, "Swift is attacking the Yahoo in each of us". Human nature is cut into two parts: The Houyhnhnms possess reason and benevolence, and selfish appetites and brutish awareness are left for the Yahoos.

The microscopic analysis of the human form that took place in the second voyage is now used to analyse the defects of man's moral nature, and it is pride that prevents man from recognizing his flaws and dealing with them. When Gulliver experiences the shock of recognition that he, too, is a Yahoo, Gulliver passes from being a "perfect example a character acting in ignorance of his condition" to experiencing "a terrifying insight into evil (which) is accompanied by all the bitterness of a profound disillusionment".

Yet, I agree with many of the critics who say that though Gulliver makes the mistake of identifying himself completely with the Yahoos, Swift and the reader do not. "For the truth, as we are meant to realise, is that man is neither irrational physicality like the Yahoos nor passionless rationality like the Houyhnhnms" but are something in between.

We are meant to be repulsed by the chilling calmness with which the Houyhnhnms accept death as described in Chapter nine as much as we are by the selfishness of the Yahoos, and it is clear Swift does not present Gulliver's comic and absurd withdrawal from people as a viable solution.

Instead, Swift wants us to be shocked out of the pride that allows us to deceive ourselves into thinking man is completely virtuous when he is not by experiencing, with Gulliver, our own limitations without making Gulliver's final mistake.

The solution to the human dilemma is not so simple as Gulliver's rejection of humanity, and Swift's final success, in terms of stimulating response, is that, after masterfully dissecting and presenting the problem, he leaves the application of his lessons to "the judicious reader." For many critics, *Gulliver's Travels* "is in a sense, a tragic work...in that it is the picture of man's collapse before his corrupt nature, and of his defiance in face of the collapse".

Yet, obviously Swift felt that humbling human pride, enabling a more honest self-assessment, was absolutely vital to addressing the suffering and injustice so prevalent in human life. Contrary to many who label Swift a misanthropist, only a man who cared deeply about humanity could have produced a work like *Gulliver's Travels*.

Weilding the scalpel of satire, Swift cuts through our self-deception to our pride, the source of our moral denial and inertia. As we travel with Gulliver through the voyages, Swift brilliantly peels away our pretensions, layer by layer, until he shows us what we are and challenges us, intensely and urgently, to be better.

In *Gulliver's Travels*, Jonathan Swift continues to vex the world so that it might awaken to the fact that humankind needs saving, but it has to save itself.

Chapter 10

Critical Reception of Swift's Gulliver's Travels

Swift's greatest satire, *Gulliver's Travels,* is considered one of the most important works in the history of world literature. Published as *Travels into Several Remote Nations of the World, in Four Parts; by Lemuel Gulliver* in 1726, *Gulliver's Travels* depicts one man's journeys to several strange and unusual lands. The general theme of *Gulliver's Travels* is a satirical examination of human nature, man's potential for depravity, and the dangers of the misuse of reason.

Throughout the volume Swift attacked the baseness of humankind even as he suggested the greatest virtues of the human race; he also attacked the folly of human learning and political systems even as he implied the proper functions of art, science, and government. *Gulliver's Travels,* some scholars believe, had its origins during Swift's years as a Tory polemicist, when he was part of a group of prominent Tory writers known as the Scriblerus Club.

The group, which also included Alexander Pope, John Gay, and John Arbuthnot, among others, collaborated on several satires, including *The Scriblerus Papers.* They also planned a satire called *The Memoirs of a Martinus Scriblerus,* which was to include several imaginary voyages. An immediate success, *Gulliver's Travels* was inspired by this work. Swift finished *Gulliver's Travels* was published anonymously, but Swift's authorship was widely suspected. Alternately considered an attack on humanity or a clear-eyed assessment of human strengths and weaknesses, the novel is a complex study of human nature and of the moral, philosophical, and scientific thought of Swift's time which has resisted any single definition of meaning for nearly three centuries.

PLOT AND MAJOR CHARACTERS

Written in the form of a travel journal, *Gulliver's Travels* is the fictional account of four extraordinary voyages made by Lemuel Gulliver, a physician who signs on to serve as a ship's surgeon when he is unable to provide his family with a sufficient income in London. After being shipwrecked Gulliver first arrives at Lilliput, an island whose inhabitants are just six inches tall and where the pettiness of the political system is mirrored in the diminutive size of its citizens.

Gulliver is referred to as the "Man-Mountain" by the Lilliputians and is eventually pressed into service by the King in a nonsensical war with the neighboring island of Blefuscu. Gulliver finally escapes Lilliput and returns briefly to England before a second voyage takes him to Brobdingnag.

There he finds himself dwarfed by inhabitants who are sixty feet tall. Gulliver's comparatively tiny size now makes him wholly dependent on the protection and solicitude of others, and he is imperiled by dangerous encounters with huge rats and a curious toddler. Gulliver, however, incurs the disdain of the kindly and virtuous Brobdingnagian rulers when his gunpowder display, intended to impress his hosts as an exemplary product of European civilization, proves disastrous.

An address Gulliver delivers to the Brobdingnagians describing English political practices of the day is also met with much scorn. Housed in a miniature box, Gulliver abruptly departs Brobdingnag when a giant eagle flies off with him and drops him in the ocean.

He soon embarks on his third voyage to the flying island of Laputa, a mysterious land inhabited by scientists, magicians, and sorcerers who engage in abstract theorizing and conduct ill-advised experiments based on flawed calculations. Here Gulliver also visits Glubbdubdrib where it is possible to summon the dead and to converse with such figures as

Aristotle and Julius Caesar. He also travels to Luggnagg, where he encounters the Struldbrugs, a group of people who are given immortality, yet are condemned to live out their eternal existence trapped in feeble and decrepit bodies. Once again Gulliver returns to England before a final journey, to the land of the Houyhnhnms, who are a superior race of intelligent horses.

But the region is also home to the Yahoos, a vile and depraved race of ape-like creatures. Gulliver is eventually exiled from Houyhnhnm society when the horses gently insist that Gulliver must return to live among his own kind. After this fourth and final voyage, he returns to England, where he has great difficulty adjusting to everyday life. All people everywhere remind him of the Yahoos.

MAJOR THEMES

Each of the four voyages in *Gulliver's Travels* serves as a vehicle for Swift to expose and excoriate some aspect of human folly. The first voyage has been interpreted as an allegorical satire of the political events of the early eighteenth century, a commentary on the moral state of England, a general satire on the pettiness of human desires for wealth and power, and a depiction of the effects of unwarranted pride and self-promotion.

The war with the tiny neighboring island of Blefuscu represents England's rivalry with France. In Brobdingnag, Gulliver's diminutive status serves as a reminder of how perspective and viewpoint alter one's condition and claims to power in society. The imperfect, yet highly moral Brobdingnagians represent, according to many critics, Swift's conception of ethical rulers.

The voyage to Laputa, the flying island, is a scathing attack upon science in the sixteenth and seventeenth centuries and reveals Swift's thorough acquaintance with the *Philosophical Transactions of the Royal Society*, the leading publication of the scientific community of his day. The third voyage unequivocally manifests Swift's contempt and disdain for abstract theory and ideology that is not of practical service to humans. But it is the voyage to the land of the Houyhnhnms that reveals Swift's ultimate satiric object—man's inability to come to terms with his true nature. In particular, the Houyhnhnms are interpreted as symbols and examples of a human order that, although unattainable, deserves to remain an ideal, while the Yahoos are found to be the representatives of the depths of humanity's potential fall if that ideal is abandoned.

Gulliver's Travels has always been Swift's most discussed work. Critics have provided a wide variety of interpretations of each of the four voyages, of Swift's satiric targets, and of the narrative voice. But scholars agree that most crucial to an understanding of *Gulliver's Travels* is an understanding of the fourth voyage, to the land of the Houyhnhnms.

Merrel D. Clubb has noted that "the longer that one studies Swift, the more obvious it becomes that the interpretations and verdict to be placed on the 'Voyage to the Houyhnhnms' is, after all, the central problem of Swift criticism." Much of the controversy surrounds three possible interpretations of the Houyhnhnms and the Yahoos.

One school of thought has traditionally viewed the Yahoos as a satiric representation of debased humanity, while taking the Houyhnhnms as representatives of Swift's ideals of rationality and order. The two races are thus interpreted as symbols of the dual nature of humanity, with Gulliver's misanthropy based on his perception of the flaws of human nature and the failure of humanity to develop its potential for reason, harmony, and order.

Another critical position considers both the Houyhnhnms and Yahoos to be the subject of satire, with the Yahoos representing the physical baseness of humans and the Houyhnhnms representing the fatuousness of the idea that humans will ever achieve a rationally-ordered existence.

The ultimate satiric intent of the work to critics who accept this interpretation is that the only truly rational or enlightened beings in existence are not humans, but another species altogether. Since the 1950s, however, a variety of critics have tempered these readings by illuminating the complexity of purpose in the fourth voyage. The Houyhnhnms and Yahoos are now most often discussed as both satiric objects and representatives of the duality of human nature. The nature of Gulliver is another much-debated element of the *Travels*. Early critics generally viewed him as the mouthpiece of Swift. Modern critics, who recognize the subtlety of Swift's creation of Gulliver, have discredited that position.

The most significant contemporary debate is concerned with Swift's intentions regarding the creation of Gulliver—whether he is meant to be a consistently realized character, a reliable narrator, or a satiric object whose opinions are the object of Swift's ridicule. This debate over the nature of Gulliver is important because critics seek to determine whether Gulliver is intended to be a man with definite character traits who undergoes a transformation, or an allegorical representative of humanity.

In general, Gulliver is now considered a flexible persona manipulated by Swift to present a diversity of views or satirical situations and to indicate the complexity, the ultimate indefinability, of human nature. Many scholars have suggested that *Gulliver's Travels* has no ultimate meaning but to demand that readers regard humanity without the prejudices of pessimism or optimism, and accept human beings as a mixture of good and evil.

Eighteenth-and nineteenth-century critics of Swift were primarily interested in aspects of his character, although a few did actually discuss the meaning and merits of his work at length. The eighteenth-century critics were most concerned with depicting Swift's perceived immorality and misanthropy, and they often argued their case with the help of misrepresentations, or deliberate fabrications of facts.

Swift's defenders, in attacking these critics, provided the first real criticism of Swift, in particular pointing out the misrepresentations of his life. Twentieth-century critics have been confronted with the task of sifting through the misconceptions to reevaluate Swift's total achievement.

There are many psychological examinations of Swift's character; the psychoanalysts, however, have often been criticized for neglecting the literary or intellectual traditions of Swift's age when associating his works with supposed neurotic tendencies. Some commentators believed that psychoanalytic critics also make an obvious mistake when they identify Swift with his characters, assuming, for example, that Gulliver's comments reflect the opinions of his creator.

Close textual analysis has demonstrated the complicated elements of Swift's works and proven that they do not always reflect his personal opinions, but are carefully written to reflect the opinions of Swift's created narrators. A master of simple yet vividly descriptive prose and of a style so direct that if often masks the complexity of his irony, Swift is praised for his ability to craft his satires entirely through the eyes of a created persona.

He is now regarded as a complex though not mysterious man who created works of art which will permit no single interpretation. The massive amount of criticism devoted to Swift each year reflects his continued literary importance: his work is valuable not for any statement of ultimate meaning, but for its potential for raising questions in the mind of the reader.

Chapter 11

On the Religious Satire of Jonathan Swift

Jonathan Swift (1667-1745), the greatest satirist of the Enlightenment Movement and of all times, worked as a churchman over thirty years. In 1694, he was ordained Anglican priest, obtaining a small parish in Northern Ireland for about a year. In 1700 Swift became Chaplain to Lord Berkeley and was instituted as Vicar to Laracor, Agher, and Rathbeggan just outside Dublin. In 1713, Swift was appointed Dean of St Patrick's in Dublin, and stayed in that position until 1742, when he resigned due to poor health.

As a cleric, he was devoted to his duty, preparing his sermons arduously, serving his congregation full-heartedly, and defending the Church of Ireland militantly. However, his attitude toward church and religion was contradictory. Christianity to him, besides being a profession, was more like a choice in dilemma. An unwavering enlightener, he never gave up his right of criticizing religion, especially the evil practices of churchmen and dissension among different branches. His criticism can be seen in his religious essays, as well as in *Gulliver'stravels*, a mastery satire of all the time.

Chapter 12

Swift on False Witness

In the first book of The "Art" of Rhetoric, Aristotle discusses the relative reliability of various kinds of witnesses in proving a judicial case, distinguishing first between ancient and recent witnesses, and then between "well-known persons who have given a decision on any point" and "those who share the risk of the trial if they are thought to be perjurers." The latter are only competent as to "whether an act has taken place or not," while on questions of quality, "witnesses from a distance are very trustworthy" and "ancient witnesses are the most trustworthy of all, for they cannot be corrupted." Nearness to the event, a positive factor in an empiricist assessment of credibility, is negative in Aristotelian thinking.

Those near to a crime scene may be involved, interested, or open to bribery; the credibility of direct witness to fact must therefore be guaranteed by punitive sanctions, such as the risk of being brought to trial. To Jonathan Swift and his friends in Hanoverian Britain, classical skepticism about direct witness would have been pertinent. Until organized police forces came into existence in the nineteenth century, convictions for felony relied heavily on the evidence of professional informers, as—so it was believed—did prosecutions for the upper-class crimes of sedition and treason. Few informers were "well-known persons," i.e., possessed of reputations solid enough to guarantee credibility; many were—certainly in Swift's eyes—quite disreputable. In any case, even the honest could bend under pressure.

Not only did those who gave the Whig ministry "informations" against Tories and Jacobites not risk being put on trial for giving false evidence; they also risked arrest if they did not give such evidence.

Printers especially were vulnerable to government pressure to inform on authors, since "any 'reflection' or criticism, whether true or false" could be prosecuted as libel. This is the subject of the section that follows, which deals with Swift's experience of the gathering and use of "informations" in the immediate aftermath of the Hanoverian succession. The second section analyzes his most systematic response to the phenomenon, the sermon "On False Witness" of 1715. Subsequently, I touch on poems written for friends who had fallen victim to informers.

I turn finally to Gulliver as both victim and perpetrator of false witness, an eyewitness narrator who both unwittingly and consciously exposes the unreliability of his tribe, of the epistemology on which his testimony is based, and of the modern literary genres, such as the novel, which entrust such witnesses with authority and truth.

In the winter of 1707-08, William Gregg, a clerk in the office of the secretary of state, Robert Harley, was found to have been selling military secrets to the French. Condemned to death, he was repeatedly offered his life in exchange for inculpating Harley. He refused, insisting that the secretary knew nothing, and eventually went to the scaffold.

Six years later, in January 1714, Joseph Addison attacked the Tory ministry in The Crisis, to which Swift anonymously replied with The Public Spirit of the Whigs. The House of Lords offered a reward of [pounds sterling] 500 for discovery of the author, and took the publisher, Joseph Morphew, and his printer, John Barber, into custody and questioned them. They refused to supply a name, but were saved from imprisonment by a Tory ruse.

Swift was to remember the treatment of Gregg, and the "uneasy Business" over his own pamphlet may have been one factor in his deciding to withdraw from London politics. Another may have been the contacts between Tory ministers and the Pretender's Court at St. Germains. If Swift knew of these contacts, it might have made him all the more vulnerable to judicial pressure, because he would not have been convinced of the innocence of those against whom he might be asked to testify.

When questioned later by Archbishop William King about his time as chief propagandist for the Tories, Swift denied that there had been any Jacobite designs. But he also said that if he had discovered any, he was "not sure I should have turned Informer"; he would rather have "dropt some generall Cautions, and immediately have retired." That was exactly what he had done, the archbishop astutely noticed: "you retired, which agrees with what you say you ought to have done in that case."

Judicial harassment was only one of the means by which the early modern governments obtained information about their subjects. Since the 1660s, the English government had been investing increasingly in domestic intelligence. There were six main sources: spies recruited ad hoc; professional informers; casual informers, often paying off old scores; county and parish officers; the Post Office; and networks of diplomatic and other sources under the secretary of state.

Interception of correspondence was a constant worry to Swift, forcing him to keep to "a most cursory Style"; nothing he wrote was "the least secret, even to a Whig footman," he warned recipients. The tone is unmistakably snobbish, but not shocked. Swift seems to have regarded leniently the Whig Isaac Manley—Postmaster General in Ireland, and suspected by Tories of intercepting letters—for the mere fact that he was a friend of Stella's. It was, in any case, not only the Whigs who used covert methods of gathering information. During his term as secretary of state, Harley had built up, in addition to the usual semi-official sources, "an elaborate network of spies and agents," who in turn recruited their own informers.

Daniel Defoe bragged to the secretary about his many pensioners, and that "'tis the Easyest thing in the World to hire people here to betray their friends." If Swift knew about his friend Harley's spies, he may well have regarded them as necessary while continuing to despise them socially. With the fall of the ministry, however, Tories found themselves at the mercy of, rather than in control of, such instruments. Swift was not personally involved in the climactic events of August 1714. By the end of the month, with Anne dead, George I on the throne, and most of the Tory ministers out of office, he had returned to Dublin to take the oaths to the crown promptly, "to prevent accidents."

The Oath of Abjuration contained a promise which is of special interest: "And I will do my best Endeavour to disclose and make known to His Majesty and his Successors, all Treasons and Traiterous Conspiracies, which I shall know to be against him or any of them."

One could not be too prudent in this political climate. Having eliminated the Tories from office and taken control of Parliament in the autumn of 1714, the Whigs initiated a phase of judicial revenge. In January 1715, the papers of Thomas Wentworth, third Earl of Strafford, and Henry St. John, Viscount Bolingbroke, were seized, followed by the seizure of Matthew Prior's papers. Impeachment proceedings were initiated against Bolingbroke in April, by which time he had fled to France, to be followed by Ormonde in July. In that month, Harley too was impeached and committed to the Tower, first for "high crimes and misdemeanours," then for high treason.

Before leaving England, Swift had burned all letters received from ministers in recent years, and later hid other compromising papers. However, in May 1715, pamphlets sent him by the Duchess of Ormonde's chaplain were intercepted, and Archbishop King claimed to have had to intercede to prevent his arrest. On 21 June, Swift told his Jacobite friend, Knightley Chetwode, about the interview with King: "I said ... that if I had been called before them [the government], I would not have answered one syllable or named one person. He said that would have reflected on me. I answered I did not value that, and that I would sooner suffer more than let anybody else suffer by me, as some people did."

He had already been "named in many papers as proclaimed for five hundred pounds," and a week later there were rumors that Swift was to be sent to England "to be examined upon these impeachments." On 7 July, he reported hearing that "the Parliament resolves to carry matters to the highest extremes," and that Prior was under pressure "to force him to accuse Lord Oxford though he declares he knows nothing, and that it is thought he will be hanged if he will not be an evidence." Prior's plight naturally reminded Swift of poor William Gregg.

Meanwhile, members of Trinity College were being expelled for disloyalty, and one, Swift heard, was to be whipped or pilloried for "speaking some words." Opportunities for eavesdroppers were expanding, as he found when, to counteract the rumors about himself, he had gone "to the Courts on purpose to show I was not run away. I had warning given me to beware of a fellow that stood by while some of us were talking. It seems there is a trade going of carrying stories to the government and that many honest folks turn the penny by it." The situation Swift describes is one of community breaking down, the "trade in stories" undermining civic life.

The Jacobite rebellion of the autumn of 1715 raised the temperature even further. On 20 November, the King's Chaplain, Thomas Greene, preached in Canterbury Cathedral a ranting sermon on The Great Wickedness of Perjury, and of the Present Rebellion. For the benefit of those in public office, including the clergy, he recited in full the text of the Oath of Abjuration, with its promise to "disclose and make known."

READING THE MATERIAL TEXT OF SWIFT'S VERSES ON THE DEATH

Most modern readers of Jonathan Swift's greatest poem encounter a text that eighteenth-century readers would never have known. When we read a modem edition of Verses on the Death of Dr. Swift, we generally find a single version, entirely printed, containing no lacunae, and with footnotes either reduced in size or relegated to the back of the book. The visual and material qualities of eighteenth-century texts often differ from modern ones, but in the case of the Verses those differences are not only in degree but in kind. In the eighteenth century there were two dramatically conflicting versions of the poem, the more authoritative of which contained footnotes printed as large as the poem's lines, as well as numerous gaps sometimes filled in by hand. Thus, the early texts of this poem survive in a bewildering array of print, manuscript, and blank space.

Having gathered evidence from over twenty eighteenth-century editions of the Verses and thirty-two annotated copies, I want to use this research to redirect the study of the poem. By drawing on the often disparate fields of literary criticism, textual criticism, and the history of the book, I point to a climate in which textual variability was sometimes accepted and in which some readers actively shared and compared manuscripts and printed texts. In this context, my title "Reading the Material Text" has four different meanings.

First, I read these documents to understand the poem's complex textual transmission, the traditional purview of textual editors. Second, I argue that Swift is primarily responsible for the unusual appearance of George Faulkner's early editions, and therefore the material text of these editions forms an integral part of Swift's intentions. Third, influenced by recent developments in textual criticism, I suggest that criticism of the poem should involve reading its material text. Fo urth, I show how the annotated copies help us understand the various ways in which eighteenth-century readers responded to the work.

Tracing the textual transmission of Swift's Verses is especially difficult because it involves not only manuscript and printed evidence, but also their intricate interaction. Significant portions of the poem's notes exist only as manuscript additions copied onto printed texts. These documents pose a number of challenging problems, such as determining who copied the manuscript material, when, and from what source. The problems are even more vexing in that no authorial manuscript survives and that, as far as we know, Swift remained silent on these textual issues. Thus, we lack a complete base text from which to compare the other versions, and in addition, no two of the thirty-two known annotated copies are exactly alike.

The singular, standardized text of modem editions masks a variability that was historically integral to the work's existence and that may have been authorially intended or at least sanctioned. Careful inspection of these documents and other kinds of evidence provides a probable sketch of this particular work's circulation, which passed through all the possible media of transmission. Though Swift apparently composed the poem proper toward the end of 1731 and the notes later that spring, he chose not to commit the work to print for at least four years. After a period of oral circulation, amusingly recounted by Laetitia Pilkington, Swift had the Jacobite poet William King arranges print publication in London.

Before doing so, however, King shared the manuscript with a select circle of Swift's friends, including at least Alexander Pope and John Boyle, earl of Orrery. Drastically edited and stripped of its notes by this group, the Verses was first published by Charles Bathurst in London in January 1739. Soon thereafter, George Faulkner, Swift's trusted Dublin bookseller, published a much longer version, containing the notes and many blank spaces that signified missing material. This material was then wr itten onto some Faulkner copies, though the ultimate sources remain obscure. The poem continued to have a complex existence even after 1739, appearing, appropriately enough, after Swift's death in The Dublin Courant and in various forms in numerous collected editions of his works.

The complex intersection between print and script, as well as the textual variability that became so central to the work's subsequent existence, begins with Bathurst's edition. In that text, six lines depicting Queen Caroline's cruelty toward Swift were deleted and replaced with asterisks. Not surprisingly, this material was judged too controversial to be printed, but as King notes in a letter to Swift, "that incident is pretty well known, and care has been taken that almost every reader may be able to supply the blanks."

Exactly what King means by "care" is unclear; readers do not have enough context to supply precisely the missing words though they may be able to infer the general point. King probably means that these lines were shared orally or in manuscript, and, in fact, ten known copies of Bathurst's edition contain these lines in manuscript. These six lines were almost certainly recorded during a period shortly after the Bathurst edition's publication, for they differ from later printed v ersions, and thus do not seem to derive from any printed edition. These copies contain no other kinds of annotation, despite the circulation of Swift's manuscript around England, passing among King, Pope, Orrery, and possibly others. The absence of further annotation suggests that, at this time, this early manuscript did not circulate beyond this select circle.

The variations among these ten copies' annotations point to the absence of a single authoritative version of these lines. The first manuscript line in figure 1 reads: "He's dead you say, why let him rot." Other copies variously supply the line as: "Well if he's dead then let him rot," or "As he is gone, so let him rot." The other variations are similar in that they do not alter the overall sense of the lines, though they point to multiple manuscripts floating around, oral circulation, or a combination of both. In general, these annotations reveal readers' interests in ascertaining these lines, and the multiple asterisks probably helped convey a sense of controversy to those ignorant of the specific contents.

Shortly after Bathurst's edition appeared and before Faulkner's edition was published, manuscripts of the Verses began to circulate, though the evidence for this activity remains indirect. On 30 January 1739, King writes to Martha Whiteway, Swift's cousin, and apologetically refers to the edited Bathurst text while also stating that "It may not be amiss to tell you, that one Gaily, or Gaillie, since this poem was printed, offered it to sale to a bookseller at Temple-bar; and I am now told that there are two or three copies more in London. Gaillie pretends that he is just come from Ireland, and that he had directions to publish the poem here; so that perhaps the whole may at last appear, whether he will or not."

Nothing else is known about this mysterious figure Gaillie, but the letter suggests that he had some kind of manuscript which he was attempting to publish and that copies began to circulate. Unless King is baldly lying, this manuscript is not the same one that he had carried to London and shared with the others. King's statement that "perhaps the whole may at last appear" shows his suspicion that Gaillie's text is complete, or at least more complete than the text edited by himself and published by Bathurst.

No manuscript copies survive, though I think that eight annotated Faulkner copies provide evidence of their existence. Significantly, these copies contain manuscript material in places where there are no blanks to be filled. Enough repetition occurs across a small number of copies to suggest that readers are correcting or supplementing their Faulkner copies from manuscripts. Most of these changes occur in the notes, none of which Bathurst printed.

For example, Faulkner's text describes Frances Charteris as "a most infamous, vile Scoundrel," whereas four annotated copies replace "vile" with "Scotch," "Scots," or "impudent Scotch". (For Swift, the epithets were synonymous, though some of his readers may not have shared the prejudice.)

Similarly, shows changes to the notes on William Pulteney and Henry St. John, first viscount Bolingbroke. Here the reader has circled the printed words rather than crossed them out, suggesting a greater toleration for variants. The bottom of the page records a printed variant: "became his Mortal Enemy" for "opposed his Measures." In fact, the former phrase appears m an early state of this page, which this reader must have seen. The other variants do not appear in print, however: the insertion of "ill" before "Administration," "to expose his Corruptions," and "perfidiously."

As these variants appear in other copies, they suggest three probable stages of textual revision in which the anti-Walpole rhetoric is gradually softened, possibly by Faulkner. The handwritten variants reflect the pre-Faulkner text at its harshest: Pulteney, described as "detesting his [Walpole's] ill Administration, became his Mortal Enemy, and joyned with my Lord.

Chapter 13

Venus Athena and Other Goddesses in "Cadenus and Vanessa"

REVOLUTION

We are in the midst of one. A radical change in the way we do business, raise our children, entertain, educate ourselves and disperse news. So when we look back at revolutions that occurred two or even three centuries ago, they seem tame and pale in the face of the current one - the digital phenomenon. Yet, when Vanessa Van Homrigh directed the release of the poem "Cadenus and Vanessa" after her death, it was a revolution because it revealed, or at least intimated, that the revered Dean of St. Patrick's Cathedral in Dublin had a romantic, human side and indeed appeared to have enjoyed a clandestine love affair.

Although this old news is still discussed and debated in Eighteenth Century studies, none of the conversations addresses Jonathan Swift's use of the pagan Roman and Greek female goddesses that scamper through the lines of this long poem. It's a theme that threads its way through all his works about women.

Because of this consistency, I maintain that Swift, just as clandestinely, tried to show that women, especially those close to him, should be considered on an equal basis with men as they reportedly once were when primitive peoples revered them as creators of life. Dominating the poem is Venus, a goddess evoked by Lucretius as the proem of his long didactic poem, "De rerum natura":

Mother of Rome, delight of Gods and men,
Dear Venus that beneath the gliding stars
Makest to teem the many-voyaged main
And fruitful lands- for all of living things
Through thee alone are evermore conceived,
Through thee are risen to visit the great sun -
Before thee, Goddess, and thy coming on,
Flee stormy wind and massy cloud away,
For thee the daedal Earth bears scented flowers,
For thee waters of the unvexed deep
Smile, and the hollows of the serene sky
Glow with diffused radiance for thee!
[...] And since 'tis thou alone
Guidest the Cosmos, and without thee naught
Is risen to reach the shining shores of light,
Nor aught of joyful or of lovely born,
Thee do I crave co-partner in that verse
Which I presume on Nature to compose [...].

If Lucretius felt compelled to call on Venus as his partner in the creation of his masterpiece, then it should not surprise anyone that Jonathan Swift, nearly two thousand years later, summoned the same goddess to create his ideal woman.

To Lucretius, Venus was the Great Mother Goddess, a deity the earliest peoples venerated. But as the ages passed, she evolved into the forerunners of the deities Swift calls on in his poetry. As patriarchy became the norm, claim Ann Baring and Jules Cashford, "everything became turned around. Male was associated with spirit, light, order and mind, which were good; while the female aspect of life became identified with nature, darkness, chaos and body, which were evil."

Swift does everything he can to refute this tragic misconception and transformation as he counters the surface historical realities with allusions to timeless, cyclical mythological women, incorporating in his poetry the very myths his contemporaries used constantly but in a much different way than they ever thought of.

We feel Swift expresses what the terms masculine and feminine should mean: a way of being or a mode of consciousness available to both men and women. It's no accident that Swift's ideal woman created by Venus received the most admirable qualities of both sexes. To him the prevailing attitude was unreasonable: that women were second class.

So he shakes up his readers through a satiric approach to the abuse of reason. Martin Price says that most of Swift's satire deals with the way in which reason is cheated, subverted and betrayed by rationalism and brutality. His ironies "are means of restoring our awareness of choices, and his subjects are error, self-deception, insanity. Men fail to see clearly because their interests and passions make them prefer something more comfortable than the truth."

"Cadenus and Vanessa" is a prime example of Swift's attempt to show the truth. Venus as the Cyprian queen, is evoked immediately. His use of "Cyprian" indicates he was aware of the histories and origins of the goddess who came to Greece from Cyprus where she was born from the foam of the sea (not from Zeus' head). So as a myth, she was ancient. But by the time she arrived on Mt. Olympus, she played a diminished role. Swift's reference to her birthplace and her birth, would indicate he knew and supported the earlier rendition of Venus as the mother goddess.

In his poem, Venus is placed in a deadlocked position unable to respond traditionally to a complaint of shepherds and nymphs that traditional love has deteriorated to the point of absurdity. The women, claiming Cupid as the culprit, say love has dwindled to intrigue, and marriage has become a money-league.

Swift's narrator, or Swift himself, states that Cupid has lost his art and that his mother can no longer instill fire in anyone's loins, questioning the power of the mythic deities themselves. The shepherds counter the nymphs' accusations by blaming the women who, they say, have destroyed love as it was traditionally perceived by the troubadours. Swift detested this convention as well because it denigrated women:

That Modern love is no such thing
As what those ancient poets sing;
A fire celestial, chaste, refined,
Conceived and kindled in the mind.
Which having found an equal flame,
Unites, and both become the same,
In different breasts together burn,
Together both to ashes turn.
But women now feel no such fire,
And only know the gross desire:
Their passions move in lower spheres,
Where'er caprice of folly steers:
A dog, a parrot, or an ape,
Or some worse brute in human shape,
Engross the fancies of the fair,
The few soft moments they can spare,
From visits to receive and pay;
From scandal, politics, and play,
From fans and flounces, and brocades,
From equipage and park-parades;
From all the thousand female toys,
From every trifle that employs
The out or inside of their heads,
Between their toilets and the beds.
(ll. 27-50)

Not only is Swift ridiculing the women who have accepted the modern conditions as well as the earlier poetry that elevates them to such a mindless state, he is saying to both men and women that the male dominated perception of love since the Renaissance, embodied in the medieval courtly love, and even in Ovid's advice to lovers, does not treat women as whole human beings who have the potential to think, make decisions and rule.

Framing the poem with powerful mythological figures - women with power, reinforces Swift's concern as he continues to juxtapose the mythological cyclical time against the historic moment.

While the following verse paragraph parodies the much

ridiculed Cooper's Hill poetry, it also satirizes the harsh perception of women:

In a dull stream, which moving slow
You hardly see the current flow;
If a small breeze obstructs the course,
It whirls about for want of force,
And in its narrow circle gathers
Nothing but chaff, and straws, and feathers:
The current of a female mind
Stops thus, and turns with every wind;
Thus whirling round, together draws
Fools, fops and rakes, for chaff and straws.
Hence we conclude, no women's hearts
Are won by virture, wit and parts;
Nor are the men of sense to blame,
For breasts incapable of flame;
The fault must on the nymphs be placed,
Grown so corrupted in their taste. (ll. 51-66)

Since women's minds only gather chaff, straws and feathers, a.k.a., fools, fops and rakes, they can't be won by virtue, wit and parts. In making this adroit comparison, Swift draws attention to the conditions women confronted in his day. These lines describe women as no more than whores. They suggest that the fault, according to the men of the poem, lies with the nymphs who either have no brains or have resorted to the streets. It also becomes clear that Swift is using his own extraordinary wit and knowledge to say something almost the opposite of what critics and the reading public have concluded over the years.

By equating the female mind with a slow moving, dull stream, Swift limits women's capabilities to attracting the chaff and straws of life; they can't control the conditions that control them. Women are, to the men, like reeds in the wind, at the mercy of the social elements.

Not only does the exaggerated picture reject those conditions, it makes the men look asinine for thinking so, an irony in itself because the men blame the women for a condition they themselves created. So to combat this abuse,

Swift calls on Venus to create his perfect woman, a creature with both masculine and feminine traits.

The poem's Venus is, of course, beside herself: mortals disdain to love. Thus Swift sets the stage for his miracle. Rather than soaring off to Cyprus, Venus remains, calling for advice from the muses and the Graces—the immortals who helped form Venus/Aphrodite.

Even with her reinforcements, Venus doesn't recognize the plaintiffs and so resorts to her law books. She rejects contemporary legal advice, as well as Ovid's counsel in the Amores and the Art of Love, both of which look upon women as sex objects. Edmund Waller and Abraham Cowley, the Seventeenth Century's respected love poets, are also tossed out of court, because they, too, place women in the same untenable position.

For almost two decades Venus listens to the briefs of each party, ultimately dismissing everything. "For sixteen years the cause was spun,/ And then stood where it begun" (ll. 124-5). Finally the Goddess of Love conceives a plan. Throwing away her law books, Venus summons other goddesses including Lucina - the goddess of light who illuminates the world and reigns over births. Venus dream of a woman who will restore her reign and vows to search everywhere for all the positive attributes of a human.

[...] From courts inclusive, down to cells,
What preachers talk, or sages write.
These I will gather and unite,
And represent them to mankind
Collected in the infant's mind. [sic]
(ll. 149-54)

Vanessa is crafted by the Graces, they nymphs who attend Aphrodite/Venus, "weaving her robes, plaiting her crown of violets, all that makes for sweetness in life." "Each breathing on her thrice, inspired/That gentle, soft engaging air,/Which in old times, adorned the fair." (ll. 177-9) And who are the fair but these early goddesses? Venus plans her strategy to ferret out the purest virtues for her creation which men claim they can't find:

Since men allege, they ne'er can find
Those beauties in a female mind
Which raise a flame that will endure
For ever, uncorrupt and pure;
If 'tis with reason they complain,
This infant shall restore my reign [...]
(ll. 142-147)

Then Venus plucks a sprig of amaranthine (unfading) flowers to assure that her creation will last and the earlier reign return.

Subtle references to the earlier goddesses are strewn casually throughout the poem. In the next section Venus, "drawn by her doves," birds classically associated with goddesses, seeks out Athena to instill wisdom and knowledge. The goddess of love decides to deceive Athena and tells her the newly created child is a boy. The Olympians were also part of the switch to patriarchal thinking, and so Swift, calling attention in still another way to the inequities his society perpetuates, allows Venus's deception to stand.

Swift's describing Athena as "The Queen of Learning" is also significant because he instills a female deity with the power to "sow within her (Vanessa's) tender mind/Seeds long unknown to womankind" (ll. 202,3),that is, the power to provide a mortal woman with the education long denied Eighteenth-Century women, indeed all women, for centuries.

For manly bosoms chiefly fit,
The seeds of knowledge, judgement, wit.
Her soul was suddenly endued
With justice, truth and fortitude;
With honour, which no breath can stain
Which malice must attack in vain; (ll. 204-9)

Venus is happy with Pallas' work and hopes that in addition to men falling head over heels in love with Vanessa, that "womankind/Would by her model form their mind." The motif of restoring the goddess's reign appears again as well in "My power shall be again restored,/And happy lovers bless my reign." (ll. 246-7). While Venus's reign ostensibly means the rule of the Queen of Love, it also has implications of the restoration of the time when she was worshiped as the Great Mother Goddsss, as a forever renewable circle that turns back on itself.

But her hopes are crushed. Pallas lets things play out as they will naturally. And naturally, the internal culture of the poem cannot accept a woman crafted with both masculine and feminine attributes just as Swift's Eighteenth Century culture finds this kind of acceptance impossible. Pallas knows this, finding "her foe's conclusions were not sound." (l. 279) Pallas and Venus are at odds with each other. Pallas chastises Venus for tricking her, informing her that she's only deceived herself and that men only worship her "for want of sense."

Although Pallas predicts that Venus's scheme will fail, Vanessa nonetheless enters the world. The next 110 lines describe Eighteenth-Century society fairly accurately. Vanessa was not accepted. Her learning was too learned; her clothes were archaic and dowdy, her tastes were academic, not laced with gossip. The women she found herself among could only stare at her and ridicule her. They called her the dullest soul, noting that "[...] none will burn her for a witch." I suggest the reference means that Vanessa was considered so dull that not even the purveyors of the Inquisition would consider her a threat.

The testing of Vanessa literally continues to diminish her as Swift alludes to, or describes in a scathing indictment, the behavior of women of his day:

Filled with disdain, with rage inflamed,
Both of her self and sex ashamed,
The nymph stood silent out of spite,
Nor would vouchsafe to set them right.
Away the fair detractors went,
And gave, by turns, their censures vent.
'She's not so handsome, in my eyes:
For wit, I wonder where it lies.'
'She's fair and clean, and that's the most;
But why proclaim her for a toast'
'A babyface, no life, no airs,
But what she learnt at country fairs;

Scarce knows what difference is between
Rich Flanders lace, and colbertine
'I'll undertake my little Nancy
In flounces has a better fancy.'
'With all her wit, I would not ask
Her judgement, how to buy a mask,'
'We begged her but to patch her face,
She never hit one proper place;
Which every girl at five years old
Can do as soon as she is told.'
'I own, that out-of-fashion stuff
Becomes the creature well enough.'
'The girl might pass, if we could get her
To know the world a little better.'
(To know the world, a modern phrase,
For visits, ombre, balls and plays.)
(ll. 404-32)

The lines reflect the details of a contemporary woman's toilet and life. Vanessa was not among those jaded women and because she was not, Swift is saying that no woman should be required, taught, or expected to behave in such a fashion. But, alas, the culture prevailed. Pallas was right; the world rejected the nymph. And so like Belinda's lock, Vanessa is consigned to the heavens, a goddess. On the other hand, Venus acknowledges that "[...] great examples are but vain,/Where ignorance begats disdain." (ll. 436-7). In other words, when people are unaware of the truth, their conclusions (often erroneous) are so ingrained in a culture, that the false notion is ultimately accepted as truth.

The mid section of the poem is Swift's poetic rendering of the relationship between Cadenus (an acronym for Decanus, the Latin word for Dean) and Vanessa and is obviously drawn from real life experiences. Cupid, trying to vindicate his mother Venus's wrongs, aims arrows at Vanessa, but Cadenus wards off the blows.

Cupid eventually pierces Vanessa's bosom with an arrow that went through a volume of Cadenus's "Poetic Works" (a volume that did not exist at the time) directly to her heart.

The narrator contrasts the pair, noting that Vanessa is young and waxing, while Cadenus is on the wane, unaware of "what was love." Cadenus compiles a litany of excuses of why he can't love his pupil although he is proud of her abilities.

He wants to share his creation with the world but then realizes that the pupil is more interested in him as a person than a teacher - "she wished her tutor were her lover." (l. 562) He prepares to "take his last adieu," feeling that all his lectures were in vain. She denies his accusations, declaring that she knew "How dangerous things were men of wit,/You cautioned me against their charms,/ But never gave me equal arms:/ Your lessons found the weakest part,/Aimed at the head, but reached the heart."

Arms must be assumed to be weapons women should carry to fend off the traditional male who would naturally seek a woman as beautiful as Vanessa but who had no interest in her intellect. Cadenus continues to resist, maintains his innocence, lacing the lines with satiric jibes at the gossips who probably concluded they were already lovers:

Appearances were all so strong,
The world must think him in the wrong:
Would say, he made a treacherous use
Of wit, to flatter and seduce:
The town would swear he had betrayed,
By magic spells, the harmless maid;
And every beau would have his jokes.
That scholars were like other folks;
That when platonic flights were over,
The tutor turned a mortal lover.
(ll. 650-59)

Vanessa of the poem, like Vanessa of the real relationship, pays no attention to Cadenus' protesting. Never intended for publication, the poem was a love letter. Ultimately it would seem that Cadenus (Swift) succumbs: "Things took a turn he never meant...And oft the dancing-master's art/Climbs from the toe to touch the heart." (l. 739; 748-9) Cadenus (Swift) says quite openly in the lines, "In learning let a nymph delight,/ The pedant gets a mistress by't," (750-1) that he allowed the unthinkable (to him) to happen. Vanessa became his mistress. These lines are not the lines of a woman hater; rather, they are part of an intricately complex poem brimming with allusions to strong, powerful goddesses, goddesses who actually created a woman perfect for Swift. It was no accident that their names were the same.

Cadenus, to his grief and shame,
Could scarce oppose Vanessa's flame;
But though her arguments were strong,
At least could hardly wish them wrong.
Howe're it came, he could not tell,
But sure she never talked so well.
(ll. 752-56)

Cadenus is proud. He now takes credit for her passion, but continuing to resist, says "love, hitherto a transient guest,/ Ne'er held possession of his breast," (ll. 776-7) until that moment. Cadenus claims he is too dignified and too old to engage in love making. But then Vanessa decides, and Cadenus allows her, to teach him how to love. He reveals he's not so inept that he can't read a lady's eyes. Then Swift writes:

But what success Vanessa met,
Is to the world a secret yet:
Whether the nymph, to please her swain,
Talks in a high romantic strain;
Or whether he at last descends
To like with less seraphic ends;
Or, to compound the business, whether
They temper love and books together;
Must never to mankind be told,
Nor shall the conscious muse unfold. (ll 826 - 35).

It will be up to the unconscious muse - i.e. the timeless mythologies themselves - that there indeed was a love relationship and that Swift embraced the various kinds of love Venus in her ancient reign represented.

The fictive portrayal of the affair between Swift and Vanessa is framed by myth. By reintroducing Venus, Swift thus unites the historical with the cyclical and the timeless. Venus, having waited out the earthly conflict, decrees against the men for having been so undiscriminating as not to fall in love with the beautiful and brilliant Vanessa.

They were a stupid, senseless race;
And were she to begin again,
She'd study to reform the men;
Or add some grain of folly more
To women than they had before,
To put them on an equal foot [...]
(ll 879-84)

The reasoning behind making women even more foolish than they had been is to make them equal to the men because the men were foolish, and "every being loves its like."(l. 887) Swift uses the word 'equal,' but he implies that for equality to occur, women must drop down to the male level. Venus finds herself in a ridiculous situation where neither men or women realize how to love. However revealing some of the lines are, however succinctly they point to the earliest times when women were not vilified, however much they state emphatically that women and men should be on an intellectually equal plane, the poem ends with Venus harnessing her doves, leaving the world "at six and seven." (l. 896)

Venus throws up her hands in disgust, leaving the mess and all its rubble to Cupid. An obvious conclusion is that until the world realizes that men and women should be equal in judgement, learning and wit, nothing will be done. And very little has. "Cadenus and Vanessa" is one of the most extensively and intensely examined of Swift's poems because of its puzzling nature, but no one is really ready to acknowledge that Swift, the satirist, the humorist, the cleric, the man, could actually be a lover. Some concede he might have had an intimate, but sexless relationship with Vanessa. Most feel he rejected her outright.

All fail to comment on the cryptic lines that refer to the conscious muse unfold her secret (ll. 832-5). Basically they dismiss or ignore the hints in the lines and between the lines, reading the poem on an historical level only. Although Peter Schakel describes the allusions in Ovid and Virgil, no one suggests or acknowledges the dichotomy between the historic presentation and the mythological references even though the goddesses and all they imply line the pages of this poem.

Louise K. Barnett's explication of "Cadenus and Vanessa" actually comes close to my position, but she, too, fails to grasp the significance of the mythical figures.Describing the poem as Swift's most comprehensive poetic treatment of the position of women, Barnett remarks on Swift's portrait of Vanessa. She says it is noteworthy because it "divorces admirable qualities from gender and unites the best of both sexes in one person.

Vanessa is not an unattainable ideal, but one that could be realized if artificial distinctions between the sexes were obliterated. Swift creates the ideal woman only to find that the perfect woman is unsuitable in an imperfect society and that "without changing both sexes, the poem concludes, there is little chance of improvement. The investigation of love, she writes, "produces an explicit statement: both men and women are guilty of foolishness." But the poem goes on to say that in order for women and men to be on equal footing, women should become even more foolish. In light of my premise, one must take that notion as satire. Women could not become more foolish than they already were perceived to be.

Absurdly, to David Nokes, providing Vanessa with masculine qualities is a reflection of Swift's own lack of sexual desire. "Vanessa emerges as the de-sexed hygienic Swiftian ideal, a woman whose cleanliness, decency and manly temperament make her a truly rational companion." He says that although Swift felt passion for Vanessa, he rejected her "with feelings of guilt and loss."

This, as Bruce Arnold, the well known Irish critic who wrote and produced an opera about Swift and his passion, and I agree, is nonsense. Why do we insist on making Jonathan Swift less than human? It is surprising that such conclusions have been drawn about this poem, given the available information and the obvious messages within the lines. These critics' readings fail to give full voice to what I have demonstrated as Swift's complex sense of the dialectic between the historical and the mythic view of women. In the poem, he graphically describes the terrible fate that awaits young women of the Eighteenth Century-little or no education, pursuit of a financially suitable marriage, generally without love.

Swift riles against the inevitable pursuit of prostitution as an alternative, or worse still, the practice of elevating women to a mindless perch on an imaginary pedestal. But this historical rendering is not just recorded as lusty satire; it is countered by the consistent use of mythologies that point to the time when women were worshiped as goddesses.

The strength of the poem lies in Swift's telling lines about making the women as foolish as the men when no swain wants her. Knowing this, Venus, the goddess Swift calls on repeatedly to open his reader's eyes and the goddess who has the power to create an ideal woman, throws up her hands in frustration. And why shouldn't she? Swift makes his point. Until both men and women understand that the sexes are equal and should be treated thus, there is no solution to the gender problem. We are still waiting.

Chapter 14

Swift and the Idea of the Primitive Church

Despite his use of a variety of disguises and tones of voice, Swift is consistent in what he writes about Christianity. The reason is that he grounds what he says on his idea of the Primitive Church, that is, the Church of the Apostles. This is not just a Church lost in the haze of antiquity, but also one manifested in the past century in the days of William Laud and William Sancroft. It is not surprising that Swift looks back to the 17th century for his points of reference in writing on religion, because he grew to manhood in that century, and the religious struggles of the 1640s, the 1680s, and the 1690s are what shaped his world.

Writing in 1726, Swift equates the Church of Laud with the Primitive Church when he accuses those who defend the Puritans of the 1640s of holding an opinion "utterly contrary" to both the "doctrine of Christ and his apostles" and to "the preaching and practice" of the "true professors" of the Church of England for "above a hundred years."

With the phrase "the doctrine of Christ and his apostles," he points to the Primitive Church, and with the phrase "the true professors" of the Church for "above a hundred years," he points to Laud as the standard of his Church. He joins the Primitive to the Laudian as the antithesis of Puritanism, for his phrase "a hundred years" take us back only to the Caroline Church.

Again, writing in 1733, he asks whether the Church of Laud, especially the "best" of the clergy did not suffer as "primitive Christians": "Were not all the remainders of the episcopal Church in those days, especially the clergy, under a persecution for above a dozen years, equal to that of the primitive Christians under heathen emperors?" He equates the Puritan regim to the reigns of Nero and Diocletian.

In the "Ode to Sancroft," Swift honors this Archbishop with the title, "Primitive Sancroft." He addresses him as "original mildness," too, the word *original* being a synonym for *primitive.* Sancroft is "Primitive" for two apparently contradictory actions: first for being one of the greatest sticklers when the Catholic King attempted to revoke the Test Acts in the 1680s, and then for refusing to take the new oath to his successors William and Mary in the 1690s.

Swift compares Sancroft's exemplary suffering to what Jesus Christ his "almighty master" suffered when the same crowds that acclaimed him "Son of God" soon afterwards "pronounced his death." Sancroft went from the Palm Sunday of June 1688, when crowds acclaimed him on the way to the Tower for resisting James II, to the Good Friday of the 1690s, when the same crowds turned on him in a "rage" for resisting King William:

None e'er but you,
And your almighty master, knew
With heavenly peace of mind to bear
(Free from our tyrant-passions, anger, scorn, or fear)
The giddy turns of popular rage,
And all the contradictions of a poisoned age... (113-8).

What Swift says about Sancroft here applies to other deprived high-churchmen of the 1690s. He declares that only fools think "holy SANCROFT's motion" was "irregular" or that he contradicted himself by resisting both kings. These fools stare at the "weathercock of state" standing on the church steeple, he explains, and as they grow "giddy" they imagine that the Church, not the weathervane, is spinning round.

In this startling image Swift gives us Lilliput in a nutshell: he pictures the State – insofar as it meddles with the Church – as a tiny weathervane on top of a great solid edifice. The Church is gigantic because it is Primitive – for it was long believed that the human race had diminished in size as it degenerated in virtue – while the State is a miniscule weathervane on its pinnacle because it is modern. He makes a similar point when he says that Henry VIII put to death Thomas More, "a person of the greatest virtue this kingdom ever produced, for not directly owning him to be head of the Church."

If More was the best Englishman who ever lived and he refused to acknowledge the king's new supremacy in religion, then it follows that Henry was wrong to make this innovation in the Church. Swift elsewhere calls Henry a "monster and tyrant" for robbing the clergy of "at least two-thirds of their legal possessions," and he charges his Tudor successors Edward and Elizabeth (but not Mary) with continuing this "rapine," which ended only with the advent of the Stuarts. In the "Ode to Sancroft," he asks plaintively:

... why the church is still led blindfold by the state?
Why should the first be ruined and laid waste,
To mend the dilapidations in the last? (177-9)

Clearly Swift is not Erastian. He believes the State can only hinder the Church from following its original laws; it cannot give the Church new laws. In his eyes, More, Laud, and Sancroft are "Primitive" because they suffered to keep the State from imposing innovations on the Church.

Swift no longer finds the lineaments of Primitive Christianity in the visible Church of his own day. In the *Argument against Abolishing Christianity,* he speaks of a recent fall from the "real Christianity" of "primitive times" – he means the "primitive times" of Laud and Sancroft – to the "nominal" Christianity of 1708.

To restore the "real" thing, he says, would require digging up "foundations," a word that implies the Primitive Church is still there, buried under ground. He complains of "bishops of the Whig species" in a *Preface* to Burnet's History, and, in the "Ode to Sancroft," of "wild reformers" who have stripped the current Church of "every ornament and grace":

Some angel say, what were the nation's crimes,
That sent these wild reformers to our times;

Say what their senseless malice meant,
To tear Religion's lovely face;
Strip her of every ornament and grace,
In striving to wash off the imaginary paint.... (245-50)

He also finds that in the twenty years since "the late Revolution, men have sat much looser in the true fundamentals both of religion and government" and in parliament the "enemies to the clergy [have been] heard with the utmost applause." This has led to atheism: "the trade of infidelity" is taken up as "an expedient to keep in countenance that universal corruption of morals," "blasphemy is freely spoken a million of times in every coffeehouse and tavern," and contempt shown for priesthood on the stage. The loss of beauty in worship has led to the loss of fidelity.

Alluding to Christ's promises, Swift remarks that "The Church is supposed to last forever, both in its discipline and doctrine," but this means that it must "observe the laws" of its "foundation." His word *foundation* again points to the Primitive or Apostolic Church below ground, for St Paul called Christianity an edifice "built upon the foundation of the apostles and prophets" (Eph 2:20).

As a way of digging up this hidden foundation, Swift urges Queen Anne to put a Laudian stress on public worship and require officeholders to attend weekly services and communicate four times a year.

He sees the English of his day as fallen as far below their forefathers of a thousand years ago as hell is from heaven, for in his "Ode to Sancroft" he exclaims, "Ah, Britain, land of angels! Which of all thy sins ... / Has given thee up a dwelling place to fiends?" With the phrase "land of angels" he refers to Venerable Bede's account of how Pope St Gregory the Great, on meeting English youths in Rome, had exclaimed, "not Angles, but Angels," and promptly sent St Augustine to convert their nation.

Gulliver's Travels, which starts in 1699, opens with a picture of the Church of England grown miniscule in stature. Swift calls it "a declining church" in the "Ode to Sancroft," and here it is, only six feet long, just on a par with the weathervane State.

When Gulliver comes to Lilliput, he is tied by a chain he could easily break to this "ancient Temple," which has been stripped of all its "Ornaments and Furniture" by "the Zeal of those People" and turned "to common Use." One of the first things Gulliver does is to crawl into the Temple as far as his six-foot chain allows and defecate at the East end, right in the sanctuary where the holy table once stood.

Such an action had been done in the past by men who regarded the sacrament as an idol. Swift's point is that an ordinary Englishman at the start of the 18th century is as nonchalantly sacrilegious as any rabid iconoclast of an earlier time. Gulliver defends himself from being unclean, but not from being sacrilegious. By using the word zeal to explain how the Temple was stripped bare, Swift hints at a new surge of Calvinism in the 1690s.

However, in the first voyage also blames Anglicans and Catholics for the ruined Church of 1700. He tells of a century-long quarrel between the Little Endians and the Big Endians, during which one king was killed and another banished, meaning Charles I and James II. In the 17th-century the egg was an emblem of the Eucharist in that it remains the same on the outside while turning to meat on the inside. The quarrel over whether the egg should be broken at the big or little end represents the controversy between Catholics and Anglicans over the *modus* of the Real Presence – whether this Presence be only within the soul of the receiver at communion (the smaller end), or also in the sacrament of the altar and thus received bodily at communion (the bigger end).

Swift regards this quarrel as having opened the way to rampant sacrilege. He remarks that the same "litigious vein" had "stopped the progress of Christianity" in the time of Duns Scotus. In one of his sermons, he warns that the modus of a mystery should not be discussed, because God requires us "to believe mysteries, while the reason or manner of what we are to believe is above our comprehension." We are to accept a mystery simply as a fact: "God himself hath pronounced the fact, but wholly concealed the manner." It is an either-or proposition: "either believe what God directly commands us" or "wholly reject the Scripture." In his letter to a young clergyman, he warns that it weakens "orthodoxy" to try to explain "the mysteries of the Christian religion," since God himself cannot explain them without giving us those "new powers or faculties of the mind" which he reserves for eternity.

The first point to be noted here is that Swift finds no analogy between the natural and the supernatural. He is a sceptic about the power of language or theological argument to defend the revealed mysteries. Thus, in the "Ode to Sancroft" he mocks at the "artillery of words" that will never "satisfy the doubt," for there is no way, he insists, "To judge of things above by things below." One has to make a leap of faith. Apart from Scripture, he finds the "best resemblance" of eternal Truth on earth in a holy man like Sancroft, whom he calls "the brightest pattern earth can show / Of heaven-born truth below".

A second point is that Swift sees the quarrel between the Church of England and the Church of Rome in the 16th and 17th centuries as scandalous because he believes they agreed on the essential point, that there is an egg to be broken, that there is a Real Presence of Christ's Body in the Sacrament. Here he follows Laud, who at his trial said that Catholics differed from the Church of England only about the "means of Christ's presence in the sacrament, a question of mere circumstance, but both accounted that Presence to be a point fundamental." Swift gives a clue about where he stands on the Lord's Supper when he uses the words bread and wine for the Presbyterian Church, but the word *elements* for his own: he says, "their manner of taking bread and wine in their conventicles, is performed with little more solemnity than at their common meals.

And ... they look upon our practice in receiving the elements, to be idolatrous." This word *elements* was the one Richard Hooker had used to define a sacrament, saying that when the "word" is added to the "elements" at the holy table the result is the "sacrament." Another clue is that Swift defends kneeling for communion, a posture Presbyterians long objected to as idolatry; he says kneeling obliges people to say "their prayers when they receive the Sacrament." A third clue is that Swift used to bow to the holy table, a practice for which Laud had been condemned.

On the other hand, the Real Presence appears to have been for him a purely interior encounter with Christ's body at the moment of communion, for he denied passionately that the Eucharistic Test for public office could result in profanation of the Sacrament if the candidate happened to be wicked or unbelieving. He insisted that receiving communion was no different than taking an oath: "For an oath is an act of religious worship as well as the Eucharist." Just as the words of an oath cannot be desecrated by a liar, so neither can the sacrament by the unworthy receiver.

The implication is that the Real Presence occurs only within the soul at communion. Yet the charge of sacrilege in the Test upset him; he returned to it several times, at one point insisting that men are assumed to receive "the sacrament" in "their own church; and if not, are hardly fit for an office." Thus he argued that the blame for sacrilege, if any, would fall on the receiver. In addition to this, Swift usually included Transubstantiation when he listed the Church of Rome's "errors," but like the Laudians, he did not condemn it as idolatry.

In *Tale of a Tub* Swift depicts the Primitive Church as three Brothers endowed by their dying Father with two legacies: a Will and a Coat that will never decay and always fit their changing bodies. The Brothers represent national churches that are equal branches of the universal Church. Laud had a similar conception when he wrote that the Church of Rome and the Church of England were two "daughters" or "particular churches" dwelling within a "great universal house," namely the "Catholic Church which is spread over the face of the earth." Swift uses the same word house for the universal Church when he has the Father admonish the Brothers to "live together in one House."

This is a reference to John 17, where Christ prays that his disciples may "be one." The Will is the Scripture, and the three Coats represent the visible worship of the Primitive Church.

The Brothers receive exterior Coats, not an interior assurance of election, because for Swift the Church requires public worship involving creed and sacrament. In this he resembles Laud, who saw the "outward profession of Christianity, and the administration of the sacraments" as the Church's main concern.

Just as Christ promises the gates of Hell will not prevail against his Church (Mt 16:18), so the Father in Swift's *Tale* promises that the original Coats will remain fresh and sound "as long as you live." In one of his sermons, Swift declares that "those mysteries held by us . . . have been ever maintained by the universal body of true believers from the days of the apostles, and will be so to the resurrection; neither will the gates of hell prevail against them." The word he uses – mysteries – includes both Creed and Sacrament.

Like Laud, Swift faults the Church of Rome for making unnecessary additions to the mysteries, but he does not accuse it of breaking with the Primitive Church. In *Tale of a Tub*, Peter's original Coat – the foundation of Primitive worship – is completely hidden under all the ornaments, but it remains intact. It is Presbyterian Jack who, from iconoclastic zeal against all ornaments, tears his Coat apart and thus loses his foundation in the Primitive Church. Thus, Swift shows Jack to have lost the basis of Christianity.

In his prose writings on religion, Swift often uses the word *fundamental.* This word does not mean the same thing as *primitive* but it is closely related. Where *primitive* means *apostolic, fundamental* means *universal or catholic.* At one point, Swift states that bishops are of "divine and apostolic institution," and then asks if they are not also "a fundamental point of religion." Elsewhere he defines fundamental as what has been "universally received by all bodies of Christians since the condemnation of Arianism under Constantine and his successors." Hence, involves the "tenets" held by virtually all Christians since the 5th century – the Greeks, the Orientals, and the Latins.

These "tenets," he asserts, "have been held inviolable, almost in all ages, by every sect that pretend to be Christian;

and cannot, therefore, with any colour of reason, be called points in controversy, or matters of speculation, as some should pretend." Note well his phrase "almost in all ages." He implies that the tenets of the 5th century are not Primitive or apostolic, but he puts them beyond dispute because they are deduced from the Primitive and have been held continuously by the universal Church.

Swift observes that "to remove opinions fundamental in religion is impossible, and the attempt wicked, whether those opinions be true or false; unless your avowed design be to abolish that religion altogether." Note well his phrase true or false; it betrays his discomfort with 5th-century deductions from the Primitive. Elsewhere he traces the decline of Christianity to the early use of philosophical language in theology: "I believe that thousands of men would be orthodox enough in certain points, if divines had not been too curious, or too narrow, in reducing orthodoxy within the compass of subtleties, niceties, and distinctions, with little warrant from Scripture and less from reason or good policy."

He faults even the Athanasian Creed for "some nice and philosophical points which few people can comprehend" and which were meant only to confute the Arian heretics, "very subtle disputers." Even so, he goes all the way back to the 5th century to defend the rights of clergy in the matter of tithes: "Let any scholar show the like precedent in Christendom for twelve hundred years past." If tithes are not Primitive or "of Divine original," he argues, they are "at least of great antiquity." They are thus sacrosanct because universally deduced in antiquity from the Primitive Church.

While he dates the fundamentals of Christianity to the 5th century, Swift dates "Popery" only to the 8th, which means he does not include in this category Pope St Gregory the Great, who sent St Augustine to convert the Angles and Saxons around 600 A.D. Writing in 1733, he declares, "As to Popery in general, which for a thousand years past hath been introducing and multiplying corruptions both in doctrine and discipline; I look upon it to be the most absurd system of Christianity professed by any nation."

If we subtract a thousand from 1733, we come close to the Second Nicene Council of 787 AD, the seventh general council. Swift claims that "Popery" arose a millenium before his own day, not before Luther's, and he calls Popery a "system of Christianity" professed by a "nation," as the Laudians did, not an Anti-Christian religion. As fore the Second Nicene Council, John Tillotson, who was Archbishop of Canterbury after Sancroft, said this council marked the fall of the Greek Church into idolatry: there "the Doctrine of the *corporal* presence of Christ was first started upon occasion of the Dispute about the *Worship of Images*."

In *Tale of a Tub*, the speaker – who tells the history of the general councils from a Presbyterian point of view like Marvell's – depicts the 8th-century council as the one where all three Brothers fell by consensus into idolatry and stopped consulting their Father's Will. They convened for this council to decide whether to add images to their Coats. At first they were stopped by an express prohibition in the Will, that is, the Second Commandment against graven images, but then they agreed to make a distinction that would allow them to use images, that is, a distinction between an image and its prototype. After the council the Brothers agree to lock up the Will, or prohibit the translation of Scripture into vulgar tongues.

The result is that one Brother begins to dominate the other two. And now, suddenly, the Brothers acquire names, for up to this point, they have lived nameless in one House and convened to make joint decisions about adding ornaments to their Coats. In the next council, which represents the Lateran Council of 1215, Peter, who stands for Innocent III, tells his Brothers they must believe, against sensory evidence, that the loaf they are having for Supper is a joint of lamb. Tillotson made this argument against Transubstantiation in the 1680s, appealing to the senses of taste, sight, and smell, although no one had actually claimed that the Real Presence was a miracle perceptible to the senses. It is doubtful that Swift, who warns against a philosophical or reductive approach to the mysteries, would go along with Tillotson.

What Swift probably means by the rise of "Popery" in the 8th century is the start of Peter's dominion over his Brothers, for he believes firmly in the equality of bishops and of national churches. He would not condemn Second Nicene, as the speaker of the *Tale* does, for encouraging religious art. Far from being an iconophobe, Swift compares those who stripped the English churches of their artistic treasures in the 1640s to "some vast army of Turks or heathens" sent "on purpose to ruin and blot out all marks of Christianity." In the third Voyage of *Gulliver's Travels,* he also shows the Dutch merchants as much greater sticklers than the Japanese for making foreign visitors trample the crucifix.

His point is that European iconoclasts have a much greater hatred of Christian images, which they condemn as idols, than non-Christians do. Swift plainly rejects the view that religious images are idols, for he calls what the Puritans destroyed in the 1640s "the most innocent ornaments both within and without" the Church. He laments that they spared "neither the statues of saints, nor ancient prelates, nor kings, nor benefactors" and broke "the tombs and monuments of men famous in their generations." Thus he shares the Laudian idea that Christian images are innocent, and yet, since he includes the "worship of images" in his list of Rome's errors, he probably means images that are only historical reminders, not ikons inviting to prayer.

One notes that the Brobdingnagians – giants representing Primitive innocence (albeit tainted by the Fall) – have a Church such as Laudians would approve of. Gulliver reports that their Temple is "adorned on all Sides with Statues of Gods and Emperors cut in Marble larger than the Life, placed in their several Niches." Another clue to Swift's personal appreciation of images in that, despite "severe criticism," he is said to have restored some monuments of earlier ages at St Patrick's, such as Tregury's gravestone.

Swift shows the three Brothers wearing their Coats down through the centuries: this indicates that Christianity has had an unbroken visibility, a lawful succession of bishops from the Primitive Church to the present. This succession is both

Primitive (or apostolic) and fundamental (or catholic), for when he observes that to "remove opinions fundamental" causes the abolition of a religion, he gives as an example the Puritans of the 1640s who "succeeded" in the "extirpation of the Church" by removing bishops, "the whole system of spiritual government, established in all Christian nations, and of apostolic institution."

When we look closely at Swift's pamphlets defending the rights of clergy, we realize that he has a sacramental view of orders closely connected to his idea of the Primitive Church. He emphasizes that the clergy has always had "powers and employments different from the laity": they alone from the age of the apostles to the Reformation had the right to pray and preach in churches and to administer the Lord's Supper. Writing against Matthew Tindal, who sees no difference between priest and layman, Swift declares: "you alter the whole method from what it was at first. We see bishops: There always were bishops: It is the old way still.

So a family is still held the same, although we are not sure of the purity of every one of the race." In this passage, he argues that the lack of purity in any age has not stopped the succession of bishops and priests: it is "the old way still," he says, the same "method" followed as "at first." His phrases *old way* and *at first* point to the Primitive "laying on of the apostles' hands," as in Acts 8:18. In another place he says plainly that "the government of bishops" was "ordained by the apostles themselves" and "continued without interruption, in all Christian churches, for above fifteen hundred years." His "fifteen hundred years" takes us from the Apostles to the Reformation.

In his *Quaeries* Swift asks pointedly whether bishops be not "essential" to "conferring holy orders." In his refutation of Tindal, he answers that they are. He explains that Christianity was first received in England as a "subordination of ecclesiastics, bishops, priests, and deacons." So from the start, bishops were "set apart" for their function by other bishops, while "presbyters and deacons" were "differently set apart, always by the bishops." His phrase set apart means separated from the laity. Swift sees priests and bishops in the Church of England as lineally descended from the bishops of the pre-Reformation Church.

While he blames medieval popes, monks and friars for wrongdoing, he defends the bishops of those times: "For the bishops were no tyrants: Their power was swallowed up by the Popes, and the people desired they should have more. It were the regulars that tyrannized and formed priestcraft."

When Swift affirms that there is not "so pure a religion as ours," he means that the national Church is closest to the Primitive in its worship. For in *Tale of a Tub,* he says the Coats the three Brothers received were originally "very plain, and with little or no ornament." In short, they received a creed and sacraments untouched by philosophical explanations. In *Tale of a Tub,* Martin comes closest to this simplicity when he removes the additions to his Coat without damaging the fundamental fabric.

He stops removing ornaments at the 5th century, at the time when there was a universal consensus about Christian worship, before the iconoclasm arose. But Presbyterian Jack continues to rip off ornaments in the hope of getting back to an apostolic state and ends up destroying the Primitive foundation of his worship.

Elsewhere Swift speaks of "rites and ceremonies, and forms of prayer" as the "ornaments" of a Church. Thus he includes a rite such as the Lord's Supper under this symbol of "ornaments." Martin's cautious paring down of his Coat represents how some national Churches – the Lutherans and the Laudians – retained the Lord's Supper almost unchanged in word and action.

Swift contends that since the worship received by "princes and states" at the end of antiquity was "*deduced* from Christ and His apostles, and the instructions of the *purest* and earliest ages," this amounts to the ancient constitution of the national Church.

The fundamentals received then remain now "as a divine law" and cannot be "justly altered or annulled," he warns, "any more than the common laws of nature." He defends the rights of the clergy by calling their convocations "an original part of our constitution ever since Christianity became national among us." Whatever the Church had in late antiquity is still its legal "patrimony." For this reason he refers more than once to the clergy's "ancient legal rights" and "ancient legal dues," and claims for the clergy "an older title" to tithes than any layman to his estate.

While he approves of Henry VIII's rejecting papal authority, he disapproves of his doing it to commit "sacrilege, in which no tyrant, since Christianity became national, did ever equal him by many degrees." His phrase "since Christianity became national" recalls the Church established in 600 AD. Henry's "misapplying" of tithes to "secular persons" Swift finds "a most flagrant act of injustice and oppression" because it violates the original constitution of that Church.

In Swift's view the best way to keep the Primitive Church as the foundation of national Churches is for these to join into a Catholic or Universal Church. He is not afraid to use the phrase Catholic Church to denote a Church spread throughout the world, in which the national Churches would be equal branches.

He pointedly defends his use of the term by saying: "Nor to me does there seem anything contradicting, or improper in this notion of the Catholic Church; and for want of such a communion, religion is so much corrupted." Note his word *corrupted.* He explains that the "necessity" of the Church's "being a corporation all over the world" is to "avoid heresies, and preserve fundamentals, and hinder corrupting of Scripture."

A national Church can go astray, but not a universal Church. Swift thinks such a worldwide communion might be inaugurated if bishops of independent national Churches would meet together all on the same footing. He compares this council of the universal Church to the assembling of "colleges in a university," which are "independent, yet, joined, are one body." But in his scheme, such a "body politic of the Church" spread through the "whole world" would have no Pope, no "visible head to have recourse to."

Just as the Father in *Tale of a Tub* commands his sons to live in one house, so, Swift reminds us, "our Saviour" in his last instructions urged brotherly love on his disciples. The "primitive Christians" at first "propagated the faith by their strict observance of that instruction."

Swift finds the present divisions of Christiandom a pressing concern, and thinks we ought at least to desire a Primitive unity – to want "to be able to communicate with all Christians we come among" and to promote this intercommunion "as much as we can."

Yet he remains doubtful it will ever come to pass: "That there might be a perfect union in the whole Christian Church, is a blessing which every good man wishes, but no reasonable man can hope." Still, he casts a kindly eye on Charles Leslie's scheme of reunion between the Gallican and the Anglican Churches. Evidently, he could live with French Catholicism, even with all its added tenets and rites, as long as it were ruled by bishops alone.

At the start of the first voyage, Gulliver defecates in the sanctuary of the Temple to which he is bound. At the start of the fourth voyage, the Yahoo elders go up a tree, or pulpit, and defecate on Gulliver because he has attacked them with a sword for no reason except that he dislikes the way they look.

In this last episode, Swift takes us into the not-too-distant future when atheism will have gained the upper hand in Britain. The Horse was an emblem of philosophical atheism, based on a line of interpretation of Psalm 32:19, "Be ye not as the horse, which has no understanding."

Donne has an entire sermon on that verse and theme. Gulliver's unprovoked attack on the Yahoo elders represents a modern hatred of the clergy about which Swift complains, but in Houynhnmland he shows it being carried to the extreme limit.

The Yahoos, who bear the name of Yahweh and are his people, represent the Church after it has been trampled for a couple of generations under the hoof of atheists. It is now reduced to Primitive silence again and its members, who are seen as vicious and dangerous, are slated for extermination.

The fourth voyage is a dark parable revealing Swift's profound fear of what is in store for Christianity at the start of the Enlightenment. His response to widespread blasphemy and hatred of the clergy, as he tells us in his "Ode to Sancroft," is to put on "anger" and "spite" and go off to battle with his pen,

To make them understand, and feel me when I write;
The muse and I no more revenge desire,
Each line shall stab, shall blast, like daggers and like fire....

Chapter 15

Swift in and Out of the Pulpit

As a spokesman for the Church of Ireland Swift's views are hardly ambiguous. He was a fierce defender of church doctrines and prerogatives. He saw the church as besieged by secular and sectarian enemies. He never tired of arguing that the church must prevail if society were to survive intact. He urged anyone who questioned the importance of an established church to think hard about the English revolution. And he identified Christianity so strongly with the church that toward the end of his life he wrote his friend Charles Ford that opposition to the church in both England and Ireland had made him give up "all hopes of.Christianity" (Correspondence 4: 505).

Dissenters, he insisted, were not motivated by theological or liturgical concerns, but by the "Spirit of Opposition" (Prose Works 2: 34.) They aspired to power, not purity. He refused to acknowledge that freethinkers might be engaged in honest inquiry, afflicted by honest doubts, in search of greater clarity. All they really wanted, he said, was freedom from moral restraint.

Swift preached sermons on the superiority of Christianity to Greek philosophy and on the need to believe in the Trinity whether one understood it or not. He wrote that the biblical account of Creation seemed "most agreeable of all others to probability and reason." He was uncompromising in his support of the Test Act and scornful of republican governments for "treating Christianity as a System of Speculative Opinions, which no Man should be bound to believe" (Prose Works 3: 49).

In his *Letter to a Young Gentleman, Lately entered into Holy Orders,* Swift argues that Christianity triumphed over Greek and Roman philosophy because it could draw on a source of power greater than intelligence or firmness of character. "The true Misery of the Heathen World," he said, was "the Want of a Divine Sanction; without which, the Dictates of the Philosophers failed in the Point of Authority" (Prose Works 9: 73).

The ancient philosophers had no notion of "relying" on Providence; they would not have understood what it meant to place one's trust in God; they "trusted in themselves for all things," and therefore, Swift said, had no sure recourse in hard times: "upon every blow of adverse fortune, [they] either affected to be indifferent, or grew sullen and severe, or else yielded and sunk like other men" (Prose Works 9: 245-46).

More importantly, the ancient philosophers were never able to posit a compelling reward for virtue. "Human nature is so constituted," he argued, "that we can never pursue any thing heartily but upon hopes of a reward." As for the notion that virtue is its own reward, Swift said that if there was "any thing in this more than the sound of the words, it is.too abstracted to.be of general use" (Prose Works 9: 244). But Heaven and Hell are concepts even the simplest person can understand; they are, Swift insists, in one of his sermons, "the great Principle for Conscience to work upon" (Prose Works 9: 156), and essential to the welfare of society.

"Great Abilities, without the Fear of God," are most dangerous Instruments when they are trusted with Power. The Laws of Man have thought fit, that those who are called to any Office of Trust should be bound by an Oath to the faithful Discharge of it: But, an Oath is an Appeal to God, and therefore can have no Influence except upon those who believe that he is...a Rewarder of those that seek him, and a Punisher of those who disobey him." (Prose Works 9: 156-57)

As a public spokesman for the church, then, Swift's views are absolutely straightforward. He sought to secure its position from attack, to discredit the motives of those who took part in such attacks, and to demonstrate that Christianity itself, particularly the doctrine of eternal rewards and punishments, is the only sure foundation of moral life. Elsewhere in his writings, though, we run up against more problematical reflections. Consider this strange entry in the disgruntled journal Swift kept at Holyhead while waiting for the weather to clear so he could get a ship to Ireland:

"...Last night I dreamt that Ld Bolingbroke and Mr Pope were at my Cathedrall in the Gallery, and that my Ld was to preach. I could not find my Surplice, the Church Servants were all out of the way; the Doors were shut. I sent to my Ld to come into my Stall for more conveniency to get into the Pulpit. The Stall was all broken; the[y] sd the Collegians had done it. I squeezed among the Rabble, saw my Ld in the Pulpit. I thought his prayer was good, but I forget it. In his Sermon, I did not like his quoting Mr. Wycherly by name, and his Plays...." (Prose Works 5: 205-06)

Looked at one way, this dream is a major psychic affront, a nightmare of impropriety, violation, and loss that assails Swift's dignity on several cherished grounds. His pulpit is usurped by Bolingbroke, who, though a friend, was also an outspoken deist. Worse yet, Bolingbroke quotes Wycherley. Meanwhile, Swift not only loses his surplice, he loses control of the Church servants, who vanish just when he needs them. As if this were not bad enough, undergraduates from his old college advertise their disrespect by wrecking his stall, leaving him to hear the offensive sermon 'squeezed among the Rabble.'

But we should not forget that while Swift is the authority mocked in this dream, he is also the one who conjures up the mockery. In dreams, Addison observed, the soul "converses with numberless Beings of her own Creation...is transported into ten thousand Scenes of her own raising...is herself the Theatre, the Actors, and the Beholder" (Spectator 487). Johnson once dreamt that someone got the better of him in argument.

He brooded over the defeat till it dawned on him that the dream was, after all, his dream. "I should have seen," he told Bennet Langton, "that the wit of this supposed antagonist, by whose superiority I felt myself depressed, was as much furnished by me, as that which I thought I had been uttering in my own character." Swift himself wrote, in memorable imitation of Petronius, that dreams are never sent downward from Jove or up from the Devil's "infernal Mansions"; they are "mere Productions" of our own brains ("On Dreams," ll. 1-5). It is perhaps worth recalling here that when an undergraduate at Trinity, Swift was cited for an unusually large number of disciplinary infractions, once for starting "tumults" in the college and insulting the junior dean, whose pardon he was forced to beg on bended knee.

So in this dream we may say that Swift is not only the insulted dean, he is also those agencies of anarchy and irreverence: Bolingbroke, the neglectful servants, the rowdy students. However scrupulous Swift's public behavior, however militant his service to the church, in the dream he goes on holiday, makes mischief in the pulpit, "loses" his surplice and refuses to look for it, creates havoc in the stalls, then squeezes in among the rabble where he is safe from detection. This final touch seems an apt metaphor for the way Swift's irony often dissociates him from unseemly thoughts.

Swift's dream of cathedral monkey business epitomizes the problem of gauging his true religious convictions. In his satires, we often rub up against things that don't square with the orthodox assertions of the religious tracts and sermons. In his ironical attack on the famous free thinker Anthony Collins, for example, Swift spectacularly ignores his own advice that clergymen should not preach against atheism. To do so, he said, is to risk perplexing "the Minds of well-disposed People with Doubts, which probably would never have otherwise come into their Heads" (Prose Works 9: 78).

Here are a few of the things Swift gives "well-disposed people" to think about as he parodies Collins: first, that many other cultures in the world have scriptures they believe to be divinely inspired, and that some of those scriptures contain striking parallels to the New Testament: "the Bonzes in China have theirs, written by the Disciples of Of-he, whom they call God and Saviour of the World, who was born to teach the way of Salvation, and to give satisfaction for all Men's Sins"; the clergy of Siam "have a Book of Scripture written by

Sommonocodum, who, the Siamese say, was born of a Virgin, and was the God expected by the Universe; just as our Priests tell us, that Jesus Christ was born of the Virgin Mary, and was the Messiah so long expected" (Prose Works 4: 32); second, that the Bible itself is so complex a work that a bishop said he thought it more "a Trial of our Industry than a Repository of our Faith" (Prose Works 4: 33); third, that learned Christians cannot even agree about such central articles of faith as original sin and the resurrection of the dead.

Swift was, of course, writing under cover of satire. In later years, Pope would tease him about the effectiveness of that cover: "your method of concealing your self puts me in mind of the bird I have read of in India, who hides his head in a hole, while all his feathers and tail stick out" (Correspondence 4: 217-218) From no work of Swift's do more feathers protrude than from A Tale of a Tub. As Voltaire recognized, the central religious allegory in which a father leaves coats to each of his three sons, with instructions not to alter them in any way, has subversive implications.

The father's most striking quality is not rectitude, or love for his children, but determination to exercise power over them after he is gone. The will he leaves instructs his sons on the care of the coats, threatens them with penalties for "every Transgression or Neglect," and warns them that their "future Fortunes will entirely depend" on following his wishes to the letter (Prose Works 1: 44). The will does not explain why such exacting care of the coats should matter.

In the "Apology" he wrote for the fifth edition of the Tale Swift said he could not understand why anybody should think the it dangerous when other books "are kindly received, because they are levell'd to remove those Terrors that Religion tells Men will be the Consequence of immoral Lives. Nothing like which is to be met with in this Discourse..." (Prose Works 1: 2). His footnotes to the story of the coats, however, tell us straightout that the father represents "the Divine Founder," and the will, "the Doctrine and Faith of Christianity" (Prose Works 1: 44).

Considering that the brothers never seem to suffer any of

their father's threatened penalties, it is hard to see how the allegory really supports belief in those salutary "Terrors" Swift says are so essential to religion. One can argue that going mad, as do two of the brothers, is penalty enough. But one can just as well argue that Peter and Jack would never have lost their wits had their father left them the coats to wear as they saw fit, or had the brothers ignored the will and gone about their business. One hard-headed moral of the story might be that the father has no power except the power his sons accord him in their minds.

Did Swift privately believe eternal rewards and punishments—that "great Principle for Conscience to work upon"—exist only in the minds of believers? Perhaps he did. In his Thoughts on Religion, Swift describes love of life as an extraordinarily irrational impulse. Were people guided by "the dictates of reason, every man would despise [life], and wish it at an end" (Prose Works 9: 263). But if there truly are terrible punishments for vice in the hereafter, and if the world is as full of knaves as Swift continually assures us, why would it be rational for "every man" to wish life at an end?

When preaching, Swift argues that the "excellency" of Christianity is that it enables ordinary people to achieve a nobility they would never otherwise attain by making virtue and self-interest one: "the primitive Christians...were altogether the product of their principles and doctrine," whereas "the great examples of wisdom and virtue, among the Grecian sages were produced by personal merit, and not influenced by the doctrine of any particular sect" (Prose Works 9:249).

While it is true, he says, "that there hath been all along in the world a notion of rewards and punishments in another life...it seems to have rather served as an entertainment to poets, or as a terror of children, than a settled principle, by which men pretended to govern any of their actions. The last celebrated words of Socrates, a little before his death, do not seem to reckon or build much upon any such opinion" (Prose Works 9:245).

Yet it is precisely the individual merit of men like Socrates (fellow master of irony) that most attracted Swift. He owned a signet ring with the head of Socrates, and often used this seal when signing important documents. Swift preached that the doctrine of future rewards and punishments was important for ordinary people, but it is by no means clear how much real efficacy he thought that doctrine had. The most immoral people Gulliver encounters on his travels, the Lilliputians, are also the only people said to believe in Divine Providence, an afterlife, and a system of rewards and punishments.

Their case for making belief in God a prerequisite for public office sounds exactly like the case Swift often made: "since Kings avow themselves to be the Deputies of Providence, the Lilliputians think nothing can be more absurd than for a Prince to employ such Men as disown the Authority under which he acteth" (Prose Works 11:44). No one else Gulliver visits even seems to have a religion, except for the Brobdingnagians, who, to judge from the description of their great temple, "adorned on all Sides with Statues of Gods and Emperors," are polytheists (Prose Works 11:98). As for the Houyhnhnms, they regard death just as Swift said reasonable people should, without "the least Regret" (Prose Works 11:258).

Swift's last, and most moving poem to Stella, written when she was gravely ill, acknowledges the importance of future rewards, then side-steps the doctrine to offer consolation of a more immediate sort:

Were future Happiness and Pain,
A mere Contrivance of the Brain,
As Atheists argue, to entice,
And Fit their Proselytes for Vice...
Grant this the Case, yet sure 'tis hard,
That Virtue, stil'd its own Reward...
Should acting, die, nor leave behind
Some lasting Pleasure in the Mind,
Which by Remembrance will assuage,
Grief, Sickness, Poverty, and Age
And strongly shoot a radiant Dart,
To shine through Life's declining Part.

Say, Stella, feel you no Content,
Reflecting on a Life well spent?
(ll. 19-22, 25-26, 29-36)

The allegory of the coats in A Tale of a Tub raises unsettling questions about the "Divine Founder's" arbitrariness and the nature of his power; the "Digression on Madness" in the Tale raises potentially unsettling questions about the origin of Christianity: "if we take a Survey of the greatest Actions that have been performed in the World," one of which is "the contriving, as well as the propagating, of New Religions: We shall find the Authors of them all" to be mad (Prose Works 1: 102). No sane person would dream of "subduing Multitudes to his...Visions" (Prose Works 1: 108).

Indeed, the importance of preserving established religion is so persistent a theme in Swift's later writings, that he insists even a change to a new, "more pure and perfect [religion] may be an Occasion of endangering the publick Peace; because, it will compose a Body always in Reserve, prepared to follow any discontented Heads, upon the plausible Pretexts of advancing true Religion, and opposing Error, superstition, or Idolatry. For this Reason, Plato lays it down as a Maxim, that Men ought to worship the Gods, according to the Laws of the Country; and he introduceth Socrates, in his last Discourse, utterly disowning the Crime laid to his Charge, of teaching new Divinities, or Methods of Worship." (Prose Works 2: 11-12)

But what of the new divinity and method of worship taught by St. Paul? Claiming certain knowledge of "things agreed on all hands impossible to be known" (p. 166) is the sure sign of madness. How are we to distinguish Jesus from other propagators of new religions? The predictable answer, and the answer Swift gives in his sermons, is, of course, that Christianity is not the vision of a single man, but the revelation of divine will. A common response to this question in the period, was to argue that we can know the apostles were divinely inspired, rather than deluded enthusiasts, because their claims had empirical support: miracles.

In his sermon On the Trinity, though, Swift reverses the

argument, saying not that miracles prove the authenticity of Scriptural revelation, but that miracles are so contrary to the "Rules of Nature and Reason" we would never believe them unless they were affirmed by Scripture: "It is against the Laws of Nature, that a Human Body should be able to walk upon the Water...or that a dead Carcase should be raised from the Grave after three Days...Yet these Miracles, and many others, are positively affirmed in the Gospel; and these we must believe, or give up our Holy Religion to Atheists and Infidels." (Prose Works 9: 165-66)

In other words, we should believe because the consequences of disbelief are unthinkable: "Men should consider, that raising Difficulties concerning the Mysteries in Religion, cannot make them more wise, learned, or virtuous; better Neighbours, or Friends, or more serviceable to their Country; but, whatever they pretend, will destroy their inward Peace of Mind, by perpetual Doubts and Fears arising in their Breasts" (Prose Works 9: 166-67). This is as close as Swift gets to discussing the need for religion from the inside. He talks about God as the ultimate authority for doctrines of imperative social importance, about crimes against social order being crimes against God, but about individual relationships to God he says remarkably little.

What comes across most powerfully in Swift's references to God is a sense of God's remoteness and unknowability. Swift dismisses people's claims to have had direct experience of spiritual agencies—good or evil—as intoxications of pride: "I laugh aloud to see these Reasoners...engaged in wise Dispute...whether they are in the Verge of God or the Devil, seriously debating...whether certain Passions and Affections are guided by the Evil Spirit or the Good....it is a Sketch of Human Vanity, for every Individual, to imagine the whole Universe is interess'd in his meanest Concern. Who, that sees a little paultry Mortal, droning, and dreaming, and drivelling to a Multitude, can think it agreeable to common good Sense, that either Heaven or Hell should be put to the Trouble of Influence or Inspection upon what he is about" (Prose Works 1: 180).

One of the few altogether personal religious rituals we know Swift observed was to read the third chapter of Job every year on his birthday. That it should be the third chapter, rather than the explanatory prologue or the celebratory epilogue, is telling. For it is in the third chapter that Job curses the day he was born and asks "Why is light given to a man whose way is hid,/ And whom God hath hedged in?" In a sermon, Swift might hold up Abraham as exemplifying the power of faith, extoll his readiness to believe "that God would raise from him a great Nation, at the very same time that he was commanded to sacrifice his only Son, and despaired of any other Issue"(Prose Works 9: 163).

But Job is a figure to touch his heart. Job epitomized the kind of undeserved suffering with which Swift identified so readily. Swift's letters and private writings are filled with complaints of unearned misfortune—from the great fish that dropped off his line when he was a little boy to the preferment that eluded him in England. The weaknesses he confesses to friends are less moral failures, than failures of power visited on him by sickness or age: loss of memory, of stamina, of invention, of the ability to do serious work. It is impossible to imagine Swift standing four hours in the rain, like Johnson, to atone for some long ago act of thoughtlessness.

It is easy to imagine him asking Job's questions—"Wherefore do the wicked live,/ Become old, yea, wax mighty in power?"—and hearing in return something like that voice of inscrutable power out of the whirlwind: "Where wast thou when I laid the foundations of the earth?" In the Essay on Man, Pope continually reminds readers to "presume not God to scan." But he reminds them with an assurance that suggests he pretty much knows what God had in mind for the world:

Why has not Man a microscopic eye?
For this plain reason, Man is not a Fly. (I, 193-94)

The God of Swift's poem "On the Day of Judgment" is much like the God of Job: aloof, implacable, something of a trickster.

Of all the stories that bear on Swift's religious outlook, I think the most haunting is Deane Swift's account of a Sunday visit to Swift two years after he had been declared of unsound mind. Swift was sitting in a chair, and when he reached for a knife that lay on the table, his housekeeper moved it away. Deane Swift recalls that Swift shrugged his shoulders, and, rocking back and forth, said, "I am what I am, I am what I am: and, about six minutes afterwards, repeated the same words two or three times over" (Correspondence, 5: 214).

The words may mean nothing. They may mean only that despite loss of powers Swift still knows who and what he is—more than can be said of Gulliver, who at the end of his travels studies himself in a mirror yet continues to think himself what he is not: a Houyhnhnm. But inasmuch as the words are St. Paul's, who Swift cites more than perhaps any other figure in the Old or New Testament, they invite a larger reading. Paul had been speaking of the promise of eternal life offered all people through Christ's Resurrection, and of his own place among those who witnessed it:

"...And last of all he was seen of me also, as one born out of due time. For I am the least of the apostles, that am not meet to be called an apostle, because I persecuted the church of God. But by the grace of God I am what I am: and his grace which was bestowed upon me was not in vain; but I laboured more abundantly than they all" (I Corinthians, xv, 8-11)

It is tempting to see flitting across Swift's mind, some deeply personal and darkly ironic sense of kinship with Paul. Like Paul, he had been "born out of due time." Like Paul he had not come early or easily to the Church. Like Paul, his writings had been misunderstood. And he, too, had tried to make up for his lateness by laboring "more abundantly than they all," fighting, as he had told Lady Worsley ten years before, "with Beasts like St. Paul, not at Ephesus, but in Ireland" (Correspondence 4: 79). This labor might well have seemed abundant to Swift because he appears to have performed it without Paul's experience of personal revelation, without Abraham's faith, which embraced impossibility and contradiction, and without clear expectation of that personal reward he assured his parishioners was the very basis of Christianity.

Chapter 16

The Satirist and His Faith

Writing about Swift, is always a difficult, but fascinating, task. And writing about him in the house built upon the site of his very own Deanery is particularly interesting. Is he listening? If he is, I hope that he appreciates that in the following paper on his early published attitude to dissenters I do not seek a window into his soul. I merely wish to look at what he wrote in the context of what his contemporaries may have understood by it in the reign of Queen Anne.

Swift, I believe, like the good public relations man (or spin doctor) that he was, always had an eye on the impression that his writing would make. And writing about dissenters for his fellow English and Irish countrymen (and women) was not merely writing about religion. It was about writing about the way they wanted the country governed and, more pertinently, who they wanted to govern it.

Faith in early 18C England was inextricably bound up with political ideology and religious practice. As a result of the civil wars, jealousy over career opportunities, and all that that entailed, loyalty to one church or other became a party statement. In this paper I will look at how this antagonism and downright sectarianism can be seen to have influenced Swift's writing about dissenters, those protestants whose refusal to accept the terms and conditions of the Established Church seemed to early eighteenth century Anglicans to be undermining the rights and privileges upon which their society was built.

During Swift's lifetime Anglicans' perceptions concerning those outside their own religion was anything but ecumenical.

If Roman Catholicism (and James II) had endangered the relationship of the monarch and his people, it was the dissenters, nominally Protestants, who through being associated with the Commonwealth had threatened the very basis of the English monarchical system. Throughout the last half of the seventeenth century they had therefore, in way or another, in the eyes of the Anglicans caused the near break up of the English nation.

During Queen Anne's reign, in less dramatic fashion, but equally insidiously, they once again appeared, at least to the Tories, to be threatening the very fabric of English society by the back door. The apparent reliance of the dissenters upon money rather than land, their infiltration of the political system and their support of the Whigs made them suspect to the land owning Tories who had considered power to be prerogative of estate.

The concessions made through the practice of occasional conformity branded them, it could be argued, as the silent enemy, far less trustworthy than even the Roman Catholics and their incompetent figure-head the Old Pretender. Nor did it go entirely without comment that the rot appeared to have started from the very top, with William III attending Dutch Calvinist services in his native Holland, and receiving dissenting ministers with some sympathy when in England. At least this was the true Blue Tory version.

I will suggest therefore, that when we look at Swift's attitude to Dissenters, particularly as 'published' through his pamphlets and journalism, it displays a distinct sensibility to the nuances of hardening Tory attitudes, even before he was designated such and certainly before he was a party writer. Clearly, Swift if only by his faith, was bound up with his support of the status quo . It is therefore a point worth making that his depiction of dissenters underwent considerable changes in his most popular works from the end of the seventeenth century until the end of Anne's reign.

It is surely no coincidence that the beginning of Swift's brilliant career in satire and A Tale of a Tub coincided with the ineffectual Blasphemy Act of 1697, which attempted, but failed to stem the flow of anti-clerical tracts and treaties. Whatever the arguments about Swift's early Whiggism, his natural Tory-ness and his therefore natural distrust of dissenters seems to have found some outlet in his *Tale of Tub* and its partner *The Mechanical Operation of the Spirit.*

If we take a longitudinal view of Swift's published opinions on dissenters, they change in tone dramatically with the balance of power. A*Tale of a Tub,* was written in the late 1690s. At this point dissenters, although distrusted by good Anglicans, were supported by the status quo. The Tory Right had not hardened into an identifiable and cohesive force. *The Tale* sits in this accommodating atmosphere as an almost cheerful satire, with a burlesque view of 'Jack' Calvin as he tears the New Testament coat into ribbons, and perverts his 'Father's' will. The scatological twinkle in Swift's eye is clearly present as Jack's ludicrous adherence to the very text of the New Testament is taken to its extreme when, unable to find the 'authentic phrase' for directions to the toilet he fouls himself, and then in equally strict, but with even dafter logic, he refuses to clean himself up, because he 'met with a passage near the bottom' – what carefully chosen words! – 'which seemed to forbid it'.

The satire, while still apparent in the 'follow up' to *A Tale, The Mechanical Operation of the Spirit* has a distinctly bitter edge. The belching and humming Aeolists, lampooned for tilting at windmills and fearing the air-gulping chameleon, become far more sinister. The trapped wind of the Banbury 'Saint' becomes the origin of the peculiar nasal tone supposedly used by puritan preachers.

Throughout this text, Swift's anger (in a metaphorically apt way) bubbles to the surface, his pen excoriates instead of teasing. In the place of allegory and symbolism, and an almost affectionate disapproval of the silly brothers, Peter and Jack, the dissenters are named, and shamed: 'John of Leyden, David George, Adam Neuster ... whose visions and revelations always terminated in leading about half a dozen sisters a-piece.'

As though intending to bring the point home, Swift shortly

after this focuses on the Quakers and their 'visionary devotion', which simply acts a spur for 'inflaming brotherly love' that inevitably proceeds to 'raise that of a gallant'. Again, this bitterness may well have been informed by the reformulation of the factions after 1697, where as the church historian G.V. Bennett describes it, the 'new High Church party' began to attack William's ministers without mercy, and no doubt to Swift's horror, the Church of Ireland seemed 'dead on its feet'. While Swift's language is strong, either in its (albeit jovial) satire or its invective, and while we can see the firm foundations of the hostility embedded in the politics of this period, Swift's texts still fall short of the anger with which Tories attacked just a few years later.

If we go forward another few years to 1708 Swift's position had now shifted so that he was beginning to be personally implicated in the balance of power between Anglicans and Dissenters. At this time he produced two pamphlets which similarly to the previous pair show two sides of his print-views about the erosion of the Church of England's power-base.

One, *An Argument against Abolishing Christianity,* shows Swift in an equally ironic, if less playful mood than in *A Tale of a Tub*. The problem of the dissenter had, however, become more urgent, and Swift's more direct strategy is politically more effective. At the time of writing, in the newly unified Britain of 1708, there was a general election in the offing or in progress, and the Pretender had just launched a lack-lustre though much feared invasion attempt. While the all-powerful Whigs continued to suggest that the Tory and Stuart causes were somehow linked, the threat to the hegemony of the Church of England seemed ever stronger from opponents from the other end of the religious scale, the Dissenters.

The Anglican's hope, Secretary of State Robert Harley (although he himself came from a dissenting family) had resigned under a cloud and the Godolphin and Marlborough Ministry was finally forced to succumb to the Whigs in order to guarantee continued funding of the War of the Spanish Succession If the *Argument* was written during this period of a likely, and subsequently confirmed, Whig landslide it is hardly surprising that Swift exhibits a disquiet for the future of the Established Church.

His opening comments that it was 'neither safe nor prudent' to support 'Christianity at a juncture when all parties appear so unanimously determined' to abolish it seem to place it perfectly at this historical moment. *Argument* is littered with ironic gems. With his tongue firmly in his cheek Swift suggests that only fifty years previously (during the hey-day of Cromwell's dissenting inter-regnum) 'a project for the abolishing of Christianity' would have been considered absurd. Is it because it would have been impossible to abolish an Established Church that no longer existed in a world of dissenters? With the same kind of double bluff he insists that he is not suggesting the restoration of the 'real' Christianity – the kind that Christ practised. Indeed, he argues, the economy, the arts and the sciences could never withstand that kind of shock – lip service to primitive Christianity is all he seeks, which he implies is all that the money-driven Dissenters give, even though they claim to be the real successors to the Primitive Church.

The *Sentiments of a Church of England Man* is altogether a more political document. Its serious tone presents as a contrast to the *Argument* just *the Mechanical Operation of the Spirit* offers the 'hard' edge to *A Tale of a Tub*. Despite his claims that he is not accusing either Whigs or Tories of any desire to alter the status quo, almost immediately he points out that since the 'Presbyterians, Anabaptists, Independents, and other sects' found themselves united against the Church in the early days of the Restoration, 'present dissenters do naturally close in with the Whigs, who profess moderation', and they will not prevent the dissenters being 'denied the privilege and profit of serving their country'.

Tory Anglicans, already smarting under the lack of opportunity for 'privilege and profit' under the Whig administration, could surely see the danger signs which Swift clearly flags for them. Sects are 'mistaken'. Dissension is 'evil'. But most significantly, dissenters should not be allowed to 'advance their own models upon the ruin of what is already established'. In a state where religion is intrinsic to the government, this is a roundabout way of saying that dissenters should have no part in legislature.

This is an attack on the Whigs who, Swift claims, are not 'over nice', that is over precise, in distinguishing between an 'unlimited liberty of conscience and unlimited freedom of opinion'. In this way they appear to be willing to allow these 'free-thinkers' to the 'highest employment so state'. After all, unlike the true Church of England man, why should these 'free-thinkers', once admitted to the 'highest employments' not take the opportunity to change the rules? A dissenter does not have the 'true veneration for the scheme established among us of ecclesiastical government'. While Swift's words say 'ecclesiastical government', do they not also imply 'government' in general? For a depressed Tory electorate, what might come next?

Earlier in the text Swift had already planted the seed that each man believes himself to have a 'real share' in public affairs. When it changes from an 'imaginary' one to an actual one, as he projects in the case of the dissenters, where can this lead? As he astutely points out, 'when those who dislike the constitution, are so very zealous in their offers for the service of their country they are not wholly unmindful of their party or of themselves'.

He suggests it is unnervingly similar to the treatment they were receiving before the Glorious Revolution when they could be coupled with the Roman Catholics in order to outflank the Anglicans. The linking continues by yoking together all the things which would raise a good Church of England man's hackles: Swift suggests the dissenters are simultaneously talking about 'our brethren the Roman Catholics' while complaining that they are still being accused of murdering Charles I. This kind of propaganda was clearly in the political air at the time.

Comparing it with a draft pamphlet that Robert Harley was also writing in 1708. Harley, later Earl of Oxford, led the Tories to victory in the 1710 election, by which time he had become a great friend and patron Swift's. In his paper Harley echoes Swift's concerns that the dissenters are being favoured by the Whigs in order to win their support. He wonders how everyone 'does not every one see how a faction [the Whigs] has been industriously kindled & perverted in the Church upon the frivolous pretences, to what other purpose but that socinianisme, Arianisme, Deisme, & all manner of absurd opinions against Christianity and common morality might flourish and encrease; while the orthodox members are discountenanced and disgraced'.

Harley was as concerned as Swift about the influence of the dissenters in national government – he suggests that it is akin to the troubles the Church of England found itself in before the Glorious Revolution. This comment on how well the dissenters were being treated in comparison to those who should have been favoured matches Swift's concession that the dissenters could have as much liberty of conscience as they like – but no power!

I finish my discussion of the *Sentiments* with this mockingly liberal attitude to dissenters before moving onto *The Examiner* because Swift's writing clearly continues to focus on them. Not surprisingly, his tone becomes more savage when he begins to write for the Tory ministry's mouthpiece. The Tory-line antagonism was undoubtedly reinforced by the sweeping political changes that had occurred in the two years between the 1708 election and the inception of the *Examiner* in August 1710.

By the time Swift took over its pages, the Tories had triumphed in the 1710 elections, partly on a 'Church in danger' ticket. The enthusiasm for the Church had continued at a high point after the commotion caused by the trial of the High Church Dr Sacheverell and his triumphant performance at his impeachment for preaching a rabidly High Tory anti-Whig ministry sermon at St Paul's in the previous year.

We have to bear these changes in mind when reading Swift's *Examiner* and particularly his heightened denunciation of the dissenters and all they stood for. We should recall his claim not to be a 'bigot in religion' that he made in *Sentiments of a Church of England Man*, because frankly, his comments on non-Anglican protestants are inflammatory. Politically, this already places Swift in the red hot Tory Secretary of State St John's camp.

Harley, clearly thinking of the damage that might have followed if he had published his earlier proto-pamphlet, had made overtures to the dissenters prior to the election. He had offered them financial inducements in an effort to seduce them from the Whigs.

Meanwhile, the other wing of the party (led by St. John, the man who was Harley's rival for leadership) were virulently attacking the dissenters. Indeed, their followers had already done it physically during Sacheverell's trial, destroying dissenting meeting-houses. Therefore, Swift's sneer in his first *Examiner*, No 14 at the early Whigs who had begun by 'caressing the Dissenters' and his continued sniping at the non-conformists continued right through Swift's period in the editor's chair. If we look at this logically, it seems quite peculiar, since it was his political patron, Harley who had just been doing precisely the same caressing.

If I finished the paper at this point, it would seem fairly obvious that Swift's personal opinion on Dissenters follows entirely in the footsteps of his published one. However, as always with Swift it's not that easy. When reading his letters, in which there are not that many opinions expressed about Dissenters anyway, it appears that this may well that this antagonism may be as much a 'political' attitude as a spiritual one.

There is no question that he is opposed to the repeal of the Test Act, which lays down attendance at Church as a prerequisite to official office. In 1703, 1708 and 1711 he vigorously denounces the move to his fellow clerics in Dublin, particularly Archbishop King. However, we should recall that this Act was primarily a political one, intended to ring fence political and official office away from Dissenters and Roman Catholics.

In terms of his attitude to dissenters on a personal level, he seems remarkably relaxed. He refers to Mr Shute, appointed Secretary to Lord Wharton ironically as a 'Moderate' man, who attends the 'Church and Meeting House indifferently', but also as a 'young man, ... reckoned the shrewdest Head in England'. To be called 'Moderate' was not necessarily a compliment at this point (it was more of a suggestion of accommodating and unscrupulous compliance) but if we can be permitted to judge Swift's tone through the letter, it is not one of bitter condemnation. It is more amused admiration at the slick operator that Mr Shute is generally judged to be.

And, even more significantly, in 1711, when he spitting venom at the Dissenters through the pages of the *Examiner* he seems perfectly happy to spend time with William Penn the Quaker, if his letters to his friend Stella in Dublin are to be believed. In fact on 7 October 1711 he was happily ensconced with Harley, Harley's son-in-law and Penn, 'drinking as good wine as you do', while only two months later he was declaring that 'while the Dissenters, to gratify their Ambition and Revenge, fell into the basest Compliances with the Court'.

Where does this leave us? I would suggest that we should not take Swift's published writing on Dissenters at face value. As so often with Swift and his journalistic contemporaries, we should not make assumptions that his heart, rather than his head, lies behind everything that he wrote. Instead, I would look at the historical context of much of it and suggest that Swift was a canny writer. He knew better than most the effect of words on the electorate. This made him a brilliant and effective propagandist, but not necessarily an inveterate hater of dissenters.

Chapter 17

Jonathan Swift's 'On the Day of Judgement'

In seeking to understand this poem by the Dean of Saint Patrick's, we might adopt any of several approaches. If we were to seize on its theme, then it would be possible to place it in a reading of the remarkably few religious poems which Swift composed. Modifying this rather limiting perspective, we might concede that in Swift's Ireland, religion was never wholly separable from politics. Read in this light, 'On the Day of judgement' would be judged in connection with its author's expressed views on the relative claims of Catholics, Protestants and Presbyterians within the state.

There again, if we refresh our memory of the poem itself, two further possibilities are opened up. First, the opening lines conjure a situation which for long was regarded as peculiarly distinctive in this poet - that of obsessive, involuntary terror, delusions amounting almost to madness, more specifically in this case, the terror of nightmare:

With a whirl of thought oppressed
I sink from reverie to rest.
A horrid vision seized my head
I saw the graves give up their dead.

Through the power of intervening tradition concerning Swift's mental state, these lines lure us to read the poem biographically. Given that there is scant evidence to associate it with Swift in his lifetime - it was first published in 1773, and no author's holograph has ever been found - it has about it an odd air of hindsight directed at the putative author.

Finally, there is the question of Swift's poetic style, his use of the higher doggerel as a vehicle for serious work.

A second detail of the text, however, rescues us from that temptation, without leading us out of all others. The repetition of Jove's name in the course of its twenty-two lines serves to remind us of the classical-pagan framework in which the Christian theme of Judgement Day is pursued. Indeed, more than half of the poem is spoken in Jove's voice.

A crucial moment in the history of Irish denominational conflict came in 1733 with the proposal to repeal the Test Act, a part of the legislative code by which members of the non-established reformed churches were controlled by government. As Christopher Fauske points out in the latest study of Swift's engagement in ecclesiastical politics, the issue had preoccupied him much earlier.

In 1708, he had circulated a pseudonymous pamphlet, *Letter from a Member of the House of Commons in England, Concerning the Sacramental Test,* this at a time when his official business on behalf of the Irish Church should have counselled greater discretion. In 1733, the question prompted the poet rather than the pamphleteer, and the result was 'On the Words Brother Protestants and Fellow Christians', a piece of invective which impressed WB Yeats two hundred years later in the hate-filled 1930s.

Reading it now in conjunction with 'On the Day of Judgement', we can readily identity the notions of theological universalism and political toleration at work behind the rhymes. This is not to conclude Swift endorsed either notion, quite the contrary. But in a manner which takes us closer to him, a third question can be addressed. Acting as a kind of vanishing mediator between the two already mentioned is the doctrine of predestination, central to the Calvinist Presbyterian churches whom Swift so particularly distrusted and disliked.

Yet, rather than explore the 1733 poem for these weighty themes, I'd like to draw your attention to an odd moment of verbal convergence between the two poems. Each poems ends with the same rhyme - wit/bit - and it is instructive to consider each:

'On the Words...'
Let folks in high, or holy stations,
Be proud of owning such relations;
Let courtiers hug them in their bosom,
As if they were afraid to lose 'em:
While I, with humble Job, had rather,
Say to corruption, 'Thou'rt my father.'
For he that has so little wit,
To nourish vermin, may be bit.
'On the Day of Judgement'
The World's mad Business now is o'er,
And I resent these pranks no more.
I to such Blockheads set my Wit!
I damn such Fools - Go, go you're bit.

The identity of rhymes should not distract us from noting the contrast in sentiment. In the first poem, it is an absence of wit among the contending factions of religion which exposes them to satiric condemnation and the further humiliation of not even knowing their condition - to be 'bit' is to be deceived, taken in by their own fine distinctions. 'Bit' in this sense is a verb which can only be used passively. But in 'On the Day of Judgement' the speaker (Jove) actively directs his wit against such blockheads, revealing to them how they have been deceived - 'bitten'. Between identity and difference in the two pieces, one might note Swift's bitter implication that the typical pale sinner who will face his Maker is an Irish bigot.

If, for Swift, there was such a worrisome thing as 'the sin of wit', then it is possessed by the presiding Deity of the poem, albeit a pagan one, or the Christian God here passing under a pagan name. And at this point we might note a deeply concealed rhyme, of a kind scarcely recognised even by the industrious and ingenious Jakobsen. By utilising the principal Roman god as spokesman in his poem, Swift achieves an audacious absent rhyme on the shortest sentence in the Bible. God is J/Love (cf 1st Epistle of Saint John 4:16).

The belief that the Christian God was all forgiving and merciful has been difficult to reconcile with those of hell-fire and eternal punishment. Calvinist teaching on the subject of predestination, though more complex than many of its detractors think, presents a God who is far from Jovial. If, as some readers feel, Swift's poem leans towards universalism - the notion that, eventually, no-one is damned - then it can be seen as directed particularly against his Irish non-conformist contemporaries.

However, Jove does not simply dismiss the congregation of Irish bigots who monopolise his Judgement Day, he says with colloquial exaggeration -'I damn such Fools'. In a poem titled as this one is, however, the particular curse can hardly be dismissed as empty. In such a reading, Swift's poem hints at a negative universalism, at least in so far as the Irish bigot is truly representative of all sinners.

Is it possible to deduce anything of Swift's theology from the poem?

The dramatic use of Jove holds Christianity at arm's length, and additionally introduces a chasm between author and speaker which we ignore at our peril. And even if one concludes that the final lines imply a rejection of every kind of future state - you are all blockheads for fighting about this vacuous issue - nothing can diminish the ample prosaic evidence of Swift's support for the sacramental test and his hostility towards presbyterianism. Universalist he just might be, political liberal he sure wasn't. And if there is a universalism implied in the closing lines, then it is one of comprehensive damnation, not comprehensive salvation.

There remains one further approach to the poem which re-asserts its literary character. This would approach the poem as one which locates Jove within the speaker's unconsciousness and emphasises an unbroken continuity between the first ten lines and the twelve which follow. If the opening lines are, in some straight forward way, addressed to the reader, then so are the other lines which - by dramatic conceit - are ostensibly addressed by Jove to the full house attendance on the Last Day. To sin is, by implication, to read - or rather to mis-read in the contentious manner of sectarian rivals with their self-serving classifications of the damned and the elect.

Jove in fact observes four groups, the first of which

incorporates the other three. The entire 'offending race of humankind' is said to be 'By nature, reason, learning, blind.' Swift's compact syntax leaves indeterminate the question as to whether mankind is blinded by nature or blind by the standards of nature; the same can be said in relation to reason and learning. Has humankind blinded itself by learning; or - more difficult to imagine - is it blind to learning in some true sense of that last term?

The strong rhyme of humankind/blind underscores a condition which absolutely prohibits or prevents an act of reading. To sham reading when one is blind would be the most ludicrous act of delusion, just as aiming to see one's rivals damned is madness in a physically blind bigot. There is a sustained and consistent imagery of sight/blindness running right through the poem, from 'the horrid vision' of line three onwards, an imagery again consistent with the idea that the reader and the act of proper reading constitute the real subject of the poem.

The three sub-groups or instances of offensive mankind are, first, those who stepped aside, that is, adopted a passive attitude towards life. Ironically such a condition places them at the mercy of wit and - ironically again - wit knows no mercy.

Second are those who 'never fell ~ through pride';

And then climactically, the groups of those who 'in different sects have shammed'.

These are a complexly structured triad of sinful human types. The passive and the shammers represent the two extremes of one polarity. The middle ground is occupied by those who never fell, but resisted sin only because it was injurious to their own pride. Or, in an equally tenable reading, those who fell, but not through pride, are lacking even the Satanic qualities described at positve length by John Milton.

In conclusion, I want to suggest that it is the reader, especially any reader blinded by learning or sectarian passion, who is curtly dismissed by Swift's Jove. Commencing to study a poem solemnly entitled, 'On the Day of Judgement', he is rash if he expects to learn of that transcendent event which lies beyond all the properties and powers of human language.

One can hardly go further than the words of the Litany preserved in that Book of Common Prayer which Swift used in these precincts - 'In all time of our tribulation; in all time of our wealth; in the hour of death, and in the day of judgement, Good Lord deliver us.'

New readers of Swift most often encounter him for the first time through a reading of Gulliver's Travels. What is to be learned about the satirist and his faith from a reading of Swift's fictional masterpiece?

In Lilliput, there is endemic social division, exploited by the Monarchs of neighbouring Blefuscu, over whether eggs are to be broken at the larger end – the 'primitive Way', we are told, where the word 'primitive' has positive connotations as in 'primitive Christianity' – or whether the edict of the present King's grandfather, that eggs will be broken at the smaller end, should be obeyed.

In chapter 54 of the Brundrecal, Lilliput's holy book, it is written that 'all true Believers shall break their Eggs at the convenient End: and which is the convenient End, [adds Gulliver] seems, in my humble Opinion, to be left to every Man's Conscience, or at least in the Power of the chief Magistrate to determine'. (1.4).

Readers don't need super powers to spot the analogies being drawn between Lilliput and England in the reign of Queen Anne. The big-endian and little-endian controversy figures that between Protestantism and Catholicism that fissures Swift's own society. To reduce this to a ludicrous quarrel over the breaking of eggs is to suggest that nothing hinges on the difference. Did Swift really think that nothing hinged on it?

The two solutions proposed, though they are connected in Swift's sentence by an effortless grammatical conjunction, the reader might consider to be dramatically disjunct: there seems all the difference in the world between leaving such a question to 'every Man's Conscience' and leaving it 'in the Powers of the chief Magistrate to determine'. To Swift, however, the former needs the corrective of the latter because, as he writes in a sermon 'On the Testimony of Conscience':

"Hence have likewise arisen those Mistakes about what is usually called Liberty of Conscience; which, properly speaking, is no more than a Liberty of knowing our own Thoughts; which Liberty no one can take from us. But those words have obtained quite different Meanings: Liberty of Conscience is now-a-days not only understood to be the Liberty of believing what Men please, but also of endeavouring to propagate the Belief as much as they can, and to overthrow the Faith which the Laws have already established...And this is the Liberty of Conscience which the Fanaticks are now openly in the Face of the World endeavouring at with their utmost Application."

Gulliver's elevated detachment from the petty squabbles of the Lilliputians is not, then, quite the broad-minded tolerance that it appears to be.

In Brobdingnag, Gulliver gives it as his opinion that bishops are chosen "...by the Prince and wisest Counsellors, among such of the Priesthood, as were most deservedly distinguished by the Sanctity of their Lives, and the Depth of their Erudition; who were indeed the spiritual Fathers of the Clergy and the People' (2.6). But the King asks whether those holy Lords I spoke of, were constantly promoted to that Rank upon Account of their Knowledge in religious Matters, and the Sanctity of their Lives, had never been Compliers with the Times, while they were common Priests; or slavish prostitute Chaplains to some Nobleman, whose Opinions they continued servilely to follow after they were admitted into that Assembly...".

The King's question is suspiciously complex and acute. Did he really need both adjectives, 'slavish' and 'prostitute', to make his point? Behind it lies a narrative voice unconvinced that in Georgian England, priests are really advanced for their piety and learning.

At the end of Book III, Gulliver posing as a Dutch merchant tries to enter Japan, a country that, since 1638, had closed its ports to all nations except the Dutch. Gaining ingress requires compliance with the ritual of Yefumi, or trampling upon the crucifix, which, it seems, the Dutch are perfectly cheerful about doing. Gulliver asks to be excused, and the Emperor 'seemed a little surprised; and said, he believed I was the first of my Countrymen who ever made any Scruple in this Point; and that he began to doubt whether I were a real Hollander or no; but rather suspected I must be a Christian' (3.11).

So the point of this episode is to satirise the Dutch? Dutch Protestants are not Christians, or at least are willing to traduce their faith in the interests of trade? Is the animus, though, really against the Dutch, or does it glance at what Swift took to be an unholy alliance of the Orange dynasty with the ruling Whig elite, who permitted such freethinkers as John Toland to prosper, Toland who was ordered to leave Oxford for "...Trampling on the Common prayer book, talking against the Scriptures, commending Commonwealths, justifying the murder of K.C[harles] 1st, railing against Priests in general.."?

In Book 4, the Voyage to the Houyhnhnms, there is a reprise of the kind of satire that we have already seen in Book Gulliver informs his Houyhnhnm 'Master' of the 'State of England' and explains the most common causes of war:

"...Difference in Opinions hath cost many Millions of Lives: For Instance, whether Flesh be Bread, or Bread be Flesh: Whether the Juice of a certain Berry be Blood or Wine: Whether Whistling be a Vice or a Virtue: Whether it be better to kiss a Post, or throw it into the Fire: What is the best Colour for a Coat, whether Black, White, Red or Grey; and whether it should be long or short, narrow or wide, dirty or clean; with many more. (4.5)...".

This is more disturbing than the reduction of two major religions to a controversy over the breaking of eggs. Here, Gulliver deliberately vacuums out the meaning of the differences between Anglicanism, Catholicism and the various dissenting sects in the way he presents the case to the Houyhnhnm. The symbols of religious difference are substituted for the substance of religious difference, and the reader feels like leaping into the text to protest that this is not fair, that Gulliver is leaving too much out. From a conventional eighteenth-century religious standpoint, one of the most disturbing aspects of the sardonic utopia that is Houyhnhnmland is the attitude to death evinced there:

"...If they can avoid Casualties, they die only of old Age, and are buried in the obscurest Places that can be found, their Friends and Relations expressing neither Joy nor Grief at their Departure; nor does the dying Person discover the least Regret that he is leaving the World. (4.9)...". We are told that a Mare and her two foals ('a Mistress and her two Children') give as an excuse for being a little late for an appointment with Gulliver's master that her husband died late in the morning and it took a little time to determine his place of rest. This sanguine attitude to death, doing away with all Christian rituals and customs, might be impeccably orthodox if there were any mention of a future state of punishments and rewards beyond the life on earth.

Refusal to consider the existence of such a state was of course one of the primary objections to the writings of those same Deists and freethinkers that Swift excoriated throughout his early writings. Houhyhynm death customs, their solemn leave-takings of their friends, seem to be represented as consummations devoutly to be wished in GT. So-called 'soft' readers of GT, who consider the Houyhnhnms to be objects of satire, might not have much trouble with this, but I have always thought hardline soft readings, so to put it, unconvincing. Swift does intend this no-nonsense attitude to death to be seductive, but it is a dangerous, lotos-eaters pull that is being exerted.

The neophyte reader of Gulliver's Travels could be forgiven for thinking that its author was one of the most tolerant men who ever lived; a figure of the early enlightenment who, looking down with Olympian detachment at the petty squabbles and controversies of the age, urges us to see the characteristic differences between faiths and churches as 'matters indifferent', occluding the fundamental Christianity that we all share.

But I have tried to indicate that in all the places singled out above, Swift's liberalism is more apparent than real. Clues are planted in the text for the careful reader. The King of

Brobdingnag, for instance, appears a smiling, good-natured, 'easy' monarch:

"...He laughed at my odd Kind of Arithmetick...in reckoning the Numbers of our People by a Computation drawn from the several Sects among us in Religion and Politicks. He said, he knew no Reason, why those who entertain Opinions prejudicial to the Publick, should be obliged to change, or should not be obliged to conceal them. And, as it was Tyranny in any Government to require the first, so it was Weakness not to enforce the second: For, a Man may be allowed to keep Poisons in his Closet, but not to vend them about as Cordials. (2.6)...".

In other words, there should be no known, declared dissenters. The state should repress them. It is difficult to imagine that Swift really believed it possible to maintain such a distinction as this between privately-held and publicly-expressed views, but in fact it is entirely consonant with statements made in many other places in his writings. Attacking the Freethinkers in The Sentiments of a Church-of-England Man (1708), Swift relates them to dissenters and to Whigs, 'because They likewise preach up Moderation, and are not so over nice to distinguish between an unlimited Liberty of Conscience, and an unlimited Freedom of Opinion'. You can think whatever you like, believe whatever you like, as long as you never anywhere express your views and in so doing rock the boat of state. 'Fair Liberty was all his Cry', Swift famously said, summing up his own career in an autobiographical late poem.

Was it? Ruth Herman's paper has eloquently shown running through all of Swift's early writings a hardening of the line against the dissenters. It's only momentarily surprising that Swift's main animus should be reserved, not for the Catholics, but for those whose beliefs were in fact closest to his own church. Dissenters were traitors within the gates. They had brought civil society towards the verge of collapse during what Swift terms, following Clarendon, the 'rebellion', and now, in the first decade of the eighteenth century, owing to their influence in trading circles, they form part of a diabolical alliance with the Whig financial paladins. In the Examiner essays, Swift deploys the same breathtaking forcing of logic as he used to persuade the very much alive almanac-maker John Partridge that he had died, to show that the Whigs and their vanguard troops the dissenters and the freethinkers, are in fact the only true Jacobites.

Supporting toleration through the Declaration of Indulgence and now through the abolition of the Sacramental Test Act, they are the backdoor through which the Pretender will creep into power. Swift's fanatical support for the Test Act was based on the conviction that writers who were foolish enough to express views at variance with those of the established, state-sanctioned church, should not have civil rights. This paragraph from Examiner 30 for 22 February 1710 sums up Swift's views on the question of keeping stumm:

"...a Man may perhaps have little or none of it [Religion] at Heart; yet if he conceal his Opinions, if he endeavour to make no Proselytes, advance no impious Tenets in Writing or Discourse: If, according to the common Atheistical Notion, he believes Religion to be only a Contrivance of Politicians for keeping the Vulgar in Awe; and that the present Model is better adjusted than any other to so useful an End: Although the Condition of such a Man as to his own future State be very deplorable; yet Providence, which often works Good out of Evil, can make even such a Man an Instrument for contributing towards the Preservation of the Church...".

The question begged by all of this is the one raised by Ruth Herman at the end of her paper. What relationship subtends between Swift's opinions on the politics of church and state, and his views on faith itself? It is raised in an acute form by Swift's finest satirical pamphlet pre-Modest Proposal, An Argument [against] Abolishing of Christianity.

Swift's satiric strategy here is to claim that "....real Christianity, such as used in primitive times...to have an influence upon men's belief and actions.." is beyond the pale of any possible discussion. We are so far out of touch with real Christianity as preached in the Gospels, the argument implies, that only a madman would attempt to re-establish contact with it. We can only debate whether to preserve, or not to preserve, nominal Christianity through the preservation or repeal of the Sacramental Test and the continuation or cessation of occasional conformity. Proposed by Swift's satirical tactics is a radical split between the institution of the Church on the one hand, and a structure of belief underlying that called Christianity, on the other:

"...I am far from presuming to affirm or think that the Church is in danger at present, or as things now stand, but we know not how soon it may be so when the Christian religion is repealed...".

But what exactly is this residue of Christianity? In all of Swift's early writings, and even in the Argument itself, the sincerely-held view is inferrable that Christianity, indeed religion of any kind, is entirely coextensive with the doctrines and practices of the church as by law established. Swift writes so often as if to be a dissenter or a Catholic is to be no kind of Christian at all.

If we were looking to define Christianity irrespective of all the specifics of worship, we would probably fall back on a stripped-down creed, and beyond that on cardinal virtues - charity in particular. Christ's teachings as expressed through the Parables and the Beatitudes again and again stress the need to turn the other cheek, to love one's enemies, to interpret the idea of the 'neighbour' as inclusively as possible. That is why it is disturbing that there is so little charity in what Swift has to say about his clerical/political enemies. His attitude towards them seems to be, in a word, unChristian.

If we turn, for example, to the sermon that Swift preached in this very Cathedral on 1st December 1717 on 'Brotherly Love', we find the cause of the 'great Want of Brotherly Love among us' to be that:

"...This Nation of ours hath for an Hundred Years past, been infested by two Enemies, the Papists and the Fanaticks, who each, in their Turns, filled it with Blood and Slaughter, and for a time destroyed both the Church and Government...".

Whereas the Papists are hobbled by the law, and have no 'Advocates or Abettors among Protestants', the 'Fanaticks are to be considered in another Light; they have had of late Years the Power, the Luck, or the Cunning, to divide us among ourselves'.

Such words issuing from the pulpit probably have more power to shock in Dublin today than they did in Dublin in 1717. At the present juncture in the twenty-first century, we would like our great writers to be apostles of liberal toleration and freedom of speech.

We would like them to be charitable to their polemical opponents, like Voltaire defending to the death his opponents' right to say those things that he rejects. Swift disconcerts because, as I have tried to show even in Gulliver's Travels, the work in which one is tempted to find an ostensible commitment to some kind of ecumenical toleration, he is an undeniably great writer who stands in opposition to tenets of Christian faith, or to political inferences from them, that underlie democratic freedoms now held to be inalienable.

Chapter 18

Swift and Sin

It is a most fitting act of historical piety that this Cathedral Church, of which Dr. Jonathan Swift was Dean from 1713 to 1745, should commemorate him with an annual discourse. And it is a great honour that the present Dean, Swift's successor, Dr. MacCarthy, has shown to me by inviting me to deliver that Discourse this year; it is an honour for which I am deeply grateful.

I JUST noted that this is an occasion of historical piety. I didn't say religious piety. Simply because of *Gulliver's Travels,* one of the greatest works in our Western heritage, Swift is one of the very best-known writers in the world. A pioneer in literary experimentation, one of the greatest satirists of all time, a prolific political propagandist, an Irish patriot - Swift is all these, but as a religious figure, a man of the cloth, he doesn't come to mind so readily. And nobody was more responsible for that obscurity than Swift himself.

On the one hand he was very self-consciously the Reverend Dr. Swift, a clergyman of the Church of Ireland, and he demanded respect for his priestly office from others. He was a very dedicated administrator of this cathedral as well, regularising services and procedures, always taking his turn to preach; and he was just as regulated in his domestic life, calling his household in the deanery - which would be his servants, since he had no family - to prayers twice a day. On the other hand, he often made fun of himself as a foolish-looking bachelor dressed in a gown like a woman.

He could also be crude in his references to human sexuality or matters of personal hygiene, in terms which many even today find revoltingly explicit. These are certainly mixed signals, and they fostered the perception that he was an irreligious parson.

Moreover, he could seem very cold in person: though he made a practice of helping beggars, for instance, his beneficence 'was not graced with tenderness', as the great Samuel Johnson put it, 'he relieved without pity, and assisted without kindness.' This kind of behaviour hardly fits our conception of a minister of the gospel. Swift was in fact a very devoted clergyman, but gave the impression that he was more devoted to the Church as an institution than to the souls that institution was intended to serve.

Swift's 'affection to the church was never doubted', one of his acquaintances observed, 'though his Christianity was ever questioned'. Indeed, when he was appointed Dean of this Cathedral, there were quite a few who regarded him as an unbeliever. According to a famous story, on the day of Swift's installation here, a rival clergyman had a poem posted on the door of the cathedral which satirised the new dean's lack of faith. If I may quote a verse or two –

This Place he got by Wit and Rhyme,
And many ways most odd
And might a Bishop be in time
Did he believe in God.
And now, whene'er his Deanship dies,
Upon his Tomb be graven;
A Man of God here buried lies
Who never thought of Heaven.

Though these verses are only clever doggerel, the reference to Swift's tomb does foreshadow the fact that there is no mention of Jesus, God, or heaven, in the famous Latin epitaph that Swift wrote for himself, and which is inscribed upon a marble tablet near the entryway of this very cathedral; instead he considered that his body would rest where savage indignation would no longer tear his heart. He may have been thinking of heaven, but he was certainly thinking of death as a release from hell on earth, from the human sinfulness that prompted his anger.

Sin fascinated Swift: in all its variety, whether petty vanities, palpable hypocrisy, or complicity in unspeakable crimes, sin was a constant subject of his poetry and prose; and even as it fascinated him it of course also horrified and repelled him.

Economists talk of "push" and "pull" motives, factors which make us want to turn away from something and those which attract us: I think sin was a very strong "push" factor for Swift, making him think of God as its opposite, a relief from the obsessive horrors of sin. With this "push" factor, he did not need a well-founded theological picture of God to "pull" him - the negative reason for believing in God was sufficient. But Christians are not supposed to be drawn to God as the opposite of sin, so much as by the source of love; so it is fair to say, I think, that Swift's contemporaries were accurate in seeing him something other than a conventional Christian.

Christianity supplied for Swift, however, a framework for restraining the common human tendency to sin. He once referred to Christianity in a sermon as the "Scripture system", perhaps an odd way to talk of the gospels, but its systematic qualities appealed to him, and he accepted even the mysteries of religion - subjects like the Trinity or the Virgin birth, which formed part of the structure of Christian belief - as mysteriously fitting for a God from whom our own sinfulness has distanced us.

Because we cannot bridge that chasm of sin, we cannot really understand very much about God, and thus it makes sense that some features of God's religion should seem mysterious. This sort of explanation wouldn't work for many modern believers, but it satisfied Swift. He professed not to find the mysteries troubling at all - they certainly trouble a good many believers - and in that sense his attitude toward religion seems to me belief, even conviction, without the flame of faith.

When he delivered sermons, for instance, he thought it sufficient to tell his congregation what they were to believe and how to apply it to ordinary life. Belief and application formed the essence of religious duty; his own and that of others. Christian belief wasn't a matter for investigation; rather, belief would act as a bulwark against the very human tendency to sin. And not only was a simple acceptance of belief fundamental to the life of a citizen, but the form of that unexamined belief should be determined by the state.

It seems genuinely peculiar to those who think of Swift as a champion of liberty that it mattered less to Swift what religion was established by law as the state church, than that there be a state church. He was devoted to the Church of Ireland, and passionate in defence of its spiritual and financial interests, but he was dedicated to it because in those days it was the church of the state. Without a church establishment, people would be left to their own devices to worship God or not; and to Swift that meant they would be very easily tempted away from the path of righteousness.

To him, belief in God makes people good citizens, because a community that worships together is less likely to succumb to sin, and sin is at the very least anti-social behaviour. Since it is the job of the state to restrain anti-social behaviour, the state needs a church to which all citizens are required to give allegiance and support. The root of it all is, for Swift, sin, something much more palpable to him than was God.

Christian believers nowadays would generally find it awkward to square the notion of a state-church with the concept of free will that commonly defines the very essence of personhood. We would probably say that forcing all citizens to support a particular church is hardly moral at all, may even be simply immoral. But that is very much a modern attitude, deriving from the comparatively recent idea that people in the main are basically good; it seems logical to us that they should have the exercise of choice, since they would probably choose the good.

But Swift felt differently: in general, in essence, people tended toward the bad, the selfish, the anti-social; the church, as the social embodiment of belief, was the best available means of restraining the sinfulness to which people in general inclined.

And if the church was fractured, it was less effective than

if it were one and comprehensive. The only way to keep the church from fracturing was to have the state, the government, look after the church. Thus there would be only the one Church of England, say, rather than a dozen sects; establishing the church by law is the means he could recognize, to keep the Church solid and whole, and thereby to reduce the opportunity for sin.

His focus on sin led Swift, then, to want to empower the Church. But did he believe in God? I would affirm that he did, but that his belief was more negative than positive – he certainly believed in sin, and wanted to believe in something that was stronger, something that would overpower sin. It is a way of believing that Christians in Swift's own day found peculiar, and that many Christians in our own time would consider exceeding strange. It is belief, I have suggested, without the flame of faith - at least not with faith arrived at through love. And since Christians identify God with love, that sort of faith wasn't his.

Yet I hesitate even to venture a reservation about Swift's form of belief, much less any judgment. For all the coldness that we may find in his obsession with sin, it kept him from the sort of self-delusion that allows us often to forget that we are all of us sinners, even those of us who profess a faith informed by love. Swift believed because he was afraid of sin, and I think he distrusted faith because he feared our human tendency to deceive ourselves, to lull ourselves into complacency. Whatever the chilliness of his belief, it was certainly not complacent.

Chapter 19

Reading Politics in Swift and Pope

In February 1727, reporting progress in the printing of their joint *Miscellanies,* Pope tells Swift that he hopes they will go 'hand in hand to posterity . . . diverting others just as we diverted ourselves' (Corr., II, 426). Both had, after all, been members, along with Arbuthnot, Gay, Parnell and Queen Anne's minister Lord Oxford, of the Scriblerus Club as it had flourished in 1713-14. After the death of Queen Anne in 1714 had put the Tories out of office, the incoming Hanoverian regime was to be in the hands of the Whig Sir Robert Walpole for most of the next forty years; and from the vantage point of this long Walpolean tyranny (as both Swift and Pope perceived it), these Scriblerian meetings would be halcyon days to look back on.

Hobnobbing with the principal ministers of state as they negotiated an end to the Whig-supported War of the Spanish Succession, and looking to a renewal of cultural prospects under a gratified Queen Anne, Pope and Swift could in these years, as never since, dedicate their writing to an ongoing, positive assertion of traditional political and cultural values. But the Queen died, the ministers were prosecuted, Swift went to Ireland, and the two friends seldom met again.

In politics, they continued to warm to the same themes and revere the same heroes, notably Oxford and Bolingbroke, the late Queen's ministers, and Bishop Atterbury, now all tainted by accusations of Jacobitism. Pope applauded Swift's defeat of Wood's coinage, which both saw as yet another corrupt piece of Hanoverian wheeling and dealing; and he did so in the provocative context of an address to the very king whose mistress had connived at the scheme in the first place:

Let Ireland tell, how Wit upheld her cause,
Her Trade supported, and supply'd her Laws;
And leave on SWIFT this grateful verse ingrav'd,
The Rights a Court attack'd, a Poet sav'd.
(*Epistle to Augustus*, lines 221-4)

When Pope elaborated the cumulative project of his own career, the *Dunciad*, into its three- and four-book forms, from 1729 onwards, it was to Swift that he dedicated it, cheering his friend with the thought that there is at least one English monopoly that benefits the Irish: England has such a monopoly on stupidity that there's none left over for Ireland (*Dunciad in Four Books*, I. 19 28).

Yet despite all this, the political commitments of the two friends have typically been very differently received by later readers; and in taking up today's topic of Swift and radicalism, I'd like to offer a few thoughts on why that might be.

'Radical' as a political term emerges only in the late eighteenth century to refer to an ideology which, while in some respects it resembled the hatred of empire and oppression that had animated Swift, stood in a clear line of descent from the Whig ideology that Swift and Pope both loathed. Swift snipes at this outlook not just in overtly political works like *Modest Proposal* but also in satires like *Genteel and Ingenious Conversation* that, once the connotations of party are left behind, may look like fairly trivial mockery of contemporary taste and manners.

To say, therefore, that Swift appeals to radicals, is to build in a rather large historical irony. The irony, and the gap in perception it represents, becomes negotiable mainly because the political configurations in which Swift's (and Pope's) texts originally made sense had effectively ceased to be meaningful by the middle of the eighteenth century.

In 1742, while both were in fact still alive, Sir Robert Walpole finally left office, and the long stand-off between government and opposition ended in a scramble for power from which the leaders of the Patriot opposition emerged with principles in tatters. Swift and Pope turned out to have spent their prime in addressing political values and identities that readers would very soon find it difficult, pointless, and in some cases counterproductive to reconstruct.

As England in the second half of the eighteenth century moved on to face an American War, the French Revolution, and the movement to abolish slavery, reviving the party politics of the age of Walpole in all its antagonistic detail became less and less attractive.

In Pope's case, the blurring of political contexts was arguably hastened by his appointed editor, William Warburton, a clergyman of humble origins with a career to make, who had in Pope's last years encouraged him towards high-minded ethical and religious conservatism rather than Tory or Patriot partisanship.

Warburton's orthodox zeal and political caution no doubt helped him rise to become a bishop; but it decisively alienated, for example, the radical satirist Charles Churchill, for whom Pope seems to have been decisively smeared by association. Swift's works arguably benefited from lacking such a doorkeeper. His politics too had become difficult to grasp once their original context had disappeared, but with the crucial difference, as Professor Mahony has pointed out, that 'Swift grew the more useful as the passage of time eroded historical anomalies to fit the simpler standard of British-Irish antagonisms characteristic of nineteenth-century nationalism, and seemed thereby to resolve his own inconsistencies'.

Just how dangerous it might be to Swift's reputation to have the original context of his politics put back on the agenda was illustrated in 1816 by the response of the Whig reviewer Francis Jeffrey to Walter Scott's edition of Swift. For Jeffrey, Swift is damned as a Tory, and a venal one at that: nothing about him can serve as any kind of inspiration to progressive thought. As for the Drapier: 'His Irish politics may all be referred to one principle – a desire to insult and embarrass the government by which he was neglected, and with which he despaired of being reconciled'.

Moreover, 'every body is now satisfied of the perfect harmlessness, and indeed of the great utility, of Wood's scheme for a new copper coinage'. Perhaps most damagingly, Jeffrey points out that by the standard of early C19 Whigs, Swift was indifferent to Ireland's greatest problem: 'to the last we hear nothing of its radical grievance, the oppression of its Catholic population'. Jeffrey's fervour for the Whig tradition casts Swift into the outer darkness of self-interested Tory bigotry.

William Hazlitt, a man of more radical views than Jeffrey, but an admirer of Swift, sees that Swift can only be recuperated for progressive readers by minimising the significance of his politics:

I do not, therefore, agree with the estimate of Swift's moral or intellectual character, given by an eminent critic, who does not seem to have forgotten the party politics of Swift. I do not carry my political resentments so far back: I can at this time of day forgive Swift for having been a Tory. I feel little disturbance (whatever I may think of them) at his political sentiments, which died with him, considering how much else he has left behind him of a more solid and imperishable nature!

In the case of Pope, there was an additional problem, namely a huge shift in poetic taste. Half a century on, Pope seems to Hazlitt an artificial and limited poet. Notably, Hazlitt makes no appeal to Pope's politics to revive the passion with which his work had been consumed within its own context of controversy. He prefers to read even his most politicised passages in terms of a lofty moralism: 'The finest burst of severe moral invective in all Pope, is the prophetical conclusion of the epilogue to the Satires'.

He quotes with admiration Pope's injunction to 'Disdain whatever Cornbury disdains', commenting 'One would think (though there is no knowing) that a descendant of this nobleman, if there be such a person living, could hardly be capable of a mean or paltry action'. Thus distinctive connotations of Cornbury's career in a rhetoric of Patriot virtue are entirely lost.

Even Byron, a more openly subversive figure and one unusual in his passionate advocacy of Pope, pitches his claim at a level of ethics so general as to transcend even nationality:

'He is the moral poet of all Civilization – and as such let us hope that he will one day be the National poet of Mankind'. As Swift's example showed, resuscitating the Toryism of dead Tories was no way to commend their work to progressive taste.

Once Swift and Pope had been surgically separated from the Whig/Tory matrix of their time, Swift proved better equipped to survive the operation than Pope. While Pope had written mainly in heroic couplets, a form that fell into relative disfavour from the mid century, *Gulliver* became a standard work, and would, in time, qualify Swift to be read as more a novelist than a satirist.

This is, of course, a reading of *Gulliver* that rests on considerable anachronisms; and one of the distinctive contributions made by Professor Donoghue's 1969 *Jonathan Swift: A Critical Introduction* is the critical pressure it applies to the by then well established assumption that Gulliver was to be read as a novel, particularly as a novel as conceived in the wake of Henry James. On the other hand, to be read as a novelist in the nineteenth and twentieth centuries was arguably the best thing that could have happened to Swift, because it kept him, however oddly, on the right side of a hierarchy of genre that was shifting decisively in favour of prose fiction.

Finally, we should perhaps ask whether, intrinsically as opposed to occasionally, Swift's work really does constitute an exemplar of anti-establishment satire. In Swift's later life the establishment was Whig, and he opposed it. It is potentially inspiring to deduce from this that he was essentially, rather than accidentally, an anti-establishment writer. This makes him easy for later opponents of established power to appropriate. To insist, on the contrary, that Swift's opposition to Walpole's Whig regime was based on specific beliefs and commitments as they were uniquely inflected in the England and Ireland of his time may seem unhelpful and even dog-in-the-mangerish.

On the other hand, the inspiration that might be drawn from Swift is not necessarily or even obviously liberal and progressive. There is plenty in Swift, after all, to comfort those who believe that most of the trouble in life is caused by newfangled nonsense. A.L. Rowse's *Jonathan Swift: Major Prophet,* its universalising moral agenda blazoned boldly in its subtitle, was published in 1975: on the title-page of the Birmingham University Library copy a student has ringed the date and written, 'this book should have stayed there' — in the context of the present discussion a somewhat plaintive appeal to the historical particularity from which Rowse works to liberate his subject for service in the present.

Although Rowse identifies Swift as a Whig and does describe aspects of early C18th politics, he proclaims at an early stage, without qualification or nuance, the universal applicability of the principles that Swift inherited from his royalist grandfather, commenting 'All his life Swift hated fanatics and doctrinaires and illusionists – quite rightly, for the troubles they bring down on sensible people'. Later he declares, 'Swift was no great favourite with Victorians, and never with liberals, with their childish illusions – but we have contemporary Ireland in ferment once more, like him, to enlighten us'.

He cites Swift's evocation of what he calls 'the authentic Puritan twang, a nasal whine, which passed over with the elect into New England'; and he adds: 'Bad as it is today to live in a society of Leftist liberal cant – about the educability of everybody, and everybody being not only equal but the same, and what not – it must have been appalling to live in the England of the Civil War and Commonwealth, when these hypocrites were on top'.

Rowse's bugbears of the 1970s are thus uncritically identified with their remote ideological ancestors: Swift's original contexts are acknowledged in name only, with no emotional distance left in which his texts' remoteness from what we can readily identify with might come into focus. In comparison with progressive readings of Swift, however, with their vested interests in seeing him as defender of the weak, exposer of corruption, prophet against empire, even proto-feminist, this unashamedly conservative approach has at least one merit: it brings us sharp up against much that is harsh in

Swift. The narrow and doctrinaire exclusiveness of much of his political and religious writing, for instance, is problematic if we want to make Swift a liberal: it is all grist to the mill if our agenda is to maintain distinctions and hierarchies, to insist on discipline.

Yet, like readings that make Swift a patriot or a radical, those that make him a conservative disciplinarian also require a degree of selectivity and of special pleading to bring him round to their agenda. Trying to co-opt Swift's fascinating exasperations for the agendas of a later age has proved an activity as questionable as it is, apparently, irresistible.

THE FULLBACK'S DILEMMA [MH]

I want to thank you for this opportunity to return to the deanery and say something about Swift, after last year happily sitting near the back of the audience reflecting on how little I knew. I hope this time I might have a few ideas to add to the discussion, but I'm wary to suggest this might be so, for as D.J. Enright says about Swift in his wonderful book, *The Alluring Problem: An Essay on Irony*, 'everything has been said already'. Of course, he offers hope to those like me, and a reason to be here today, when he points out that nonetheless 'we can scarcely not say something ' about Swift.

So here goes...

Or, rather, doesn't...

For I don't particularly want to say something about Swift. I'd like, instead, to say something about some of the people who have said something about Swift, not so much as a way of understanding them but to reflect on the chimera-like qualities of satire, which is a kind of glass wherein we observe every face but our own. But you knew that, of course.

Or, as the Dane put it, the ironist

Knows only that the present does not match the idea. He is the one who must pass judgment...The ironist...has stepped out of line with his age, has turned around and faced it.

—Not Hamlet, but that other great contrarian Dane, Søren Kierkegaard. What was offered as a definition of irony works just as well as a definition of satire.

Swift himself seems at times to conflate the two terms, as when in his verses on his death he suggests that:

Arbuthnot is no more my friend,
Who dares to irony pretend;
Which I was born to introduce,
Refined it first, and showed its use.

But either way, the interesting point, at least for me, and at least for the purposes of this talk, is the idea that the ironist 'knows only that the present does not match the idea. He is the one who must pass judgment.'

And pass judgment Swift does. Again. And again. And again.

You can't miss the judgment.

You certainly can miss the proposed solution. It often is not there.

Sometimes, as in *An Argument Against Abolishing Christianity*, a solution is implied. More often not. Just judgment. Swift perhaps knew *that* Dane, Hamlet, well enough to avoid the self-paralyzing connecting of the recognition of a time out of joint with the self-absorbed reflection 'O cursèd spite that ever I was born to set it right'. But perhaps not.

It's not entirely clear Swift ever intended to set anything right. For what use is an ironist when the time matches the idea?

That aside, I want to use Kierkegaard's definition of irony, which skill Swift claimed for himself, not to ask, or answer, the question 'who was Swift, "about whom everything has been said already" '? but to look briefly instead at something we once knew but have largely forgotten: Jonathan Swift, Dean of St Patrick's, Dublin, might have claimed for himself the title scourge of the oppressor, vindicator of liberty—to make not too liberal a translation of his own epitaph—but he was no radical, as that towering Whig of a later generation demonstrated by 'a single fact...While [Swift's] friends were in power, we hear nothing of the grievances of Ireland; and to the last we hear nothing of its radical grievance, the oppression of its Catholic majority.' And he was right, was Francis Jeffrey, writing in 1816.

So why, irony of ironies, was Swift's reputation preserved for us for so long not by those with whom he would have claimed kinship but by those he would most have despised, the social, political, and cultural heirs of that fine Ulsterman, John Toland?

The answer lies in Kierkegaard's definition, in the fact that Swift wrote on the cusp of mercantilism and before modern economic theory was a settled discourse, and, of course, in Swift's power as a demagogue.

Mark this, though, William Hazlitt, Percy Bysshe Shelley, Lord Byron and others knew their Swift. Knew him and used him as surely as Jeffrey did in another cause, Used Swift as they saw fit, and did not let that bother them one bit. It was not a trait confined to a particular period of the nineteenth century.

Listen to these words:

He had a horror of state tyranny and ...an uncanny presentiment of totalitarianism and all the torture it would brand on body and mind...He knew what crawling self-seekers politicians could be, but he knew too that politics was concerned with the great question of the rich and the poor.

Perhaps it is that last qualifier which gives away that these are the words of a man whose wit and learning—in both the classic and the modern sense—offer a stark reminder of their absence among so many of his ilk, the former leader of the British Labour Party, Michael Foot, always a champion of socialism and of personal dignity, a shining rebuke to those who would conflate socialism with tyranny. A man who offers the most resounding defence of Jonathan Swift I have ever read.

Foot, in this same essay, dismisses Jeffrey's attack on Swift as a 'brilliant libel'. It is a charge which could be applied with as much justice against those who praise Swift for his radicalism.

But the passion of Foot's defense still leaves unanswered the great question: how did the radicals see in Swift what they saw?

Well, one answer, Foot suggests, is found in Sir Herbert

Grierson's account of Byron's publication of *Don Juan*, for, as Byron had said in Canto III, 'words are things'. And, says Grierson Milton and Swift are the only other Englishmen of Letters whose writings have been not only literary works but deeds...Swift was a pamphleteer, but his pamphlets ended a European war and shook the government of Ireland, and it was not the satire alone which did so but the personality, the fearless pride and strength of the man who launched them.

I'm not sure Swift's pamphlets did achieve any such political results, but, as Grierson says, they accomplished something far more important than that; they suggested words and actions are potentially commensurate.

It was this which inspired Byron, Hazlitt, and, later, of course, George Orwell, to claim Swift for their camp: these writers who were, or dreamed of being, men of action.

But while the motive for the radicals' adoption of Swift as a mascot might be clear, the means was surprisingly uncomplicated for a man who had a coherent center, one that was conservative not reactionary, principled but occasional. Hardly a centre of gravity conducive to radical sympathies, except that Swift was most certainly opposed to what today we call the establishment, at least the establishment post-1714, opposed to what William Cobbett called 'the Thing'.

The 'Thing' was the political idea of the time in which he lived, manifested in economic and political restructuring that Swift was unwilling to condone and unable to collaborate with. The present did not match the idea. Which is exactly the claim that Byron, Hazlitt, and their ilk wished also to make?

Here is Byron on the death of Castlereagh:

Of the manner of his death little need be said, except that if a poor radical...had cut his throat, he would have been buried in a cross-road...In his death [Castlereagh] was necessarily one of two things by the *law*—a felon or a madman-... and in either case no great subject for panegyric...It may at least serve as some consolation to the Nations, that their Oppressors are not happy, and in some instances judge so justly of their own actions as to anticipate the sentence of mankind.

Hardly more temperate than Swift on Chief Justice Whitshed who had '*libertas & natale Solum* [liberty and my native country] written as a Motto on his Coach, as it stood at the Door of the Court, while he was perjuring himself to betray both.'

Swift had a point of view and he expressed it, even when decorum might have suggested he should do otherwise. It is hard for the dedicated oppositionist not to admire that trait in another.

But the sympathy of the radicals for Swift was not simply about my enemy's enemy being my friend. There is another matter: language changes, ideas change. And in those changes lies the opportunity for misreading, whether intentional or not.

On 25 August 1816, that most appropriately named journal, *The Examiner*, published a letter from William Hazlitt on the subject, supposedly, of Edmund Burke and the ignorance of the world: 'One reason we do not grow wiser,' Hazlitt cautioned, 'is that we forget what we have learned.' Burke might well have read *Gulliver's Travels*, Hazlitt conceded, but when he pointed out that ' "if the poor were to cut the throats of the rich, they would not get a meal more for it" he seems not to have recollected what that very popular Author says on the subject.'

Which author was Swift, whose sixth chapter of the Voyage to the Houyhnhnms, Hazlitt writes, 'may show that Swift's Toryism did not, like Mr Burke's Anti-Jacobinism, deprive him of common sense.'

Hazlitt knew his man. Knew at least his politics, was 'even prepared to forgive him for being a Tory,' says Foot. But I don't think Hazlitt spotted a greater paradigm shift than the possibility that a Tory might retain his common sense.

The passage Hazlitt has in mind is that wherein 'my master was yet wholly at a loss to understand what motives could incite this race of lawyers to perplex, disquiet, and weary themselves by engaging in a confederacy of injustice'.

Gulliver goes on to observe that:

England (the dear place of my nativity) was computed to produce three times the quantity of food more than its inhabitants are able to consume...and the same proportion in every other convenience of life. But in order to feed the luxury and intemperance of the males, and the vanity of the females, we sent away the greatest part of our necessary things to other countries, from whence in return we brought the materials of disease, folly, and vice...Hence it follows of necessity, that vast numbers of our people are compelled to...beg, rob, steal, cheat, pimp, forswear, flatter, suborn, forge, game, lie, fawn, hector, vote, scribble, star-gaze, poison, whore, cant, libel...and the like.

Which may well sound like the sort of argument heard outside the halls of wherever the WTO last met, a damning counter-argument to the rational economics of the Chicago School. But it is not.

This is not the argument Swift was making.

And radicals of almost every generation since Swift, from William Godwin to Michael Foot, have taken advantage of the language and have ignored the intent, whether deliberately or not.

If he had a point of view when it came to finance and markets, Swift was a full-fledged mercantilist. Land and people were wealth, money a measure of them only, if it were to have any real value. In modern economic parlance, Swift would have thought M_0 mattered, might have considered M_1 significant, but certainly would have held M_2, and M_3 to be chimeras of fabulists. But that's an anachronistic argument.

He did believe this: people were an asset. Labour was wealth producing and so for him had value. Full-employment was not just a worthy goal. It was a moral fundamental.

Swift's castigated the English administration because of the effect of those policies on the Irish economy not by pity on behalf of those who deserved better. He was outraged not so much by the consequences of the policies as by the fact that the policies were so flagrantly out of synch with the ideas he thought should form the basis of sound government. The suffering he saw around him proved only that the present was out of synch. The anger of *A Modest Proposal* is so startlingly vituperative precisely because it lashes out at a polity so insane as to make the rearing and eating of babies appear logical. It wasn't the hunger that moved Swift half as much as it was the cause of the hunger. That the ideas he defended by implication had run their course and the beast slouching toward Babylon to be born would become modern economic policy was of no import to him. He knew 'only that the present did not match the idea'.

Here is not the place to consider just what exactly changed in 1688, D.W. Jones does that quite handily in his short essay 'Sequel to revolution: the economics of England's emergence as a great power'. Suffice it to say, as Jonathan Israel demonstrates exhaustively and lucidly, the Dutch Republic, whether by design or by necessity, reconceptualised the ideas of wealth, society, and property, and in 1688 England and, soon thereafter, Scotland seized hold of the experience of the new economics, if not yet fully aware of the consequences of such a wholesale rethinking of social structures.

[If any of Swift's contemporary polemicists saw it coming, by the way, it wasn't so much Bernard Mandeville, whose *Fable of the Bees* is as much a moral allegory as it is an economic argument, but Daniel Defoe, whose writings on political economy are badly in need of a decent modern airing.]

Swift did not understand, and did not wish to understand, the *whys* of the destitution and, to his mind, financial failures of his time. He simply intended to use those failures to his own ends. He knew the problem, even if he did not understand the cause of that problem.

And for the radicals of later eras this interest of Swift's in the value of labour was vital. But to understand how separate was the contemporary understanding of people such as Swift from later thinkers, it is instructive to look at what Swift's peers were saying.

Here is David Bindon arguing in 1738 that It is certain, that the power and Riches of a Nation depend not upon its having Mines of *Gold* and *Silver*, but upon its having *a numerous and industrious People.*

Bindon is quite clear about the ill consequences of a supply of the former and a dearth of the latter:

Spain and *Portugal* are rich in Mines...but thin of inhabitants; and the few they have are idle or luxurious: Therefore neither of them has any great Power, and the Riches their Slaves dig from the Bowels of the Earth, are yearly sent out for supporting the Idleness and luxury of their people. On the contrary, *Britain* and *France* have no Mines of *Gold* ands *Silver*; but they have Multitudes of People *usefully employed*, and consequently are rich and powerful.

It does not matter here whether Bindon is right about wealth or power, still less whether his analysis of *causes* of wealth, poverty, power are correct. What matters is the clarity with which he makes his case, and the fact that this opinion was the dominant trope of the period and so the one least in need of analysis and elaboration.

Here is archbishop King in a 1721 letter to archbishop Wake in Canterbury:

Y^r South Sea [Bubble]...has surely made us miserable to the highest degree, if starving be a misery...I was of the opinion before that one Third of this City needed Charity; but [I find] that at least one Half are in this lamentable state...& the cry of the whole People is loud for Bread.

Notice how King connects speculative, stock-market capitalism with destitution.

[I should pause here for one moment, if I might, to observe how frequent is the phrase the 'whole people' in accounts of this time in the papers of King, Synge, Stearne, Brodrick, and others. Swift's use of the phrase in the fourth Drapier's letter was not some radical innovation. Nor, even, was his appending 'of Ireland' to the first two words.]

Anyway.

The political and economic ramifications of the South Sea Bubble to Irish polity were not the same as in England and Scotland, and this can perhaps be seen most clearly in the debate over the Bank of Ireland, which debate also helps demonstrate the crucial significance to modern understanding of Patrick Hyde Kelly's point that

The unquestioning assumption of earlier scholars that sixteenth-, seventeenth-, and early eighteenth-century writers were simply grasping with greater or lesser success after the categories which came to dominate [modern economic theories]...has given way to a realisation that there is a radical discontinuity between the two forms of discourse.

This 'radical discontinuity' was not apparent to those who later claimed Swift for their own radical agendas. It is too often overlooked today.

Two 1723 tracts from Ireland make clear the nature of that disconnect. Their titles make their premises clear, but to today's reader their arguments are shockingly at odds with their presumed tone. Molesworth's title says it all: *Some Considerations for Promoting the Agriculture of Ireland and Employing the Poor*. Francis Hutchinson wrote *A Letter to a Member of Parliament Concerning the Imploying and Providing for the Poor*.

Molesworth's solution, anticipating by some considerable period Gresham's Law (if labour and wealth are co-terminous in a mercantilist analysis), was to deport any indigent labourers. Hutchinson thought this view extreme, preferring instead (*vide* Swift) to badge beggars, employ them upon public works, and confine them to their home parishes unless they had gainful employment elsewhere (when, presumably, they would cease to be beggars).

Swift's third Drapier's letter would be addressed to Molesworth and, in *Some Arguments Against Enlarging the Power of Bishops...*, Swift would describe Molesworth's *Considerations* as an 'excellent discourse'.

The Londonderry MP Hercules Rowley took full advantage of the popular conception of economic reality in his *Answer to a Book Entitled 'Reasons Offered for Erecting a Bank in Ireland'*:

> Whenever the importation of consumable commodities destroyed at home exceeds the exportation of the manufactured or unmanufactured products of any country, then it must be daily impoverished. Lessening our Importation and encouraging our manufactures would feed the hungry, clothe the naked and relieve the oppressed.

Or, as Swift put it in *A Short View of the State of Ireland*:

> The first cause of a Kingdom's thriving is the Fruitfulness of the Soil, to produce the Necessaries and Conveniencies of Life; not only sufficient for the Inhabitants, but for Exportation into other Countries.

In modern parlance, this is the argument of the autarkist, and Nicolai Ceauçescu's Romania and modern North Korea demonstrate the deficiencies of autarky in a contemporary setting, but precisely because the discourse of Swift's time was mercantilist not capitalist these failings were not only inconceivable but theoretically impossible. Then, as now, the failure of an economy was proof only that the idea had been inadequately applied to the problem. Hence, David Bindon again:

> Both [wholesale and retail drapers] are a Sort of Middle-Buyer, or what Mr *Locke* calls Brokers between the manufacturer and Consumer, it is, according to that great Man's Opinion, inconsistent with the public Good, to encourage their Trade, or increase their Numbers.

Bindon talked of economies dependent upon slavery—corrupt, indolent, impoverished and, more importantly, injurious to their own people. Molesworth, Hutchinson, Rowley, and Swift of the need for work, of the value of labour, not simply for its own sake but for the public good.

Recall Jeffrey's damning dismissal of Swift: 'to the last we hear nothing of [Ireland's] radical grievance, the oppression of its Catholic majority'. True, as I said, but also fundamentally wrong.

As King wrote to Wake, as Swift would famously say in the fourth Drapier's letter, the 'whole people of Ireland' were an integral part of any financial analysis of Ireland. Catholic, Anglican or Dissenter, a man's production added value to society.

As the industrial revolution dawned, as cities grew, land was enclosed, and the rights of the old yeoman class as imagined by William Cobbett during his *Rural Rides* vanished, it was no wonder that the radicals found something to admire in Swift. [Though here I should point out that Cobbett himself derided Swift as 'an eccentric sort of misanthrope...and a disappointed politician of great ambition'. Which, actually, might not be too ill-considered a description of that Tory turned radical, William Cobbett himself?]

Swift shared with the likes of Hazlitt, Byron, and Shelley, a remarkable ability to claim to speak on behalf of individuals in a society gone mad, while at the same time demonstrating some quite unappealing cant on the matter of particular individuals.

More to the point, however, later radical writers recognised a fellow stylist and polemicist of great accomplishment when they saw one, and—here's the rub—gleefully recognised that although his sentiments and motives might have been unbecoming, the argument still sounded, even resounded, for was it not Swift who had pointed out that the 'question is whether People ought to be Slaves or no'? That he asked this question in defence of the right of the Church of Ireland Convocation to meet, presumably to seek to undo social and political changes he saw as inimicable to preserving the power of the church, did not matter.

This sentiment could be co-opted, even if the cause had changed. But, then again, Hazlitt who was no friend of the established church was also not shy about reflecting of catholicism that 'nothing is to be said against [it] but that it is contrary to reason and common sense'.

—You are wondering, perhaps, about the title of this talk or, at least, about the sub-title, 'the fullback's dilemma'. The explanation for that lies in these concluding thoughts: I was asked last year by the fullback of the university rugby team I coached, *a propos* of what, I don't know, 'was Swift a radical?' This is not an easy question to answer at the best of times, and most definitely not when you have wandered over from the pack to consult with your fullback about the possibility of catching the occasional high ball. But I could not quite put the question aside, perhaps not only because of its unlikely provenance.

A few days later, I mentioned to a friend and colleague, who had been a prop, that I had been taken aback by the question and its circumstances. His response, quite wisely, was that that's the problem with fullbacks, they have way too much time to think about things. Which is probably true of all of us here today.

Was Swift a radical?

It might well be too complex a question for all but the fullbacks of life. And fullbacks, of course, should not be encouraged.

Quite what some of the radicals saw in him, that we might be able to answer, even the props of the world, who, like the radicals girding themselves for another fierce encounter, can't help but think that the 'present does not match the idea'.

Chapter 20

Swift, The Wild Boy of Hanover, and Queen Caroline

In early March 1726, Swift set sail for England, full of anticipation. His visit was designed to do more than to catch up with his old Scriblerian friends Pope, Arbuthnot and Bolingbroke. He carried with him the manuscript of *Gulliver's Travels*, published by Benjamin Motte that October. And he also came with a political mission.

The recent success of the *Drapier's Letters* had made him a hero in Ireland and a redoubtable political player. During this stay in England Swift planned to seek audiences with important court and ministerial figures to advance the cause of Ireland and Irish economic affairs. In early April he dined with Robert Walpole, not, as some suspected, to negotiate for himself an English bishopric, but in order 'to represent the affairs of Ireland to him in a true light'.

The maverick Tory Bolingbroke, conscious of his friend's new political stature, tried to recruit him to another cause – his new offensive again the Walpole ministry. Bolingbroke, alongside the dissident Whig William Pulteney, had just launched *The Craftsman*, a major propaganda tool in the war against Walpole, and hoped to persuade Swift to write for it .The opposition to Walpole found a focal point in the heir to the Hanoverian throne, George, Prince of Wales. Prince George, later George II, had long been at war with his father.

He and his wife, the clever and ambitious Caroline of Anspach, held high-spirited gatherings at Leicester House, their winter residence, an attractive focus for opposition politics. Leicester House became a magnet for the politically disaffected who hoped for an end to Whig oligarchy in the new reign. Out of office Tories and discontented Whigs were welcome there, as Prince George flattered their hopes that on the death of George I, he would dismiss Walpole and offer the Tories a share in power.

Swift was one of many drawn to the Hanoverian court-in-waiting, with its hopes of the 'reversionary' interest. Today I want to talk about Swift's complicated relationship to that court, particularly Princess Caroline and her lady-in-waiting, Henrietta Howard, also Prince George's mistress. Despite Bolingbroke's best efforts, Swift was less interested in participating in opposition politics than in using the royal connection to advance the Irish cause.

He tried to inveigle Mrs Howard, and through her, Princess Caroline, publicly to champion Irish manufacture. He commissioned some Dublin weavers to make an especially fine Irish plaid or poplin, woven after the fashionable Indian manner, which he sent as a gift to Mrs Howard, hoping that the fashion would catch on at court. To his delight Princess Caroline also wanted some - what better advertisement for Irish wares than to see Irish dresses worn by the numerous little princesses?

'Are you determined to be national in everything', asked Pope, 'even in your civilities?'. There were also deeper personal factors woven into Swift's relationship with these two women. He was undeniably attracted both to Mrs Howard, a charming, witty woman, 'a most unconscionable dealer' who had learned the consummate courtier's art of knowing how to please, and to Princess Caroline herself, whose boundless energy, intelligence and sense of humour drew many admirers. Caroline could take a joke against her own husband. On reading *Gulliver's Travels* she 'laughed heartily' at the account of the hobbling prince in Lilliput, a representation of Prince George's ungainly efforts to keep a foot planted in both the Tory and Whig camps. Princess Caroline's attentions flattered Swift's personal vanity and revived his latent ambition for royal recognition and a superior living in England.

He enjoyed playing hard to get with the Princess, boasting that she had had to send for him eleven times before he would obey the royal summons. He described his exchanges with her involving 'Civility' on her side and a roguish 'Freedom' or familiarity on his own.

It is precisely this easy intimacy which he vaunts in his *Pastoral Dialogue between Richmond Lodge and Marble Hill,* in which the two houses, one owned by Caroline, the other by Mrs Howard, talk about imminent changes in their situation on the coronation of 1727. Swift depicts himself 'tattling' in the gardens with the future queen, 'stunning her Royal Ears with talking; / His *Rev'rence* and her *Highness* walking'.

Yet Swift's attitude to courts and power was always deeply ambivalent. Despite his early admiration for Queen Anne, he never forgot that, offended by his indecency, she had failed to reward him for his efforts promoting the Treaty of Utrecht: 'The Queen, a royal Prude / Incens'd by him, his services forgot'.

And Caroline, who belonged to an alien 'foreign' dynasty, was perhaps, despite her apparently good inclinations, to be viewed with greater suspicion. There is a teasing parallel between Swift's relationship to Caroline's court and that of another foreign 'visitor' who arrived in England the month before he did, in February 1726.

This was Peter, the so-called 'wild boy' of Hanover. Peter, a feral child, had first been seized in a forest near Hamelen in Germany in the summer of 1724. Aged, at a guess, somewhere between 11 and 15, he was found wearing the remains of a shirt, living off raw vegetables, grass and sap. Alert and suspicious in the early days after his captivity, he was unable to speak and moved at times on all fours, like a dog. In October 1725 he was sent to Hanover, then in February 1726 to London as a 'guest ' of George I's court. His care entrusted to Swift's friend Dr Arbuthnot, the royal physician, by April Peter had become annexed to Princess Caroline's court. Swift recorded that

> ... he is in the keeping of Dr Arbuthnot, but the king and court were so entertained with him, that the Princess could

not get him till now. I can hardly think him wild in the sense they report him.

Peter created an enormous stir in England. His 'freakshow' status, half-man, half-beast, made him one of the most celebrated 'rareties' flooding mid-18th Century London, second only to Mary Tofts, the woman who apparently gave birth to live rabbits. He also fuelled contemporary philosophical debates concerning man's superiority to beasts, and the true nature of 'savage' or natural man - debates which inform Swift's own *Gulliver's Travels* particularly Book 4, with its account of the Houyhnhms and Yahoos. Swift was fascinated by wild Peter, recognising a kind of kinship with him. He recalled 'I was informed she [Princess Caroline] loved to see odd persons, and that having sent for a wild boy from Germany, she had a curiosity to see a wild dean from Dublin'.

The parallels between Germanic and Irish 'wildness' are provocative. Swift is here, just for once, claiming to have imbibed some of the 'wildness' or savagery of the Irish. Irish 'wildness' supplies a healthy antidote to court dependency and political sycophancy: the 'wild Dean' is the antithesis of the 'tame' Dean. The 'taming' of Peter the wild boy becomes a trope for Swift's anxieties about his proximity to the new Hanoverian court.

Swift recognised in his comparison that Peter was a 'curiosity', one of the 'odd persons' or objects collected by Queen Caroline, who was acquiring a reputation as a virtuoso, or collector of arcana and rarieties - coins, shells, busts. She 'took up' Peter just as she was later to 'take up' Stephen Duck, the untutored Wiltshire farm boy and poetic genius who became her tame grotto keeper at Richmond park. Peter's relationship to the court was, at one level, one of humiliating dependence.

Prodded, measured and scrutinised, his wildness was gradually emasculated. Soon after the coronation of George and Queen Caroline in early 1727 the court seems to have tired of his novelty value: Peter was pensioned off to live with one of Caroline's chamber women and later with a farmer in Hertfordshire. His very limited acquisition, or perhaps reacquisition of language, marked him as a cast-off royal dependent. Peter's neighbours in later years, the novelist Maria Edgeworth and her father, noted that he 'had all his senses in remarkable perfection', but could 'only articulate imperfectly a few words', in particular 'Ki Scho' [King George] and 'Qui Ka' [Queen Caroline], which words he always accompanied by an imitation of bells, which rang at the coronation of George II'.

Yet some contemporaries viewed Peter in a different relationship to the court – not as a humble dependent, grateful recipient of the maternal royal bounty, but as a standing rebuke to courtly sophistication and decadence. This was the tenor of at least five satirical pamphlets inspired by Peter's presence at court.

His 'wildness' becomes a sign not of barbarism, but of moral integrity and independence. The 1726 poem 'The Savage' describes Peter as an 'innocent and free' creature in danger of being contaminated by courtly vice. True 'savagery' - backbiting, treachery, cruelty - belongs to the 'civilised' world he encounters.

The liveliest of these pamphlets, *It Cannot Rain but it Pours; or, London Strew'd with Rarities,* was once thought to have been written by Swift's friend and Peter's mentor Dr Arbuthnot, but recent evidence points to Swift himself. Its subtitle once again draws analogies between Peter and Swift, including among its promised descriptions of London 'rarities' an 'Account of the Arrival of a White Bear, at the House of Mr. Ratcliff in Bishopsgate-Street ... And of the Copper-Farthing Dean from Ireland.

And Lastly, Of the wonderful Wild Man that was nursed in the Woods of Germany by a Wild Beast, hunted and taken in Toyls; how he behaveth himself like a dumb Creature, and is a Christian like one of us, being call'd Peter; and how he was brought to Court all in Green, to the great Astonishment of the Quality and Gentry.' The pamphlet bears striking similarities to *Gulliver's Travels.*

The depiction of Peter is politically loaded. An ironic foil to throw into relief the benefits of 'civilisation', Peter borrows elements of the Yahoo and the Houyhnhm. In a play on the Lockeian idea of the untutored mind as a *tabula rasa,* we are told that Peter 'receiv'd his first Impressions at Court: His Manners are, first to lick People's Hands, and then turn his Breech upon them; to thrust his Hand into every body's pocket; to climb over Peoples Heads; and even to make use of the Royal Hand, to take what he has a mind to ... these are manifest tokens of his innate Ambition; he is extremely tenacious of his own Property, and ready to invade that of other People'.

Yet the mode of irony switches, and Peter becomes a 'naif' whose arrival at court becomes a catalyst for dissolute mores. The young ladies-in-waiting await his entrance with a frisson of sexual anticipation: but his 'being so young was the Occasion of the great Disappointment of the Ladies, who came to the Drawing-Room in full Expectation of some Attempt upon their Chastity: So far is true, that he endeavoured to Kiss the young Lady W—le, who for that reason is become the envy of this circle'. One recalls the young Brobdingnagian ladies-in-waiting 'playing' with a naked Gulliver.

The fantasy of sex with a savage other highlight the sexual innuendo surrounding Princess Caroline's circle of pretty young ladies-in-waiting, a 'fast set' who had already earned a reputation for lewdness. Above all, Peter's 'naturalness' is a foil for court affectation.

He acquires a primitive, figurative language which penetrates social facades: he calls a young lady a 'peacock', 'old women magpyes and owls', 'a beau with a toupee a monkey', 'blue, red and green ribbons [colours of the Orders of Merit] he calls Rainbows, an Heap of Gold, a Turd'. Just like the Houyhnhms first encountering a clothed Gulliver, he at first believes clothes to be 'the natural skins of the creatures that wore them'. Above all, Peter, like Gulliver on his return to England, prefers equine to human company: 'He takes vast Pleasure in Conversation with Horses ... He expresseth his Joy most commonly by Neighing'.

Which version of Peter – the 'tamed' court dependent or the 'wild boy' – did Swift opt for in the end? George I died suddenly and unexpectedly in Osnabruck on 12 June 1727, and Bolingbroke persuaded Swift to stay on England with a kind of breathy anticipation that everything was about to change, and that Swift was set to be given an English bishopric. But the splendid coronation which transformed Prince George to George II, and Princess Caroline to Queen Consort, dashed opposition hopes that Walpole would be replaced by a new administration embracing Tories as well as Whigs. Swift's hopes that Caroline might do something on behalf of Irish affairs, and for him personally, came to nothing.

He rapidly distanced himself from Mrs Howard, and his admiration for Caroline turned to an emotion far more bitter and intense than the indifference he feigned. In a letter to Gay, who had recently been offered, and declined, the lowly court of a post as Gentleman Usher to the two-year old Princess Louisa, Swift wrote 'I always told you Mrs Howard was good for nothing but to be a rank Courtier, I care not whether she writes to me or no, she may go hang herself, and so may her presumably 'Her Majesty'.

The *Verses on the Death of Dr Swift*, written between 1731-3, finally published in 1738, harp endlessly on Caroline's failure to reward him for his gift to her of Irish plaid. This small episode – blown up to epic proportions in over sixteen lines of footnotes detailing the exact cost of the fabric, Swift's refusal of payment, Caroline's promise of a medal and her forgetting to give it to him – points to his deep-seated grudge against royal ingratitude, as well as to a characteristic self-pity. 'Instead of Favour or Medals, [he] hath been ever since under her Majesty's displeasure'. Swift imagines Lady Suffolk's malicious, and Caroline's brutally frank reaction to the news of his death.

Kind Lady Suffolk in the Spleen
Runs laughing up to tell the Queen.
The Queen, so gracious, Mild, and Good,
Cries, "Is he gone? 'Tis time he shou'd.
He's dead you say; why let him rot;
I'm glad the Medals were forgot.
I promis'd them, I own, but when?

I only was the Princess then;
But now as Consort of the King,
You know 'tis quite a different thing".

And Swift returns the compliment in his satirical account of fawning court panegyrics, 'On Poetry, a Rapsody'. He starkly juxtaposes anodyne poetic fictions of royal immortality with the brutal physicality of an imagined, even wished for, royal death. 'May Caroline continue long / Forever young and fair - in Song. / What though the royal carcass must/ Squeezed in a coffin, turn to dust'. Whereas Peter, the former 'wild boy of Hanover', retired uncomplaining to suburban obscurity, Swift, the 'wild Dean' of Dublin, refused to be tamed by any king, queen or court.

SWIFT'S THOUGHTS ON RELIGION [MH]

Jonathan Swift was installed as Dean of St. Patrick's Cathedral on June 13, 1713. Much to his dismay, indeed: he had hoped for a much greater appointment. In one of his letters he referred to "the deanery they thought fit to throw me into.." (Corr: I: 380). "At my first coming [to Dublin]," as he wrote to Esther Vanhomrigh on July 8, 1713, "I thought I should have died with discontent and was horribly melancholy while they were installing me, but it begins to wear off, and change to dullness." (Corr: I: 373). But he felt no pleasure at the prospect of passing his years in Dublin.

Swift took up his duties on his return from England several months later. His main duty, as he construed it, was to defend the interests of the Church of Ireland against attack by sundry dissenters, papists, deists, freethinkers, and mischievous men in high place. He did this work mainly in pamphlets, but also, more cautiously, in sermons. He did not take his sermons as seriously as sermons should be taken: he didn't bother to print them or even to retain them for a later day. Many of them were lost when they should have been safely in his keeping. It is unlikely that the lost ones contained much that he did not include in his more formal writings, but they should have been preserved.

Swift did not regard preaching as a crucial part of his

vocation. Sermons were expected to be useful, though more often the preacher was content to have them commonplace: they were no longer the strenuous activity they had been in the days of John Donne and Lancelot Andrews.

It was widely felt, after the settlement of 1688, that the best thing an Englishman or an Irishman could do was live a decent life and a quiet one. If he had doubts of conscience and belief, he should keep them to himself. "The want of belief," Swift said, "is a defect that ought to be concealed when it cannot be overcome." In a sermon on the martyrdom of King Charles the First, he asserted that if a man had "any new visions of his own," it was his duty "to be quiet, and possess them in silence, without disturbing the community by a furious zeal for making proselytes." There was enough contentiousness at large without adding the acrimony of theological dispute.

Besides, Swift turned himself into a moderate man on questions of religion. In the sermon "On Brotherly Love" he took pains to distinguish true from false moderation: "A Man truly Moderate is steady in the Doctrine and Discipline of the Church, but with a due Christian Charity to all who dissent from it out of a Principle of Conscience; the Freedom of which, he thinketh, ought to be fully allowed, as long as it is not abused, but never trusted with Power.

He is ready to defend, with his Life and Fortune, the Protestant Succession, and the Protestant established Faith, against all Invaders whatsoever."

The main characteristics of false moderation were indifference to all religion and contempt for the clergy. The man of false moderation "thinks the Power of the People can never be too great, nor that of the Prince too little." His devotion consists "in drinking Gibbets, Confusion, and Damnation; in profanely idolizing the Memory of one dead Prince [King William III] and ungratefully trampling upon the Ashes of another [Queen Anne].

In The Sentiments of a Church-of-England Man, written in 1708, Swift said that "in order to preserve the Constitution entire in Church and State; whoever hath a true Value for both, would be sure to avoid the Extreams of *Whig* for the Sake of the former, and the Extreams of *Tory* on Account of the latter."

Swift's Christianity insisted on principles, but kept itself resolutely distant from hard questions in theology, divinity, and doctrine. He was prepared to leave to others of a more metaphysical disposition the elucidation of problems and definitions.

"I have been better entertained," he said, "and more informed by a Chapter in the Pilgrim's Progress, than by a long Discourse upon the *Will* and the *Intellect*, and *simple or complex Ideas*." Others again, he said, "are fond of dilating on *Matter and Motion*, talk of the *fortuitous Concourse of Atoms, of Theories, and Phaenomena*; directly against the Advice of *St. Paul*, who yet appears to have been conversant enough in those Kinds of Studies."

Swift had virtually nothing to say about God, and was pleased to observe that Christ, too, was silent on that august theme. "Neither did our Saviour think it necessary to explain to us the Nature of God; because I suppose it would be impossible, without bestowing on us other Faculties than we possess at present."

The only sermon in which Swift commented on a mystery of the Church was one "On the Trinity." He took as his text the first epistle of St. John, chapter 5, verse 7: "For there are three that bear record in Heaven, the Father, the Word, and the Holy Ghost; and these Three are one." The text is doubtful: it is taken from the Vulgate, but it does not appear in any of the early Greek manuscripts, or any early translation, or in the best manuscripts of the Vulgate.

Swift was not at ease – nor should he have been – in commenting on the mystery. He recited the doctrine, "as it is positively affirmed in Scripture: That God is there expressed in three different Names, as Father, as Son, and as Holy Ghost; that each of these is God, and that there is but one God.

But this Union and Distinction are a Mystery utterly unknown to Mankind." This much is enough, Swift says, "for any good Christian to believe on this great Article, without ever enquiring any farther: And, this can be contrary to no

Man's Reason, although the Knowledge of it is hid from him."

Why God thought fit to "communicate some Things to us in Part, and leave some Part a Mystery," it is impossible to know. God has pronounced the fact, "but wholly concealed the manner." We are not commanded by God to believe "any Doctrine which is contrary to the Reason he hath pleased to endow us with; but for his own wise Ends has thought fit to conceal from us the Nature of the Thing he commands; thereby to try our Faith and Obedience, and encrease our Dependence upon him."

Faith is therefore "an entire Dependence upon the Truth, the Power, the Justice, and the Mercy of God; which Dependence will certainly incline us to obey him in all Things."

Swift was clearly ill at ease in that sermon. He was relieved to be done with it. He was ready to talk about religion, so long as religion meant actions, how his flock might be encouraged to live from day to day. Religious principles were available through the collaboration of conscience and church. In a sermon "On the Testimony of Conscience" Swift maintained "that there is no solid, firm Foundation of Virtue, but in a Conscience directed by the Principles of Religion." Considerations of reward or punishment in the next life are also vital. "When Conscience placeth before us the Hopes of everlasting Happiness, and the Fears of everlasting Misery, as the Reward and Punishment of our good or evil Actions, our reason can find no way to avoid the Force of such an Argument, otherwise than by running into Infidelity."

In the sermons, as in the pamphlets, we find religion becoming indistinguishable from politics. Swift does not keep the categories of discourse separate. It is hardly surprising that he ends his sermon on the martyrdom of King Charles by showing where the middle ground between the two alluring extremes is to be discovered: "..To avoid all broachers and preachers of new-fangled doctrines in the church; to be strict observers of the laws, which cannot be justly taken from you without your own consent. In short, *to obey God and the King, and meddle not with those who are given to change.*

Even for Swift, it is a bold collocation, God and the King

together in a short sentence. If you take one further step along that road, you find yourself thinking that religion is indistinguishable from morality, law, civics, sociology, and – why not? –psychology. If you add Swift's belief in the degeneracy of the age —"men degenerate every day, merely by the folly, the perverseness, the avarice, the tyranny, the pride, the treachery, or inhumanity of their own kind—" you are inevitably seeing him as a personage, an image, perhaps an emblem of a terrifying fate.

At this point in Swift's "Further Thoughts on Religion" we are moving close to the Dean who has become a lurid if charismatic personage in the folklore of Dublin. We find him in Yeats's play The Words upon the Window Pane and in his early story "The Tables of the Law" where the narrator says to Owen Aherne: "It is not necessary to judge everyone by the law, for we have also Christ's commandment of love"; and Aherne answers, looking at the narrator with shining eyes: "Jonathan Swift made a soul for the gentlemen of this city by hating his neighbour as himself."

James Joyce was an early reader of Yeats's story and he recalled it in the third chapter of Ulysses when Stephen Dedalus is walking along Sandymount Strand and thinking of the days he spent in Marsh's Library "reading the fading prophecies of Joachim Abbas." Think of the terrible Dean: "The hundredheaded rabble of the cathedral close. A hater of his kind ran from them to the wood of madness, his mane foaming in the moon, his eyeballs stars. Houyhnhnm, horsenostrilled...Abbas father, furious dean, what offence laid fire to their brains?"

It would be impertinent to attempt an answer to that question. Maybe it was the offence, on Swift's part, of telling himself, hoping against hope, that everything in life could be tamed, domesticated, by a rational, Augustan prose, common sense, moderation, and as much silence as possible; till he came to the fourth book of Gulliver's Travels and discovered that these devices were not enough to subdue what Yeats called "the terrors that pass before shut eyes."

Bibliography

Donoghue, Dennis, *Jonathan Swift: A Critical Introduction* (Cambridge: Cambridge University Press, 1969)

Jeffrey, Francis, review of Walter Scott's edition of Swift, *Edinburgh Review* 27, no. 53 (September 1816), 1-58

Laver, James, ed., *Poems of Charles Churchill*, 2 vols. in one (London, Methuen, 1970; reprint of New York: Barnes and Noble, 1933)

Mahony, Robert, *Jonathan Swift: The Irish Identity* (New Haven and London: Yale University Press, 1995)

Nicholson, Andrew, ed., *Lord Byron: The Complete Miscellaneous Prose* (Oxford: Clarendon Press, 1991)

Rowse, A.L., *Jonathan Swift: Major Prophet* (London: Thames and Hudson, 1975)

Wu, Duncan, ed., *The Selected Writings of William Hazlitt, 9 vols (London: Pickering and Chatto, 1998) (Lectures on the English Poets in Vol. 2).*